CONSTRUCTION CONSTRUED AND CONSTITUTIONS VINDICATED

Da Capo Press Reprints in

AMERICAN CONSTITUTIONAL AND LEGAL HISTORY

GENERAL EDITOR: LEONARD W. LEVY
Brandeis University

CONSTRUCTION CONSTRUED AND CONSTITUTIONS VINDICATED

By John Taylor

DA CAPO PRESS • NEW YORK • 1970

A Da Capo Press Reprint Edition

This Da Capo Press edition of *Construction Construed and Constitutions Vindicated* is an unabridged republication of the first edition published in Richmond, Virginia, in 1820. It is reprinted from a copy of the original edition owned by the Library of the University of North Carolina.

Library of Congress Catalog Card Number 77-117311

SBN 306-71983-5

Published by Da Capo Press
A Division of Plenum Publishing Corporation
227 West 17th Street, New York, N.Y. 10011

CONSTRUCTION

CONSTRUED,

AND

CONSTITUTIONS

VINDICATED.

BY JOHN TAYLOR,

AUTHOR OF THE ENQUIRY, AND ARATOR.

RICHMOND:

PRINTED BY SHEPHERD & POLLARD.

....

1820.

TO THE PUBLICK.

The crisis has come, when the following work " may do the state some service."

The *Missouri Question* is probably not yet closed. The *principle*, on which it turns, is certainly not settled. Further attempts are to be made to wrest from the new states, about to enter into the American confederacy, the power of regulating their own concerns.—The *Tariff* question is again to be agitated.—It is time to bring the policy and the power of a legislature's *interfering with the judicial functions* to the bar of publick opinion.—The usurpation of a federal power over roads and canals is again to be attempted, and again to be reprobated.—That gigantick institution, the Bank of the United States, which, while yet in the green tree, was proclaimed by the republicans a breach of the constitution, " stands now upon its bond ;" but that charter, bad as it is, has been justified by the supreme court of the United States, on *principles* so bold and alarming, that no man who loves the constitution can fold his arms in apathy upon the subject. Those principles, so boldly uttered from the highest judicial tribunal in the United States, are calculated to give the tone to an acquiescent people, to change the whole face of our government, and to generate a thousand measures, which the framers of the constitution never anticipated. That decision

—— will be recorded for a precedent,
And many an error by the same example
May rush into the state. It cannot be.

Against such a decision, it becomes every man, who values the constitution, to raise his voice.

ii

In truth, we have arrived at a crisis, when the first principles of the government and some of the dearest rights of the states are threatened with being utterly ground into dust and ashes. When we look to the original form of the government, we are struck with its novelty and beauty. It presents to us one of the grandest experiments that ever was made in political science. We see in it an attempt to ascertain, how far power could be so distributed between two governments, as to prevent an *excessive concentration* and consequent abuse of it in one set of hands ; at the same time, that *so much power* was conveyed to each, as to enable them to accomplish the objects to which each of them was *best adapted.* The federal government was to watch over our foreign relations ; that of the states, was particularly to take care of our internal concerns. The great secret was, to have these functions so wisely regulated, as to prevent the general government from rushing into consolidation ; and the states, into a dissolution of the union. The first extreme would infallibly conduct us to great oppression, and probably to monarchy : the last would subject us to insults and injuries from abroad, to contentions and bloodshed at home. To avoid these extremes, we should never have lost sight of the true spirit of the federal constitution. To interpret it wisely, we should have rigidly adhered to the principle, laid down by George Clinton, when he, from the chair of the senate of the United States, gave the casting voice against the renewal of the first bank charter : " In the course of a long life, I have found that " government is not to be strengthened by the *assumption* " of *doubtful* powers, but a *wise* and *energetick* execution of " those which are *incontestable ;* the former never fails to " produce suspicion and distrust, whilst the latter inspires " respect and confidence. If, however, on fair experience, " the powers *vested* in the government shall be *found* in- " competent to the attainment of the objects for which it " was instituted, *the constitution happily furnishes the means* " *for remedying the evil by amendment."* This maxim deserves to be written in letters of gold upon the wall of the capitol in Washington.

But, we have been almost deaf to the voice of wisdom. We have nearly forgotten the principles of our fathers. In repeated instances, we have suffered the constitution to be trodden under foot. We have been lately rushing rapidly towards the gulph of consolidation. We have even seen the purest triumphs of the republican party in 1800-1, (when an alien and sedition law were shivered into atoms by an indignant people,) almost forgotten. We have seen a decision promulgated from the federal bench, which is calculated to sweep down the dearest rights of the states. The infatuation of the day has been carried so far, that we have just seen an attempt made, and bolstered up by the seriatim opinion of five eminent counsellors, to humble the powers of the state governments at the feet of the District of Columbia!

The period is, indeed, by no means an agreeable one. It borrows new gloom from the apathy which seems to reign over so many of our sister states. The very sound of State Rights is scarcely ever heard among them; and by many of their eminent politicians, it is only heard to be mocked at. But a good citizen will never despair of the republick. Among these good citizens, is John Taylor, of Caroline. Penetrated by the conviction, that the constitution is in danger; that the balance has seriously inclined towards the side of consolidation; he comes forward to commune with his countrymen, and to state to them frankly his impressions and his fears.

If there be any book that is capable of rousing the people, it is the one before us. Bold and original in its conceptions, without passion, and with an admirable ingenuity to recommend it, it is calculated, we should think, to make a deep impression. Its author is far removed from the temptations of ambition. He holds no office. He wishes for none. He writes, for he has thought much; and the present is a sort of last legacy to his countrymen. It is unnecessary iv

to dwell upon the particular traits of this work; yet the finger upon the wall is not to be mistaken. We here see the spirit which breathes in the pages of " Arator," and of the "Political Enquiry." The first has made him known throughout America : The last is less generally read ; but unless some intelligent men are much mistaken, it is yet to win its way to distinguished reputation. They have all one trait, without which genius exists not. *The man, who writes them, dares to think for himself.*

EDITOR.

Richmond, November, 1820.

PREFACE.

THE author of the following work earnestly wished to remain unknown; but circumstances having rendered it impossible, his alternative was reduced to an avowal, or an affectation of concealment: he hopes, however, that no one will believe him to have been influenced by money, or fame, or any personal consideration, except that kind of feeling experienced when about to take a last leave of our friends, we say to them "God bless you."

He does not solicit the indulgence of his readers, as he wishes his errors to be corrected; nor does he expect any, except from those whose interest is not disunited from that of the society.

The end of fostering eleemosynary families has evidently suggested a mode of construing our constitutions, which requires that such phrases as the following should be reconciled: "Sovereign servants. Supreme equality. Unlimited limitations. Consolidated divisions. Inferior superiority. And desirable misery." Thus, representative power may be made despotick; a co-ordinate sphere may be made supreme; convenience, like the waves produced by a pebble thrown on smooth water, may be made to undulate indefinitely; a subordinate judicial power may start up into a dictator to the state governments; divisions and limitations of power may be confounded and abolished; and English follies are converted from objects of our abhorrence, into models for our imitation. Under a reconciliation between republican and despotick principles, effected by the new idea of "sovereign servants," our legislatures are converted into British parliaments, daily new-modelling the substance of our government, by bodies politick, exclusive privileges, pensions, bounties, and judicial acts, comprising an arbitrary power of dispensing wealth or poverty to individuals and combinations, at their pleasure.

If our system of government produces these bitter fruits naturally, it is substantially European; and the world, after having contemplated with intense interest and eager solicitude the experiment of the United States, will be surprised to find, that no experiment at all has been made, and that it still remains to be discovered, whether a political system preferable to the British be within the scope of human capacity. But, if these fruits are not its legitimate offsprings, but of foreign importation, we ought to fulfil the hopes of mankind, by returning to those principles in construing our system, by which it was dictated. Let us remember, that the lucrative partialities of a government, instead of being destroyed by use, like the splendid fabricks of the loom bespangled with gold and silver to gratify pride and luxury, become richer and stronger, the longer they are worn by ambition and avarice.

The habit of corrupting our political system, by the instrumentality of inference, convenience and necessity, with an endless series of consequences attached to them, is the importer of contraband principles, and the bountiful grantor of powers not given, or withheld by our constitutions. It is, therefore, the natural enemy of our home-bred form of government, and ought to awaken the resistance of all legislative and judicial departments, and the detestation of every person not enriched by this ruinous commerce. Every lover of our institutions ought to be a vigilant custom-house officer, and do his utmost to prevent a heavy government from being brought in gradually by these seemingly light skiffs. It is convenient for the transmission of taxes, that congress should create banks; but the constitution does not delegate to the federal government a power to create political combinations, invested with a power to regulate the wealth and poverty of individuals. This new power of indefinite magnitude is, however, said to be conveyed, as a consequence of the convenient mode of removing money.

Again : congress have a power to regulate commerce ; but the constitution does not delegate to thé federal government a power to make several states tributary to one, nor a power to make the people of all the states tributary to a combination of capitalists, constituting in fact a body politick, materially affecting the interests of all persons. In this case also, the inference is made to bestow a far greater power, than that from which it is extracted.

The nourishment of exclusive interests, in all its forms, is the universal cause which obstructs the progress of political science, and has placed that which ought to be the first, in the rear of human improvements. The emoluments, attached to the administration of civil government, are unhappily a sufficient suggestion to avarice and ambition, that fraud and oppression may afford them gratifications. Even this excitement was viewed by Doctor Franklin as so dangerous to liberty, that he wished for its suppression, and refused to receive any compensation as president of Pennsylvania ; and Washington would only receive his expenses for all his services. However impracticable these speculations may be, yet the opinions of these great men are weighty authorities against the policy of superadding to an unavoidable temptation, a host of unnecessary solicitors in behalf of avarice and ambition, retained by exorbitant fees paid by the people, whilst no reward whatever is offered to the advocates for integrity and moderation. By this pernicious policy, an union is formed between the administrators of government, and corrupted combinations, creating an impulse towards oppression, which abstract principles, however good, have hitherto been unable to withstand. As the brightest beacon may be extinguished by throwing some hostile element on the flame, so the best principles are destroyed by fostering their foes.

Yet the argument in favour of exclusive privileges is, that it is the best mode by which knowledge can be advanced, and arts perfected. Under colour of this assertion, it is said, that maufactures have never been introduced into any country, except by the coercion of the government. Thus a despotick power of distributing wealth and poverty, as the caprices and vices of individuals may dictate, is artfully covered by the pretext, that it is the best mode of advancing arts and sciences; but the truth is, that they have flourished in proportion as industry has been free and property safe. The gratitude of knowledge is, therefore, due to that power, which has selected industry and philosophers for its communication. The claim of governments to be considered as the apostles of knowledge, is precisely the same with their claim to religious apostolick power, and experience has sufficiently proved, that both powers beget oppression.

This is a subject which would fill a book of no small size, and, therefore, a limited plan would not admit of its full application to the manufacturing art, selected to establish the pernicious general principle, that governments ought to have a power of granting exclusive privileges. Yet, it is highly worthy of publick consideration. Privileges imply a general deprivation. To take away in order to bestow, is merely to pull down with one hand for the purpose of building up with the other, if the deprivation discourages as much industry, as the privilege will excite. These political contradictions would then neutralize each other. But, if the discouragement operates upon greater numbers than the privilege, as is always the case, a balance arises unfavourable to industry, arts and sciences. Hence, they have flourished as exclusive privileges have decreased, and dwindled where they abound. The abolition of a vast number of feudal and hierarchical privileges gave them a great impulse in England, and a gradual multiplication of pecuniary privileges since has brought the same country to a state of misery, which may involve them in some general convulsion. Is this misery, or the mysterious advances of knowledge and liberty, the best hostage for their improvement? These have co-extensively pushed forward all arts and sciences, aided or unaided by the patriotism of governments, and agriculture has kept pace with the rest, under exactions, and without bounties. This concomitancy ascertains a common cause, establishes the ascendancy of knowledge, and explodes the necessity for the partialities of governments, or the policy of dispensing general evil, to enrich selected sects. After the dark ages, a manufacturing superiority appeared in Italy and France, without any special patronage from their disorganized governments, because those countries surpassed the rest of Europe in knowledge ; and several English kings tried unsuccessfully to rival it by legal coercions. The revocation of the edict of Nantes at length expelled a great mass of manufacturing knowledge from France, and supplied England with the leading cause of manufacturing prosperity; from this epoch, she dates hers. The improvements of machinery in England were the works of individual knowledge and industry, after her prohibitory system had become nominal. The wonderful art of ship-building, carried to such perfection in the United States, proposed to be checked by commercial restrictions, proves, that when the knowledge of an art is obtained, it is only necessary that it should correspond with the interest of individuals. Compute and compare the progress of the United States in the arts and sciences, in about thirty years, with the progress of Europe during a similar space, and anticipate its reach in six centuries, during which Europe has been employed in effecting her attainments. To what can the vast difference in velocity toward excellence be ascribed, but to a greater freedom of intellect and industry ? Why, then, should we substitute for these, avarice and fraud, as better teachers of arts and sciences ?

Alexander of Russia, a few years past, asserted the right of all states to internal self-government, and entered into a treaty with the cortes of Spain, to guaranty the constitution they had made. Now, to advance the interest of a combination of monarchs, he renounces his principles and his honour, and even forbids the penitent Ferdinand to acknowledge what he had asserted, and to confirm what he had guarantied. The federal constitution as expressly guaranties to the states the right of internal self-government ; but a mode of construction is introduced to advance the interest of mercenary combinations. Is not the analogy between the Russian and this mode of construction, apparent? The differences are, that Alexander proposes to overturn principles and a compact by force, and construction acts by sap; he adheres to the interest of hereditary monarchs ; construction, to the interest of exclusive privileges. The importance of these differences may be ascertained by comparing force with fraud, and a confederacy of foreign kings, with a confederacy of domestic parasitical privileges. Whatever may be the result of this comparison, it can offer us nothing but the old alternative between monarchy and aristocracy ; and almost all writers have agreed, that the former is to be preferred.

Against all such modes of construction, as being adverse both to republican principles, and our positive institutions, the humble reasoning of the following work is levelled.

SECTIONS.

CONSTRUCTION CONSTRUED,

AND

CONSTITUTIONS VINDICATED.

———

SECTION 1.

THE PRINCIPLES OF OUR REVOLUTION.

THESE are the keys of construction, and the locks of liberty. The question to be considered is, whether our revolution was designed to establish the freedom both of religion and property, or only of the former.

It is strange that the human mind should have been expanded in relation to religion, and yet should retain narrow notions in relation to property. Objects unseen, and incapable of being explained by the information of the senses, afford less perfect materials for the exercise of reason, than those capable of being investigated by evidence, within the scope of the human understanding. As the difficulties opposed to the correction of religious fanaticism seemed less surmountable, whilst its effects were more pernicious, the zeal of philosophers was condensed in an effort to relieve mankind from an evil the most distressing; and their attention was diverted from another, at this period the most prominent. But having wrested religious liberty from the grasp of fanaticism, it now behooves them to turn their attention towards pecuniary fanaticism, and to wrest civil liberty from its tyranny also. Between an absolute power in governments over the religion and over the property of men, the analogy is exact, and their consequences must therefore be the same. Freedom of religion being the discovery by

which religious liberty could only be established; freedom of
property must be the only means also, for the establishment of
civil liberty. Pecuniary fanaticism, undisciplined by constitutional principles, is such an instrument for oppression, as an undisciplined religious fanaticism. A power in governments to
regulate individual wealth, will be directly guided by those
very motives, which indirectly influenced all governments, possessed of a power to regulate religious opinions and rites. If
we have only restrained one of these powers, we have most improvidently retained the other, under which mankind have
groaned in all ages; and which at this time is sufficient to oppress or enslave the European nations, although they have
drawn some of the teeth of religious fanaticism. An adora-
tion of military fame, specious projects and eminent individuals, has in all ages brought on mankind a multitude of evils;
and a sound freedom of property is the only mode that I
know of, able to destroy the worship of these idols, by removing beyond their reach the sacrifices upon which themselves,
and their proselytes, subsist.

Many princes have patronized literature, but none have patronized knowledge. Augustus was celebrated for the former
species of munificence; yet the temporary splendors of impe-
rial patronage were soon obscured by the bad principle of a
tyranny over property; a principle, unpropitious to knowledge,
because it was hostile to individual liberty. We must reason
from a comparison between general or universal facts, and not
from a contemplation of temporary exceptions, to come at truth;
and when we discover that an absolute power over property,
though occasionally exercised for the attainment of praise-wor-
thy ends, is yet constantly attended by general evils, infinitely
outweighing such particular benefits; we forbear to draw our
conclusion from the partial cases, or decide erroneously. A
truth, established by its universality, ought to be an overmatch
for the sophistries of cupidity. The best general principle, under the destiny of mankind, is capable of producing partial
evils. The freedom of the press, of religion, and of property,
may occasionally produce inconveniences; but ought mankind
therefore to transfer their approbation from these three founda-
tions of civil liberty, to the instruments by which it is destroyed?

No form of government can foster a fanaticism for wealth, without being corrupted. The courtiers of republicks, able to exercise an absolute power over the national property, are more numerous and more vicious than the courtiers of kings, because access to patrons is easier; they have more occasion for partisans, and a multiplication of despots over property multiplies the channels of fraud. New ones also are frequently opened by a revolution of parties, and of patrons, who with their favorites and dependants, are in haste to bolster power or amass wealth, during the continuance of a fleeting authority. Against a propensity so mischievous, and so fatal to republicks, there seems to be no resource, but a constitutional prohibition of the power by which it is nurtured ; and a rejection of precedents, by which infringements of so wholesome a prohibition are usually justified. Both reason and morality unite to impress upon nations, a necessity for imposing restraints upon a propensity, which may so easily be concealed under the most glittering robes of patriotism. What real patriot would feel himself molested, by restraints upon avarice and ambition ? Are not both unfriendly to human happiness ? Some patriots have sacrificed their lives for the happiness of their country. Is the sacrifice of an error, by which fraud and avarice are nurtured, too much to expect of ours ?

A love of wealth, fostered by honest industry, is an ally both of moral rectitude, and national happiness, because it can only be gratified by increasing the fund for national subsistence, comfort, strength and prosperity; but a love of wealth, fostered by partial laws for enriching corporations and individuals, is allied to immorality and oppression, because it is gratified at the expense of industry, and diminishes its ability to work out national blessings.

Look for a moment at Congress, as a power for creating pecuniary inequalities, or for striking balances between favours to states, combinations and individuals. If it could even distribute wealth and poverty, by some just scale, which has never yet been discovered, justice itself would beget discontent, and sow among its medley of courtiers, a mass of discord, not more propitious to the safety of the union, than to the happiness of the people. All would weigh their own merits, and none would be convinced that they were light. Even the distribution of those preferences, necessary to civil government, is liable to defects and productive of inconveniences. Where then is the wisdom of extending the power beyond the limits of social necessity, to the despotick principle of a gratuitous distribution of wealth and poverty by law; and of converting a small evil, abundantly counterbalanced by the blessings of government, into a calamity by which these blessings are diminished or destroyed?

To answer this question, turn your eyes towards a government accoutred in the complete panoply of fleets, armies, banks, funding systems, pensions, bounties, corporations, exclusive privileges; and in short, possessing an absolute power to distribute property, according to the pleasure, the pride, the interest, the ambition, and the avarice of its administrators; and consider whether such a government is the servant or the master of the nation. However oppressive, is it not able to defy, to deride and to punish the complaints of the people? Partisans, purchased and made powerful by their wealth, zealously sustain the abuses by which their own passions are gratified. I discern no reason in the principles of our revolution, for investing our governments with such of these instruments for oppression, as were both unnecessary for the end in view, and even inimical to its attainment; and no such reason existing, it is more difficult to discern the propriety of investing our governments with these superfluous and pernicious powers, by inference and construction. Would liberty be well established in England, if her hierarchy was destroyed, whilst the government retained the absolute power of distributing wealth and poverty? Is not that establishment merely one of the modes for exercising this species of despotism; and what substantial or lasting remedy could arise from abolishing one mode, whilst others remained amply sufficient to establish the same pernicious principle? Is not a power of transferring property by pensions, bounties, corporations and exclusive privileges; and even of bestowing publick money by the unlimited will of legislative bodies, as dangerous to liberty, as a power of doing the same thing by the instrumentality of a privileged church? Is the casuistry consistent, which denies to a government the power of infringing the freedom of religion, and yet invests it with a despotism over the freedom of property? A corporation, combination, or chartered church for one purpose, in its pecuniary effects, is analagous to corporations for effecting the other. It has been said, that government in its best form is an evil. This absurd idea seems to have been suggested, by its being usually invested with an army of supernumerary powers wholly unnecessary for effecting the end of preserving social tranquillity and safety. Against these supernumerary powers, the United States waged a long war, upon the ground, that governments are instituted to secure, and not to bestow the freedom of property ; and it would be highly absurd to suppose, that having established their great principle, they directly became contented with an unfruitful theory, and surrendered the idea of its application. It was tyrannical in the English government, said the colonies, to insist upon taking away their property, and giving it to placemen and pensioners ; and they very justly considered life and liberty as so intimately connected with property, that the rights of the latter could not be invaded, without invading the other rights also. They fought for a revolution, and established governments to secure all three of these natural rights, because a loss of one was equivalent to a loss of all, in a national view.

I see no infallible criterion for defining the nature of a government, except its acts. If the acts of a monarchy, aristocracy and democracy are the same, these forms of government are to a nation essentially the same also. To contend for forms only, is to fight for shadows. The United States did not go to war for nothing but forms. A government is substantially good or bad, in the degree that it produces the happiness or misery of a nation ; and I see but little difficulty in finding a mode of detecting the fallacy of form, and the frauds of profession. If we can ascertain the quality in human nature, from which political evil has chiefly proceeded under every form of government, this quality is the cause which can corrupt any form ; and instead of amusing ourselves with these new forms, not to be confided in, it behooves us to search for a remedy, able to remove or control the cause itself.

Cupidity, avarice or monopoly, both in the savage and civilized state, is the quality of human nature, always requiring control, and always striving to break down the restraints imposed upon it. To resist this quality, the United States endured the evils of a long war with a powerful nation. They had

seen a limited monarchy tried in the parent country, as a remedy for this bad quality of human nature ; but ineffectually ;
because a considerable power remained with the king, and an
absolute power was conceded to or usurped by the government,
of distributing property. The hostile principles, of leaving
men to be enriched by their own industry, or of enriching them
by the favours of the government, were to be weighed against
each other ; that which made many poor to enrich a few was
rejected, and that which encouraged industry was preferred, in
the most distinct manner, as I shall hereafter endeavour to prove.

Almost all governments have espoused and nourished the
spirit of avarice, which they were instituted to discipline by
justice; and have betrayed the weak, whom it was their duty
to protect. In assuming a power of distributing property by
law, they have reduced it in a great degree to a destiny, ap-
proximating to its savage destiny, when subjected to force. From
this cause have arisen the most pernicious imperfections of society. Aristocracies and democracies, by usurping this despotick
power, in imitation of monarchs, have driven nations into a circle of forms, through which they have perpetually returned to
the oppression they intended to escape. Had the essentials,
rather than the structure of governments, attracted the attention of mankind, they would not have trusted to any theory,
however excellent, asserting it to be the duty of a government
to protect rights; under a system of legislation, by which governments of the worst forms destroy them. They would have
discovered, that a power of distributing property, according to
its pleasure, has made governments of the best forms, bad ; and
that a remedy for an evil, poisonous to the best theories, ought to
awaken their solicitude and ingenuity. For want of this remedy, republicks, of the finest theoretical structure, have universally died more prematurely, even than absolute monarchies ;
because, the more numerous the depositaries of an absolute
power over property have become, the more widely has the spirit of avarice or monopoly been excited. If this universal cause
of oppression must exist, that government which afforded the
most channels for its operation, is the worst ; and hence has arisen the general preference of mankind for monarchy. Governments of all forms having exercised an absolute power over property, they have experimentally ascertained, that the oppression

derived from this source was the most tolerable, when the tyrants were the least numerous.

If the age has at length arrived, in which knowledge is able to break the fetters forged by fraud and credulity, political enquiry, as in other sciences, may take its stand on the eminence of truth, hail with exultation the happy advent, and direct its arrows straight forward against an error fraught with plagues to mankind.

To define the nature of a government truly, I would say, that a power of distributing property, able to gratify avarice and monopoly, designated a bad one ; and that the absence of every such power, designated a good one. Of what value is an exchange of one system of monopoly for another? How shall we estimate the difference between noble and clerical orders, and between combinations of exclusive pecuniary privileges? Is pure avarice better than some honour and some sanctity? The encroachments upon property by noble and clerical combinations, once fixed by law, remained stationary; and each individual could calculate his fate with some certainty: but pecuniary combinations, once sanctioned as constitutional, will perpetually open new channels, and breed new invaders, whose whole business it will be, to make inroads upon the territories of industry. Legislatures will become colleges for teaching the science of getting money by monopolies or favours ; and the deluge of laws will become as great in the United States, as was once the deluge of papal indulgences in Europe for effecting the same object. What an unaccountable feature of the human character it is, that it should exert so much ingenuity to get the property of others, and be so dull in finding out means for the preservation of its own?

The morality of the gospel and that of monopoly, seem to me, not to bear the least resemblance to each other. A christian " loves man. His light must shine before men. He keeps judg- " ment and does justice. He trusts in the Lord and does good. " He lives in goodness and honesty. He is a doer and not a " hearer only of the divine law. Whoever doeth not right, is " not of God, neither he that loveth not his brother. Repen- " tance and an avoidance of sin, constitute the claim to the " atonement of a saviour. By their works ye shall know them." The pope of Rome for many centuries persuaded the people

of Europe, that he fulfilled all these texts of scripture, by uttering annually a great number of indulgences, to cheat the people
of money.

Is there a man who could be so infatuated, as to foster zealously both bible and missionary societies, and also a spirit of
avarice and monopoly ? Geographical malice, combined frauds,
individual deceit, and civil commotion, some of the effects of
this latter policy, suggest the idea, that the same person is
equally zealous to convert the heathens to christianity, and the
christians to heathenism. This ideal character may be also a
philosopher, who ridicules the notion of being saved by faith
without works; and yet contends that the people ought to confide in forms without acts, and take it for granted that their
property will be safe under a theory, which exercises an absolute power over it. If he should make an eloquent speech, one
half in favour of the theory of equal laws, and the other half
in favour of actual exclusive privileges, what should we think ?
that it was like placing Christ on the car of Juggernaut, and
dressing the United States in British regimentals.

There are sundry points of resemblance between the English
revolution in the time of Charles the first, and ours, replete
with edification. Let us go into a comparison. The English reformation of religion, by compromising with the rapaciousness of
individuals, and by retaining sundry of the principles and habits of popery, inoculated the government with a poison, which
diffused its virulence throughout the body politick, and contaminated the blessings promised by the experiment. Those who
resisted the frauds of selfishness, and the artifices of ambition,
were called puritans ; and the derision of a nickname, united
with the excesses produced by oppression, to render the doctrine
of a freedom of religion, both ridiculous and detestable. Those
who contended for it, were successfully represented as wild
visionaries, whose views were unnatural and impracticable.
Yet to these puritans the United States are indebted for the
religious freedom they enjoy ; and the whole world, for a refutation of the arguments advanced by ambition and avarice, to
obstruct the progress of political improvement, and the advancement of human happiness.

The same contrivances practised in England to destroy religious freedom, are using in the United States to defeat civil liberty. The puritanism of republican principles is ridiculed : it is called democracy; and violations of the freedom of property (an important principle of our civil puritanism) are providing combustibles for some calamitous explosion. Our political reformation is daily corrupted by the principles and habits of the English system, as was the English religious reformation, by the principles and habits of popery; and we are exchanging the pure principles of the revolution, for the garbage of aristocracy, and compromises with venality. By disregarding these principles, our fluctuations of parties invested with power, have been made to resemble the bauble called a Kaleidescope, which at each revolution exhibits new scenes of glittering delusions, whilst the pebbles from which they are reflected, remain substantially the same. The remedy for an evil so mischievous, is that by which religious freedom has been established. Freedom of property will beget civil liberty, as freedom of conscience has begotten religious. The success of one experiment proves the other to be practicable. Every man, except he belong to a privileged combination, is as much interested to effect a freedom of property, as he is to maintain a freedom of religion, except he could become a priest of an established and endowed hierarchy.

The English protestants had adopted a variety of imaginary habits and opinions. The several American States also entertained a variety of opinions and habits, fixed by real interest, more reasonable and more stubborn, as being derived from natural and unconquerable circumstances. Each of the sects in England, after the religious revolution was established, as power fluctuated among them, endeavoured when uppermost, to impose its own opinions and habits upon the others. The apparel of the clergy, surplices, tippets, caps, hoods and crosiers; and ceremonies ; such as the sign of the cross in baptism, the ring in marriage, the mode of administering the sacrament, and the consecration and powers of bishops ; all inconsiderable compared with the cardinal end of religious freedom ; became subjects of controversy in England. The endowment of certificate holders, banking corporations, exclusive privileges, compulsory laws over free will in the employment of the earnings of industry, and violations of the local interests and habits of States, more materially affecting the cardinal end of civil liberty, have become subjects of controversy in the United States. In England, the force of opinions, less substantial, produced a frightful civil war. In the United States, opinions, better founded, have already produced awful ideas of dissolving the union. In England, the religious controversies terminated in an act of uniformity, by which a majority of the people are cruelly oppressed ; there are more meeting-houses than churches, and more dissenters than conformists ; yet by bribery with publick money, so as exorbitantly to increase taxation, the majority are both excluded from civil offices, and subjected to the payment of tithes for the suppression of their own opinions and interests. In the United States, the majority of the people of each state, are subjected to the payment of more than tithes, to deprive themselves of free will as to their own interest, and to foster exclusive privileges. Our division into state governments of great extent, and embracing a great variety of local circumstances, will render a compulsory uniformity of temporal interests, habits and opinions infinitely more difficult, than a religious uniformity in England ; and require means, more coercive and severe to effect it. A very powerful standing army, so necessary in England for one purpose, would be more indispensable here for the other. Whole states will more sensibly feel, and be more able to resist burdens, inflicted to enrich privileged civil sects, bearing heavily on their local interests and habits, than individuals only combined by the slight threads of ceremonials and speculative prejudices. Had the freedom of religion been established in England at the Reformation, a mass of civil war, national inquietude and oppression would have been avoided. A greater mass of these evils was foreseen by the framers of the Union, and attempted to be avoided, by restricting the powers given to Congress, and by retaining to the states those powers united with the local interests, habits and opinions of each state ; in fact, by securing the freedom of property.

This wise precaution was suggested by the character of human nature, sound reason, substantial justice, and unequivocal experience drawn from the consequences of the different policy pursued by England in her religious revolution. Why ought not industry to enjoy a freedom of will, similar to that demonstrated in the United States, to be so wholesome and happy in the case of religion? How can an expensive, compulsory uniformity in one case, generate blessings, when it has generated curses in the other? It was not intended by our revolution to destroy the freedom of will, in relation either to speculation, actual habits or personal interests. It designed to draw a plain line between the foreign relations of the United States, and the internal concerns of each state; and the vitality of the union, as well as the vitality of religion, lies in a strict adherence to the same principle. Each state, however different in its habits and interests, like each sect however different in its tenets and ceremonials, has its liberty and happiness embarked and hazarded upon its preservation; and if any are tempted by the bribe of delusive advantages to abandon it, they will, like the religious sects which yielded to the temptations of pride, enthusiasm and avarice, when possessed of the majority, produce civil war, forge chains for themselves, and obtain a toleration of property instead of its freedom. A combination of corporations, exclusive privileges and pecuniary speculations, assails republican puritanism, as protestant puritanism was assailed by a combination of Roman Catholick princes, and for the same reason. It obstructs frauds.

The maxim of James the first, " no bishop no king," was a political truth; not limited to the idea of hierarchical orders, but an exemplification of the necessity of intermediate orders between an individual and a nation, for the support of a despotick government. It applies to all intermediate orders or exclusive privileges between a nation and a government, whether pecuniary, civil, religious, or military; whether they be called lords, mandarins, bashaws, generals, bishops, bankers, exclusive privileges, corporations, or companies. Adhering to the maxim in its amplified sense, the English government, for its own security, has extended it gradually from bishops and a nobility, to an army and to a vast pecuniary order; which, though compounded of various corporations, companies and exclusive privileges, as the noble order is compounded of a variety of titles, is united in the support and defence of the government, whatever it may do, as being dependant upon it for all the privileges, however denominated, enjoyed by its favour. These dependant orders are even better props of an oppressive government than a hereditary nobility. Accordingly, they are more ardent in defence of political severities, and more rapidly create the evil of excessive taxation, than the orders of ancient coinage. Hereditary titles were more honorable than lucrative, embraced and corrupted fewer individuals, and extorted less from the savings of industry, than dependant privileges entirely mercenary, and only capable of being fostered by perpetual drafts from the majority of nations. And, therefore, the latter have accomplished in England a degree of oppression, which the former could never effect. Did our revolution meditate an intermediate order between the government and the people? Are not privileged mercenary combinations, dependant on the government, both such an order, and of the worst species? Have we then adopted the essence of James's maxim, and subscribed to the opinion, " no exclusive privileges, no republick?"

During the reigns of the Stuarts, there existed two kinds of puritanism; one for purifying religious, the other for purifying civil government. The natural affinity between the two objects, combined the individuals devoted to each ; and although the imperfect state of political knowledge, and a spirit of fanaticism obstructed their efforts, and prevented their complete success, yet the English were indebted to this double impulse for some accessions both of civil and religious liberty, which constituted a platform upon which we have raised a more perfect superstructure. The civil and religious patriots of that period were united by the conviction, that a despotick power over the mind will absorb a despotick power over property ; and that a despotick power over property will absorb a despotick power over the mind. The English government, by retaining such a power over property, has been enabled to retain a similar power over the mind. Our revolutionary patriots evidently entertained the same opinion, and therefore endeavoured to destroy both kinds of despotism ; and their complete success in the establishment of religious freedom, ought not to render the freedom of property hopeless, especially when it is considered, that if the latter is impracticable, the former, in time, will become abortive. The consideration of the principles of our revolution will be resumed in several of the succeeding sections.

SECTION 2.

CONSTRUCTION.

It is necessary, before I proceed, to appropriate a short section to this art or artifice. There are two kinds of construction; one calculated to maintain, the other to corrupt or destroy the principles upon which governments are established; one visible to common sense, the other consisting of filaments so slender, as not to be seen except through some magnifying glass; one which addresses the understanding, the other which addresses prejudice or self-interest. When a man splits his mind, and glues one half to certain principles, and the other to a mode of construction, by which the same principles are subverted, it is no easy matter to find arguments which will please both halves. There was in old times a God, said by his worshippers to be blind and lame and foolish, but who seems to me to be more quick-sighted, active and acute in the arts of construction than Minerva herself. But his inspirations are unhappily partial; for, if this deity would but open the eyes of every one to his own interest, the mode of construction most conducive to the general interest would be elected by a republican majority.

Next to this influence over construction, is that of governments. In all, except our own, the people have nothing to do with it; but ours is modelled with an intention that they should have much to do with it; and what is better for current use, that the members of the government themselves shall be strongly induced, individually, to give it fair play. But as the pride of power, the temptations of self-interest, and even the consciousness of good intentions, might crook or sharpen this terrible weapon, those invested with most power, hold their offices for short periods; and are exposed to frequent returns to private life; that the people might straighten or blunt its edge occasionally. This dependance, and our affection for children and relations, whose fate we are dealing out, unite to chasten and restrain the unlimited power of construction ; and though the solicitations of pride, vanity, or avarice, may in a few cases prevail, yet, under our form of government, a great majority of legislative bodies must feel an honest loyalty to correctness.

All other governments, as expositors of power, are influenced by motives exactly the reverse of these. With them, construction is not a science to preserve the rights of mankind, but an art for extending their own power. Its business is to forge wealth for individuals or combinations, and chains for majorities : To make payment for usurpations, in fulsome flatteries, and insidious projects : To substitute successive, vacillating, eccentrick meteors, for steady planets of fixed orbits : To promise future blessings for present innovations, with the prophetical truth of those prospective chronologists, who have so often foretold the arrival of the millenium : And to furnish parties, factions, combinations and individuals, with concealed dirks to stab liberty.

The framers of our constitutions exerted all their faculties, to exclude from our policy this pernicious species of construction, by specifications and restrictions. Its wonderful acuteness in misinterpretation, was understood, and sedulously guarded against. It had often perverted the Scripture, and converted patriotism into treason. Russel and Sidney fell under the edge of constructive treason. The day on which the former was beheaded, the wise and learned university of Oxford, convinced by its doctors in the art of construction, declared every principle by which a free constitution can be maintained, to be "impious and heretical," especially the doctrine, that "all civil authority is derived from the people." Sidney had maintained it. Thence it was inferred, that he meant to excite the people to enforce it; that this would cause insurrection ; that insurrection was treason; and that Sidney was therefore guilty of treason. He had also asserted, that tyrants ought to be deposed and punished, as in the cases of Nero and Caligula. Thence it was inferred, that he was a traitor in imagining, that the king of England, if a tyrant, might be justly deposed and punished. Which can do most harm to mankind, constructive treasons or constructive powers? The first takes away the life of an individual, the second destroys the liberty of a nation. The machine called inference can act as extensively in one case as in the other. A government, by an unlimited power of construction, may stretch constitutions as Jeffries did laws, or interpret them as synods do scripture, according to the temporal interest of the predominant sect. Yet it often happens, that whilst our hearts glow on recollecting the political and religious martyrs, who have fallen by the edge of this destructive weapon ; our heads freeze when it is applied to our constitutions, by forgetting its ability to destroy the political as well as the natural body.,

The Stuart family, in three successive reigns, pertinaciously adhered to the ingenuity of conceding principles, and then construing them away. Thus they craftily endeavoured to extend their powers ; and two of them paid the forfeits of the experiment. An admission of a line of separation between the powers of the state and federal governments, followed with its obliteration with the sponge of inference, would bear a close resemblance to many of the stratagems practised by this construing family.

SECTION 3.

SOVEREIGNTY.

I do not know how it has happened, that this word has crept into our political dialect, unless it be that mankind prefer mystery to knowledge; and that governments love obscurity better than specification. The unknown powers of sovereignty and supremacy may be relished, because they tickle the mind with hopes and fears; just as we indulge the taste with Cayenne pepper, though it disorders the health, and finally destroys the body. Governments delight in a power to administer the palatable drugs of exclusive privileges and pecuniary gifts; and selfishness is willing enough to receive them; and this mutual pleasure may possibly have suggested the ingenious stratagem, for neutralizing constitutional restrictions by a single word, as a new chymical ingredient will often change the effects of a great mass of other matters.

Neither the declaration of independence, nor the federal constitution, nor the constitution of any single state, uses this equivocal and illimitable word. The first declares the colonies " to be free and independent states." The second is ordained to "secure the blessings of liberty to ourselves and our posterity:" And the rest recognize governments as " the servants of the people." In none, is there the least intimation of a sovereign power; and in all, conventional powers are divided, limited and restrained. There is, I believe, an instance in a bill of rights, in which a *state* is declared " to be free, sovereign and independent." But it was the state and not its government which was the object of this declaration; and the reference was to other nations. The language of all these sacred, civil authorities, is carefully chastened of a word, at discord with their purpose of imposing restrictions upon governments, by the natural right of mankind to establish societies for themselves. It could not be correctly used as a vehicle of power, either external or internal. The idea of investing servants with sovereignty, and that of investing ourselves with a sovereignty over other nations, were equally preposterous. Sovereignty implies superiority and subordination. It was therefore inapplicable to a case of equality, and more so to the subordinate power in reference to its creator. The word being rejected by our constitutions, cannot be correctly adopted for their construction; because, if this unanimous rejection arose from its unfitness for their design of defining and limiting powers, its interpolation by construction for the purpose of extending these same powers, would be an evident inconsistency. It would produce several very obvious contradictions in our political principles. It would transfer sovereignty from the people, (confining it to mean the right of self-government only,) to their own servants. It would invest governments and departments, invested with limited powers only, with unspecified powers. It would create many sovereignties, each having a right to determine the extent of its sovereignty by its own will. And if two sovereignties over the same subjects could never agree, it would propose for our consideration what was to be expected from an army of sovereignties. Our constitutions, therefore, wisely rejected this indefinite word as a traitor of civil rights, and endeavored to kill it dead by specifications and restrictions of power, that it might never again be used in political disquisitions.

In fact, the term "sovereignty," was sacrilegiously stolen from the attributes of God, and impiously assumed by kings. Though they committed the theft, aristocracies and republicks have claimed the spoil. Imitation and ignorance even seduced the English puritans and the long parliament to adopt the despotism they resisted; and caused them to fail in accomplishing a reformation for which they had suffered the evils of a long war. By assuming divine rights, because they had been claimed by kings and popes, and drawing powers from an inexhaustible store-house, they aggravated the tyranny they intended to destroy, and merited the fate which they finally experienced. Presbyteries and synods snatched the keys of Heaven from popes and bishops, and the long parliament, those of property from the king; and both demonstrated what man would do with the powers of Providence. By our constitutions, we rejected the errors upon which our forefathers had been' wrecked, and withheld from our governments the keys of temporal and eternal rights, by usurping which, their patriots had been converted into tyrants; and invested them only with powers to restrain internal wrongs, and to resist foreign hostility; without designing to establish a sovereign power of robbing one citizen to enrich another.

Sovereignty is neither fiduciary nor capable of limitation. Accordingly, the long parliament asserted, that "there were two sovereignties in England, their's and the king's," and left us a specimen of what may be expected from two sovereignties here, state and federal. Two sovereignties or supremacies over the same subjects have often appeared. Two or more emperors frequently existed in the Roman empire, each claiming the absolute powers of sovereignty. Several popes have existed at the same time, each claiming the absolute powers of supremacy, and both pretending to keep the keys of Heaven. But sovereignty being by its nature a unit, its division implied usurpation, and therefore the king, the parliament, the emperors and the popes, in exercising it, were all usurpers; and hence an allotment or division of the powers of sovereignty by our governments among themselves, would also be an usurpation. If we must use terms, taken from the deity to adorn the brows of men, we cannot still divest them of their meaning; and as sovereignty implies individuality, we are reduced to the necessity, to satisfy its meaning, of looking for this essential quality. I admit that it may be found among us, either in congress or in the people; but I deny that it can exist in both. Chastened down to the signification of a natural right in nations to institute and limit their own governments, it only embraces the principle by which alone social liberty can be established; extended to the idea of a power in governments to regulate conscience or to distribute property at its pleasure, it includes the principle by which social liberty is destroyed.

Oppression is universally caused by pecuniary fanaticism. If the proposition be true, the remedy is indicated. Does the indication point to a sovereignty in governments over property, or to its security against a power so despotick? As the evil has eluded and corrupted all political theories hitherto, it required a remedy at its root. Sovereignty was its root, and we endeavoured to eradicate it by establishing governments invested with specified and limited powers. But the evil, restless and persevering, requires a perpetual activity and jealousy on the part of nations, to keep it from shooting up new scions. Protean and plausible, its shrubs must be grubbed up as they appear, or they will soon grow into trees. As the love of wealth is common to all civilized men, and governments are composed of men, laws to protect the property of nations against governments are as necessary, as laws to protect the property of one man against another. Jugurtha's exclamation against the government of Rome was foolish. The influence of avarice even at that early age was not a novelty. What ground then was there for surprise, because ' Rome was for sale?' The government exercised an absolute power over the national property. How then could he have doubted, whether this power could find purchasers ? I discern no age, no country, no government, wherein these sales of the rights and properties of mankind have not abounded. Though the modes of this political traffick are multifarious, yet the result is as certain as a mathematical conclusion ; and a remedy which can reach all modes can only be effectual.

Lycurgus, sensible of the cause by which governments were corrupted, excluded it entirely ; and surrendered the amenities of life, the acquisition of knowledge, the elegancies of taste, the fine arts, the circle of the sciences, and almost civilization itself ; because he computed a loss so enormous as a cheap sacrifice, to get rid of an evil so calamitous. The Athenians, unwilling to surrender the blessings of life, but sensible of the evil, endeavoured to restrain it, by the ineffectual expedient of the ostracism. The Romans long resisted the avarice of the senate, vainly depended upon elective tribunes to abolish frauds in which they participated, and at length fled from the avarice of many, to the avarice of one. The ignorant northern conquerors saw no better remedy against oppression, than to yield the utmost scope to the principle of sovereignty, by an absolute transfer of themselves and their property to feudal kings and barons. As the Europeans became more enlightened, they became sensible of the tyranny of avarice, and after a series of ineffectual struggles to emancipate themselves from its grasp, have only changed the form of its operation, without diminishing its oppressions. England, the most successful in theory, has nothing to boast of in practice ; and even the improvements in the form of her government, have become instruments for avarice, by which it has effected as much at least as the feudal system could accomplish. By the confidence derived from representation, united with the power of a sovereignty in the government over property, avarice is enabled to draw from the people all they can possibly spare. Thus they owe to the wisest political discovery, the greatest political evil ; and representation itself, the last refuge of hope, is contaminated and rendered abortive, by its union with a sovereign power over property. The means used by a sovereignty in the English government, are monitors to us. They consist of a long catalogue of exclusive privileges, and legal donations, bestowed by the power of sovereignty, and taken from private property. The nation, tutored by the domestick usurpations of sovereignty, have been taught to believe, that it was as right to sacrifice foreign nations to its own avarice, as it was, that themselves should be sacrificed to the avarice of domestick combinations ; and have suffered a second series of calamities from the same unjust principle, because the spoils of oppression are always intercepted by the instruments for inflicting it. The same thing arises universally from the most specious domestick combinations, under pretence that they will advance the national good. The managers of the pretext absorb its fruits, and the majority of the nation get regret for their loss. The people of England have gazed at the wealth amassed by the bounties, the pensions, the monopolies, the exclusive privileges, the tithes, and the contracts of their sovereign government, until, being undeluded by the argument of sensation, and deceived no longer in the promises of projects to diffuse blessings, they are only restrained from subverting society itself by the force of a mercenary army.

A love of property is the chief basis of civil society ; but like all other passions it ought to be regulated and restrained, to extract from it the benefits it can produce, and to counteract the evils it can inflict. All honest politicians have acknowledged the necessity for constitutional restrictions, to curb the fanaticism of ambition ; and as the love of wealth is a passion of wider influence, being often even the primary motive by which ambition itself is awakened, that also demanded constitutional restrictions, at least as forcible, to operate upon the individuals who composed a government. If a society is so constituted, as to invest a government with a sovereign power over property, restrictions upon the passion of ambition must become abortive, because the government will possess the means by which it is excited and nourished.

The distribution of wealth can only be regulated by industry, by fraud or by force. Fraud and force are of equal weight in the scales of justice. Theoretically, they are of the same character; practically, fraud has been by far the most pernicious in distributing property. Yet pecuniary fanaticism or exclusive privileges, can abhor a resort to force, and admire a resort to fraud for the same purpose. What could be objected to the exercise of a sovereignty in the people, forcibly to distribute property? Nothing stronger than may be objected to a sovereignty in the government, to do it fraudulently. If pecuniary morality, or the freedom of property is the basis of a good government; and if a distribution of property by the power of the government or even of the people would designate a bad one; no remedy which would reach only half the evil, could make the government good. If it deprived the people of this pernicious power and gave it to the government, or if it deprived the government of the power, and gave it to the people, the social principles would either way be imperfect, because neither expedient would be bottomed upon the natural right of mankind to the fruits of their own labour. We must extract principles from facts, and the experience of the whole world supplies them in abundance. England alone, the admired model of a sovereignty in government over property, supplies facts enough to establish the principles, and to justify the conclusions for which I have contended ; and would prove, that an artificial sovereignty for taking away that which belongs to others, cannot be better, than a natural sovereignty, for keeping that which belongs to ourselves.

The use of a hyperbolical word, suggested by a laudable zeal, has exposed philosophers to some degree of ridicule; and their exertions for benefiting mankind, have been considerably counteracted, by insisting upon our "perfectibility." If the exaggerated word "sovereignty" can be successfully used to disencumber our governments in general, or the federal government in particular, of the restrictions imposed upon them by the people; it would be peculiarly hard, that one extravagant word should arrest the improvement of man's state, and also that another should deprive him of the improvements he has made; though both as being hyperbolical, would seem to merit an equal share of ridicule.

Suppose, however, we admit the hyperbolical claim of sovereignty to divine origin, and concede the consequence, that as its origin is divine, its powers must be boundless; it will then be necessary to enquire upon whom the splendid donation has been bestowed, whether on kings, on governments, or on the people; on one man, on a few men, or on all men. Now, as the two first of these competitors are artificial beings, and the last only natural beings; and as we know of no other channel, except that of nature, through which this divine boon has been conveyed; and as mental and bodily faculties, common to all men, are the only evidences of it; the enquiry would seem very clearly to terminate in the conclusion, that the rodomontade " I alone am king of me" was considerably more modest, than that other, now contended for, " I alone am king of you."

This is a concession conformable to the doctrine of the highest-toned advocates for sovereignty which have ever appeared; but it would be uncandid to confine the enquiry to a ground which would only propose for our election, liberty on one hand, or the utmost conceivable degree of despotism on the other. The modern and more moderate advocates of sovereignty have ceased to contend for its divine origin; and have rather struggled for its powers, than defended the genealogy so much insisted upon by their predecessors. They seem tacitly, but by no means plainly, to admit that sovereignty is not a divine, but a conventional right. They must assume one of these grounds in asserting the sovereignty of governments, and as the latter is the strongest, I will yield it to them. Having gotten upon this ground, chosen by the advocates for sovereignty, I now ask them to shew me the conventional sovereignty for which they contend. Far from discerning any glimpse of the powers of sovereignty in our constitutions, I see nothing but long catalogues of limitations, restrictions, balances and divisions of power, and if this young political family can be ground back into the old hoary traitor sovereignty, in the mill of construction, it will be just reversing the ancient prodigy of grinding old men into young ones.

I do not however admit that " sovereignty and the right of self-government" are equivalent things, except it is supposed that both reside in the people, and neither in a government. Under this supposition it follows, that sovereignty or self-government are natural rights, and that governments cannot participate of either, because their rights are all conventional. This opinion is so firmly fixed in our country, however in some cases exterior politeness may subsist with internal contempt, or verbal concession with practical disavowal, that I may safely assume the principle, that the right of self-government, and sovereignty also if it came from God, resides in the people. This being a natural right, like the right to our own labour, no existing generation can deprive another of it, and convey it to kings or governments, upon any better ground, than it could decree, that the heads of all future generations, as fast as they arrived to manhood, should be taken away from them. If no conventional act can deprive man of life, liberty and property, and if sovereignty in governments would have this effect, it follows that sovereignty cannot be conventionally established ; and that whether gentlemen deduce it from this source by hyperbolical inferences, or from a divine origin, it is still a useless, foreign and perplexing word to our political system. But supposing the rights of sovereignty and of self-government to be inseparably united with each other; and that a number of men assembled to exercise one right, are also invested with the other ; yet I see no reason why they may not establish a government with limited powers, and retain this imaginary sovereignty if it is real; and instead of uniting with these limited powers, the indefinite powers of sovereignty, agree that they shall be subordinate to their will, restricted by their constitutional mandate, and liable to their revision. This was actually done in the establishment of all our constitutions; and as these conventional acts, far from bestowing sovereignty on governments, have actually retained it in the hands of the people, if it existed at all, and if sovereignty may have a conventional origin, it is so deposited, I shall therefore disregard the distinction between the rights of sovereignty and of self-government in the progress of this enquiry, and in accordance with common language, use the term " sovereignty" as an attribute of the right of self-government, and only applicable to the people.

We must then return to the old idea of sovereignty, in order to compare it with the new one. The sovereignty of kings, presumptuously derived from the same source, from which mankind derive the right of self-government, long puzzled philosophers and patriots before it was exploded; but no sooner was the usurpation wrenched from kings, but other men, with other titles, seized upon it for their own use. Thus the enquiry glided into an immaterial controversy, and instead of considering the question, whether any man or set of men ought to exercise the absolute power of sovereignty, the only contest was, whether it ought to be exercised by a monarchy, aristocracy or a republick. In such a contest the people could never gain any solid or permanent victory ; for, sovereignty was the prize of the victor, in any event, at their expense. In England, it has circulated among all these combatants. It has been exercised by kings, by occasional aristocracies of barons, by lords and commons, by the commons alone, and by a protector of the liberties of England ; by governments, regal, aristocratical, elective and hereditary. All of them exercised its despotick powers; granted franchises to the nation or to any section of it; bestowed, revoked and modelled representation; created monopolies, corporations and exclusive privileges, and managed commerce as a means for defrauding labour and gratifying avarice. First the barons, and then the lords and commons, transferred the crown from one man or family to another; and finally, this fluctuating sovereignty has settled, not upon the people, but upon king, lords and commons, with a power unlimited, except as lord Coke observes, that it is unequal to impossibilities. Its capacity to effect any political changes or innovations, is demonstrated, by its having extended the power of a house of commons elected for four years only, to seven. These facts are constructions of the word " sovereignty," displaying the consequences of its adoption into our political vocabulary. By referring to the English books and practices, from which it is borrowed, for its interpretation, it turns out to be synonimous with despotism. How then can it be incorporated with our political system, without investing our governments with a power of encroachment; without freeing them from constitutional restrictions; and without subverting the sovereignty of the people? No English sovereignty regal, parliamentary or republican, recognized sovereignty or a right to self-government in the people. The long parliament loved sovereignty as well as any other form of government. All the usurpers of sovereignty used favours and penalties to sustain it, and the acceptance of the former was a voluntary acknowledgment of a right to bestow them. Among a people jealous of their liberty, this mode for procuring a confession of the existence of a sovereign power in government, will undoubtedly be preferred as the safest, and selected as the most successful; but as it is the most seducing and dangerous, it ought to be restrained with the greatest circumspection. Exclusive privileges will make more proselytes to despotism, than the severest punishments.

But it may be objected, if sovereignty and despotism are synonimous terms, that the sovereignty of the people is also a despotism. The objection is answered by the following considerations. If societies are instituted by consent, the objection fails, because the despotism objected is converted into free will and in fact becomes the very opposite of despotism. If by the majority; it is then to be considered, whether this species of despotism or sovereignty, is preferable or not, to despotism or sovereignty in one person or in a minority. An alternative, arising from comparison, constitutes the scope for the range of intellect. In theory, it is probable that much fewer causes will exist, which would induce the majority of a nation to invade the rights of a minority, than such as solicit one or a few to invade the rights of the nation or of some of its parts. In fact, the first have been extremely rare and evanescent; the latter, continual and lasting. It is true that many wise and good men, whilst they intuitively admit the right of self-government to reside in nations, suffer imagination to conjure up a tumultuous populace, discharging its fury upon life, liberty and property, and shrink from the terrifick spectre; whilst they cannot see any danger in a sovereign government, discharging its frauds against liberty, property and individual happiness, by monopolies and exclusive privileges. Such apparitions appeared to devout men, and caused them to deprecate the introduction of religious freedom. They were also seen by no small number during our revolutionary war, and even disfigured the declaration of independence into an ugly monster. But having, in these cases, rubbed off the rust, spread over the sovereignty of the people by ignorance and monopolies, it ought not to be lost under a new incrustation composed of phantoms, kneaded by selfishness, and spread by construction and inference. Let us recollect that this composition, if left undisturbed, indurates with wonderful celerity.

It is however superfluous to consider, whether the sovereignty of the people is a better or worse political maxim, than the sovereignty of the government; because the question to be settled for application as we proceed, is, which of these competitors is sovereign in fact. If the government created the people, that is, organized them into a nation, there can be no doubt but that the government is sovereign. The kings of England had a claim to sovereignty upon this ground. They created a nation (lords and commons) by successive charters and franchises. But unhappily for the argument, our nation created their governments. Yet it suggests an observation of no little weight. Had the lords or commons, or bodies politick, or corporations, exercised a right of creating other lords, or commons, or bodies politick, or corporations, it would have been a usurpation of the king's sovereignty, and must gradually have subverted it. The application of this remark is obvious.

It has been observed, that sovereignty implies a correspondent inferiority ; and required, that the subject for a sovereign power in our governments to operate upon, should be pointed out. Does it reach the sovereignty of the people, or is the government only sovereign over itself? Is the foolish boast, " I alone am king of me," converted into sound sense, by being applied to a state or federal government? Our governments must, if they are sovereigns, have the people, or only themselves for subjects. To avoid a collision with the sovereignty of the people; to find subjects for the sovereignty of a government; and to avoid the absurdity of a sovereignty without subjects ; it has been conceived, that some of our political departments are sovereigns over others, and one over all. This anomalous sovereignty, whilst it pretends to respect, directly assails the sovereignty of the people. All our political departments hold their power under this authority, and not under the authority of the government. But this new species of sovereignty proposes to take away all its subjects from the sovereignty of the people, and reduce it to the state of a king whose sovereignty was admitted, but who had no subjects. The pope of Rome manages this affair admirably. When he wishes to get a troublesome bishop out of his way, whom he fears publickly to disgrace, he transfers him to a cure of souls in foreign parts, where there are no souls to cure; still leaving to him the title of bishop. So if congress have any sovereignty over the political departments called states, the sovereignty of the people would lose a great portion of its cure of souls, although congress should politely leave them their title.

Our state constitutions confer upon a state majority, a power over every department of government, either directly by election, or by an influence over elective departments, entrusted with appointments. In this elemental basis, we discern clearly a positive conventional power, designed to exercise and to retain the sovereignty of the people, or the right of self-government; and we as clearly discover in the governments themselves, the subjects over which this conventional power was to be exercised. The federal constitution established three conventional powers over the federal government, lodging one in the majority of the people of each state; another in the state governments, comprised in the appointment of federal senators; and a third in the state governments also, comprised in a mode of amending the federal constitution. A conventional sovereignty being thus retained by the people over the state governments, and by the people and the state governments also, over the federal government, neither of these governments can legitimately acquire any species of sovereignty at all, because it would be contrary to the conventional sovereignty actually established. The positive supervising powers bestowed by the compact of the union, upon the state governments, over the whole federal government, flatly contradicts the idea, that the same compact designed constructively to bestow a supervising power upon congress, a department only of the federal government, over the state governments.

The divinity of sovereignty, and the natural right of self-government, are therefore really the competitors for our preference. As the latter has been evidently selected as the basis of our conventional associations, the former is the only foundation upon which any of our governments can establish a right to sovereignty. Before the American revolution, the natural right of self-government was never plainly asserted, nor practically enforced; nor was it previously discovered, that a sovereign power in any government, whether regal or republican, was inconsistent with this right, and destructive of its value. Then the divine sovereignty claimed by governments of every form, was completely exploded or reclaimed by the natural or divine right of self-government, not to be again surrendered, but to be retained and employed in creating and controling governments, considered as trustees invested with limited functions, and not as sovereigns possessing powers derived from that source of despotism.

The difference between the right of self-government, and the sovereignty of governments, is very material. Under one principle the people bestow limited powers; under the other, they receive limited franchises. The sovereigns of England sparingly and partially bestowed rights upon the people, and retained all the powers they did not surrender. Here the people or the states retain all the powers they have not bestowed. It would be as absurd in the one case as in the other, to infer from limited grants, a transfer of the sovereignty itself. Whenever such inferences were made, the king was substantially deposed, until the inference itself was exploded; and similar inferences will in like manner depose the sovereignty of the people here.

In the hurry of a revolution, before this subject had been well considered, and in imitation of the English practice of receiving franchises from kings, a bill of rights was annexed to several of the state constitutions; but it was soon discovered, that this was both superfluous and dangerous; superfluous, as according to the right of self-government, powers not bestowed, remained with the people; dangerous, as it seemed to imply that the people, as in England, derived their rights from the government. In England, residuary rights not granted, remained with the government, and therefore it was important to the people to extend such grants as far as possible; here, such ungranted rights remain also with the grantors, but these are the people. This distinction put an end to the custom of annexing a bill of rights to state constitutions, and caused a proposition of the kind to be rejected by the sages, statesmen, and patriots, who framed the constitution of the United States. It can only be correct upon the ground, that neither the state nor federal governments received any powers except as trustees, or specified ; and of course it was thought that the term " sovereignty," and its coadjutors "supremacy and prerogative" were inapplicable to our governments, and incapable of defeating the reason, upon which a bill of rights was rejected. Otherwise, this rejection must be considered as a stratagem (for they cannot be charged with a want of knowledge,) invented by a considerable number of our wisest and best men to enslave their country.

The patience of the reader is solicited, whilst I am endeavouring to establish the principles by which we ought to be guided in construing our constitutions. Unless this is done before we enter into that intricate field, as the soundest minds cannot suddenly and intuitively understand new and intricate questions, they will never be understood at all ; nor construction confined within any range. To prove that the right of self-government, or sovereignty, if the right should be so called, resides in the people, may be thought a waste of time, as it is generally admitted ; but in my view it seemed necessary to consider the point, both to sustain the arguments to be extracted from it as I proceed ; and because an inattention to its consequences has, I think, caused several unpremeditated deviations from that loyalty to this primary principle of our whole political system, which our governments both feel and profess.

SECTION 4.

THE UNION.

Who made it? "We, the people of the United States." But who were they? The associated inhabitants of each state, or the unassociated inhabitants of all the states. This question is an exposition, either of the ignorance or the design of construction. If there is no difficulty in answering it, construction ought to be laughed at for playing the fool; but if it gives the wrong answer, as supposing it to furnish contrary inferences to the right one, it ought to be suspected of playing the knave. At least an attempt to construe away a fact, known to every body, is a very fine specimen of its character when aiming at an accession of power. It has been imagined, that by considering the union as the act of the people, in their natural, and not in their political associated capacity, some aspect of consolidation might be shed over the country, and that the federal government might thereby acquire more power. But I cannot discern that the construction of the constitution will be affected in the smallest degree, by deducing it from either source, provided a sound authority is allowed to the source selected. Every stipulation, sentence, word and letter; and every donation, reservation, division and restriction, will be exactly the same, whichever is preferred. A man, having two titles, may distinguish himself by which he pleases, in making a contract; and whichever he uses, he remains himself. So the people having two titles or capacities, one arising from an existing association, the other from the natural right of self-government, may enter into a compact under either, but are themselves still; and their acts are equally obligatory, whichever they may select. Politicians may therefore indulge their taste in deducing the constitution of the union from either, but whichever they may fancy, no sound ground will thence result for their differing in the construction of it.

Nevertheless, to take away the pretext, however unsubstantial, for a different construction of the constitution, on account of the capacity or title under which the people acted in its establishment, it is material to ascertain the meaning of the phrase " we the people of the United States ;" towards which, let us run over most of the state constitutions.

New Hampshire. " The people of this state have *the sole and exclusive* right of governing themselves as a free, *sovereign* and independent *state.* Every subject of this *state.* In the government of this *state.* The people inhabiting the territory formerly called the province of New Hampshire, do hereby solemnly and *mutually agree with each other* to form themselves into a free, *sovereign* and independent *body politick or state.* That the *state may be equally represented.* I do swear that I will bear faith and true *allegiance to the state* of New Hampshire."

Massachusetts. " The body politick is formed by voluntary *association of individuals.* The people of this commonwealth have the sole right of governing themselves as a free, *sovereign* and independent *state.* The people do hereby *mutually agree with each other,* to form themselves into a free, *sovereign* and independent body politick *or state.*"

New York. " This convention, in the name and by the authority of the good *people of this state.* The legislature of this *state.* No members of this *state* shall be disfranchised. Delegates to represent this *state* in the general congress of the *United States.* Be it enacted by the people of the *state.*"

Pennsylvania. " *We the people* of the commonwealth of Pennsylvania ordain. The legislature of a free *state.* All government originates from the people and is founded in compact only."

Delaware. " The people of this *state.* The government shall be called the Delaware *state.* The legislature of this *state.* The general assembly of this *state.* There shall be no establishment of any one religious sect in this *state.*"

Maryland. " The *people of this state* ought to have the sole and exclusive right of regulating the *internal government* thereof. The *legislature of this state.* The delegates to congress from this *state* shall be chosen by joint ballot of both houses of assembly. I will be faithful and bear true allegiance to the *state.*"

Virginia. "All power is derived from the people. Magistrates are their trustees or servants. A well regulated militia is the proper defence of a *free state.*"

North Carolina. "The *people of this state* have the sole and exclusive right of regulating the *internal government* thereof. Monopolies are contrary to the genius of a free *state.* All commissions shall run in the name of the *state* of North Carolina. The legislature of this *state.* The constitution of this *state.*"

South Carolina. "The legislative authority of this *state.* The several election districts in this *state* shall elect. The style of process shall be " The *state* of South Carolina, and conclude against the peace and dignity of the *state.*" I swear to preserve the constitution of this *state* and of the *United States.*"

Georgia. "Members of the legislature shall swear to promote the good of the *state,* to bear true allegiance to the same, and to observe the constitution. To make laws necessary for the good of the *state.* Citizens and inhabitants of this *state.*"

Vermont. "The people are the sole source of power. They have the exclusive right of *internal government.* All officers of government are their servants. Legislative and executive business of this *state.* The people have a right to exact from their legislators and magistrates the good government of the *state.* The legislature of a free and *sovereign state.* Shall be entitled to all the privileges of a freeman of this *state.* Every officer shall swear to be faithful to the *state* of Vermont, and to do nothing injurious to the constitution or *government* thereof."

Without further quotations, let us demonstrate the force of these, extracted from a majority of the state constitutions, to fix the meaning of the term " state" according to the publick judgment, by substituting the word " government" for it. They would then read as follows."

" The people of this *government* have the sole and exclusive " right of governing themselves as a free, *sovereign* and inde- " pendent *government.*"

" In the government of this *government.*"

" That the *government* may be equally represented."

" The people of this *government* ought to have the sole and " exclusive right of regulating the *internal government thereof.*"

" The legislature of this *government.*"

" I will be faithful and bear true allegiance to the *government.*"

" The several election districts in this *government* shall elect."

" Members of the legislature shall swear to promote the good " of the *government* and to make laws for the good of the *go-* " *vernment.*"

" Citizens and inhabitants of this *government.*"

" The people have a right to exact from their legislators and " magistrates the good government of the *government.*"

" Commissions shall be in the name of the freemen of the *go-* " *vernment.*"

It would be an incivility to the reader, to subjoin to these quotations, many arguments, to prove, that the term " state" is not in any one instance used in reference to all the people of the United States, either as composing a single state, or as being about to compose a single state. Used geographically, it refers to state territory ; used politically, it refers to the inhabitants of this territory, united by mutual consent into a civil society. The sovereignty of this association, the allegiance due to it, and its right to internal government, are all positively asserted. The terms " state and government" far from being synonimous, are used to convey different ideas ; and the latter is never recognised as possessing any species of sovereignty.

It next behooves us to consider whether the term " states" has changed its meaning, by being transplanted from its original nursery, into the constitution of the United States ; and is there used to designate all the inhabitants of the United States, as constituting one great state ; or whether it is recognised in the same sense in which it had been previously used by most or all of the state constitutions.

The plural " states" rejects the idea, that the people of all the states considered themselves as one state. The word " united" is an averment of pre-existing social compacts, called states ; and these consisted of the people of each separate state. It admits the existence of political societies able to contract with each other, and who had previously contracted. And the

words " more perfect union" far from implying that the old
parties to the old union were superseded by new parties, evidently mean, that these same old parties were about to amend
their old union.

But the parties, though recognised as being the same, were
not strictly so. The authority of the people of each state is
resorted to in the last union, in preference to that of the government of each state, by which the old confederation was
formed. This circumstance by no means weakens the force of
the last observation, because the recognition of existing political parties able to contract, remains the same. The states, in
referring to the old union, only admit themselves to have been
bound by their governments, as they possessed the right of
making treaties. But as the state governments were the parties to the first confederation, and as such, had a mutual right
to destroy that treaty, this danger suggests another reason for
the style and principles of the new union. Among its improvements, that by which it is chiefly made " more perfect," was
the substitution of the authority of " the people of the United
States" for that of the governments of the United States; not
with an intention of excluding from the new union the idea of
a compact between the states, but of placing that compact
upon better ground, than that upon which it previously rested.

The term " union" has never been applied to describe a
government, established by the consent of individuals; nor do
any of our state constitutions use it in that sense. They
speak indeed of individuals " uniting" to form a government,
not to form a union; and I do not recollect that a single compact between individuals for the establishment of a government, has ever been called a union; though a multitude of
cases exist, in which that name has been given to agreements
between independent states. If therefore this term comprised
the whole evidence, to prove that our union was the act of distinct bodies politick, composed of the people within different
geographical boundaries, and not of a number of people, en-
circled by one line, without any such discrimination, it would
be sufficient.

But the constitution itself furnishes the plainest correspondent evidence, in its origin, establishment and terms. The
members of the convention which formed it, were chosen by

states, and voted by states, without any regard to the number of people in each state. It was adopted by thirteen votes, without respecting the same principle. Now what was represented by these voters; the territory of each state, or the people of each state? The terms " United States" must refer to one or the other. If to the former, then the territories of each state entered into a compact " to form a more perfect " union, establish justice, insure domestick tranquillity, provide " for the common defence, promote the general welfare, and " secure the blessings of liberty to *ourselves* and our *posterity.*" *The posterity of territories.* If to the latter, it was the people of each state, who by compact in their political capacity, by giving one vote each, formed the union.

The concords with this opinion present themselves at every step, throughout the compact.

The house of representatives are to be chosen by the people of the *several states,* not by the people comprised within the territories of all. The right of choice is confined to the electors of the most numerous branch of the *state legislatures.* Thus the right of suffrage is placed upon different grounds in different states. Had the constitution of the United States been the act of all the people inhabiting the territory of the United States, this right would have been made uniform; but being the act of the people of each state, in their existing political capacity, the right of suffrage of course remained as it had been settled by each in forming its society.

Each state may elect these representatives by a general ticket, as some have done ; and however they may have districted themselves by their own act for their own reasons, the recognizance of state individuality by the constitution is as strong, as if they had not done so. The modes of choosing both the president and senate, coincide also with the opinion, that the constitution considered the union as the act of bodies politick called states ; and not as the act of a consolidated nature ; and it seems to have settled its own construction, by providing in the case of no election of a president by electors, that he shall be chosen by the house of representatives, " the votes to be taken by states, the representation from *each state having one vote.*"

As the great political departments of the federal government, legislative and executive, emanated from the societies called states, so they are made dependant upon them, in the mode prescribed for amending the constitution of the union; because the authors had the right of altering their own work. Had this constitution originated from, or been made by the people inhabiting the territories of the whole union, its amendment would have remained to them, as the amendment of the state constitutions belongs to the people of a state. But as such a body of associated people, did not exist, the amendment of the union is left in the hands of the existing bodies politick, to which, as its authors, it obviously belonged. No majority in congress can either call a convention, or amend the constitution; but the legislatures of two-thirds of the states may compel congress to call one, and those of three-fourths, may amend it. Thus a supremacy of the states, not only over congress, but over the whole constitution, is twice acknowledged; first, by their power over the legislative and executive departments instituted for executing the union; and secondly, by their power over the union itself. I cannot conceive that the constitution could have contained any thing more hostile to the doctrine " that the sovereignty or supremacy over the govern-
" ment of the union, rested in the people of the United States,
" not in their political, but natural capacity." It clearly discloses an opinion, that there were no such people, politically speaking; nor can I discern a vestige of the people inhabiting the territories of the United States, having ever formed themselves, or attempted to form themselves, into any political society or civil government. By this new doctrine, however, the checks provided to controul the powers of the government of the union are ingeniously evaded. It asserts, that the government of the union is responsible to the sovereignty of the people residing throughout the union, and not to the sovereignty of the people residing in each state. Now as an effective sovereignty of the people can only result from their having constituted themselves into a civil society, and the first people having never done so, an acknowledgment of a sovereignty which does not exist, only annuls that which does; and escapes altogether from any species of loyalty to this superior authority. It brings us back to the old ground of a tacit compact between governments

and subjects. The people of each state invested their government with limited powers. They have also established a government of the union with powers infinitely more limited, than those originally bestowed on the state governments. But if a tacit social compact between this last government, and the people individually of all the states, should be admitted, all these specifications would be abolished ; because, as it is unwritten, the government of the union might construe it as was most convenient to itself, as all governments have done, which have condescended to acknowledge implied obligations only. The only difference between the Europeans and ourselves would be, that though some of their governments hardly allow of this silent social compact, none acknowledge the sovereignty of the people ; whereas here this sovereignty would be denied, where it operatively exists, and acknowledged, where it does not exist at all ; so that we should still possess over the government of the union, all the advantages generally reaped from " we are, gentlemen, your most obedient servants," whilst the story of Saturn would be gradually reversed.

The eleventh amendment prohibits a *construction* by which the rights retained by the people shall *be denied or disparaged ;* and the twelfth " reserves *to the states respectively or to the people* the powers .not delegated to *the United States,* nor prohibited *to the states.*" The precision of these expressions is happily contrived to defeat a construction, by which the origin of the union, or the sovereignty of the states, could be rendered at all doubtful. " Powers are reserved to the *people.*" " The people," says Johnson, are " those who compose a community." In a political instrument, the term *exclusively* possesses a collective, inclusive, and social sense, and is never used to describe a number of men in a state of nature. A people is a collective being. No people or community has ever been composed in the United States, except by the inhabitants of each state, associating distinctly from every other state, by their own separate consent. Thus a people in each state was constituted, and these separate communities confederated, first by the instrumentality of their separate governments, and secondly by the separate authority of the people composing each state. Common consent is necessary to constitute a people, and no such consent, expressly or impliedly, can be shewn, by which all the inhabitants of the United States have ever constituted themselves into one people. This could not have been effected without destroying every people constituted within each state, as one political being called a people cannot exist within another.

The rights of a people are indivisible; and if a great people be compounded of several smaller nations, as it inherently possesses the right of self-government, it must absorb the same right of self-government in its component parts; just as the rights of individuals are absorbed by the communities into which they constitute themselves. Therefore had a people been constituted, by melting down the little nations into one great nation, those little nations must have lost the right of self-government, because they would no longer have been a people. As it was never imagined, that the individuals inhabiting all the states had constituted themselves into one people, so there has never appeared from this imaginary body politick, the least attempt towards claiming or exercising the right of self-government; nor is the government of the union subjected to its controul or modification. Not a single one of the United States would have consented to have dissolved its people, to have reunited them into one great people, and to have received state governments or unrestricted legislation from this great people, so ignorant of local circumstances, and so different in local habits. This reasoning would I think have been sufficient to ascertain the people by whom the constitution was made, had it contained no internal evidence of the sense in which it uses that term. But if the phrase "we the people of the United States" refers to the people of each state, the argument is superfluous, and the decision of the constitution itself, decisive.

The powers reserved are those "not delegated by the constitution." They could only be *reserved* by those who possessed them. They were not powers possessed by a consolidated people of all the states, but by a distinct people of each state; and as those who reserved were those who delegated, it follows, either that the reservation was to a consolidated people of all the states, or that the delegation of powers flowed from the people of the separate states. Perhaps the interpolation of a grantor and reserver of powers into the constitution, who had nothing either to grant or to reserve, may have arisen from an erroneous construction of the word " or." If the remark just made is correct, consistency decides its true meaning. "Are reserved to the states respectively *or* to the people." This word is used either to couple synonymes, or to denote opposition. The words " states and people" had the same, and also a different meaning: The same, as an associated people constituted a state; and a different meaning, from the right of self-government attached to mankind. But another construction seems to me to be the true one. " Or" is used merely to conjoin two words considered as completely synonymous; and the latter is introduced as an expletive of the former, lest it should be interpreted to mean " governments." The word " states" had been so often used in the constitution, that it was necessary to fix its meaning; and this amendment was intended to remove the suspicion of a tendency in the constitution towards consolidation, with which it had been charged previously to its adoption; by defining " states and people" as words synonymously used, effectually to defeat the pretence, that the term " people" meant the people of all the states, instead of the people, "*respectively*" of each state. A construction which supposes that all the inhabitants of all the states, and not the people of each state, were meant, would produce consequences which never could have been contemplated. The reservation would have been in favour of two incongruous objects, and therefore both could not reap its benefits. Being in the disjunctive, it might have been fulfilled by acknowledging the right of either, although the other should get nothing. By selecting the inhabitants of all the states in one mass, as the assignee of the reserved powers, the government of the union might extend their own powers; since there could be no loss, in conceding powers to those who could neither receive, exercise, nor preserve them.

In one other view, highly gratifying, these two amendments correspond with the construction I contend for. Several previous amendments had stipulated for personal or individual rights, as the government of the union was invested with a limited power of acting upon persons; these stipulate for political conventional rights. But different modes are pursued. By the first, certain specified aggressions are forbidden; by the second, all the rights and powers not delegated are reserved. The first mode is imperfect, as the specified aggressions may be avoided, and yet oppression might be practised in other forms. By the second, specification is transferred to the government of the union; and the states, instead of being the grantees of limited rights, which might have been an acknowledgment of subordination, are the grantors of limited powers; and retain a supremacy which might otherwise have been tacitly conceded, as has been often done by the acceptance of franchises from monarchs or other sovereigns. Thus the powers reserved are only exposed to specified deductions, whilst those delegated are limited, with an injunction that the enumeration of certain rights shall not be construed to disparage those retained though not specified, by not having been parted with. The states, instead of receiving, bestowed powers; and in confirmation of their authority, reserved every right they had not conceded, whether it is particularly enumerated, or tacitly retained. Among the former, are certain modes by which they can amend the constitution; among the latter, is the original right by which they created it.

When we have discovered who made a treaty, we have also discovered where the right of construction resides. Mr. Jefferson, Mr. Pinkney, Mr. Marshall, and Mr. Gerry, in their negotiations with revolutionary France, have furnished us with an admirable treatise, both to fix the residence of the right, and to display the wantonness of construction, assumed without right. Presidents Washington and Adams, all the successive members of the cabinet and congress itself, concurred in the principles advanced by these gentlemen. They prove, that an exclusive right of construction in one party, is a degradation of the other to a state of inferiority and dependance. Their arguments might be applied with great force in many views to our subject. If the states made the union, they demonstrate, that the same consent, necessary to create, is necessary to construe. Whereever the creating consent resided, there we are directed to look for the construing consent. It would be a much grosser violation of their principles, for no party to a treaty to usurp an exclusive right of construing it, than for one party to do so. As neither the executive, legislative nor judicial departments of the state or federal governments have ever consented to the union, no one of these departments can have an exclusive right of construing it. But if they did consent, and by that consent are parties, still the right is mutual. And if they are all to be considered as the co-ordinate departments or creatures of "the people of the United States," they derive a mutual right of construction, from the mutual right possessed by the states which they represent. Suppose our legislative and judicial departments had fixed their own rights by a treaty between themselves, in the words of the general or state constitutions; would not each have possessed an unsubservient right of construction? If this right would be mutual in the case supposed, what hinders it from being also mutual, if these departments are created by an authority superior to both, and invested with distinct and limited agencies. Each trustee is subject to the supervision of his employer, and neither liable to a usurpation of another, any more than several co-ordinate ambassadors, would be to a claim of one to prescribe the duties of the rest, and regulate their consciences. It is easiest for an exclusive power of construction, where the limits of respective territories are hardest to define, to make conquests which will destroy balances, and break down restrictions; and therefore its interdiction in such cases is more necessary, than in others.

I conclude this section with a quotation from the Federalist. " The assent and ratification of the people, not as individuals " composing one entire nation, but as composing the distinct " and independent states to which they belong, are the sources " of the constitution. It is therefore not a national, but a fede- " ral compact."(a)

(a) Fed. 206. M. The quotations from the Federalist are taken from the edition of 1817, which designates the writer of each essay ; and I have added the letters M. or H. to inform the reader which are cited from Mr. Madison, and which from Mr. Hamilton.

SECTION 5.

DIVISION AND LIMITATION OF POWER.

In this and the following section, I shall endeavour to establish principles vitally important to our system of government, and however the subject may be handled, particularly worthy of the publick consideration.

Human societies were originally constituted with a view to the interest of one or a few, and governments were consequently founded in the simple principle of subordination. They were splendid statues, the people were pedestals, and a succession of convulsions, occasioned by a gas too sublimated or too heavy, constantly overturned, only to set them up again. Monarchy, aristocracy, and democracy succeeded each other; but all being founded in the principle of subordination to unlimited power, it ran like the blood of the Stuarts through the whole family, and made each individual a scourge to mankind. As knowledge advanced, philosophers sought for alleviations of a condition so unhappy; and having only seen those three forms of government, called them natural principles, and expected a remedy for the defects of each, from a mixture of all. It was seen and admitted, that the formation of a government, after the model of an army, by a series of subordination from a king to a constable, from a general to a corporal, made tyrants and slaves; and checks and balances were contrived to prevent both consequences, by poizing the three supposed natural principles against each other, fraught with co-ordinate, distinct and independent powers. Thus the principle of a necessary series of subordination was exploded; but as the discovery was new, and as the dogma " that monarchy, aristocracy, and democracy comprised all the ingredients of government" was still believed; it was imperfectly cultivated. Hence absolute sovereignty continued to be assigned to mixed governments, and absolute subordination to the people. This first effort of political improvement was however recommended by a considerable portion of practical success. The checks, collisions and balances, though imperfectly contrived, produced effects, which exalted and invigorated several nations, above those which had neglected similar political modifications. But still the error of retaining absolute power in the government, and inflicting absolute submission on the people, caused no small degree of oppression, which excited mankind to search for a better remedy. Locke and others at length discovered, that sovereignty in governments and passive obedience in nations, far from being natural or necessary principles for civil societies, were arbitrary and pernicious notions, capable of being supplanted by opinions more natural ; and that civil government, constructed upon different principles, and subjected to responsibility and control, might be made more productive of national happiness. But the natural right of self-government, and the consequent rights of dividing and limiting power, might have slept forever in theory, except for the American revolution ; which seems to have been designed by Providence for the great purpose of demonstrating its practicability and effects. We seem to have been propelled by necessity and commanded by fate, to stride beyond the principles of absolute sovereignty in a government, and absolute subordination in the people ; and beyond the ineffectual project of mixing monarchy, aristocracy, and democracy together ; quite up to the sound political doctrines of limitation, restriction, and division of power. Far from allowing sovereignty to governments, or confiding our rights to a balance between arbitrary and artificial political principles, we were obliged to feel and to act upon the genuine and natural principle of self-government ; to extract from it the obvious truths " that sovereignty resided in the people, and that magistrates were consequently their trustees," and to vindicate these rights by creating co-ordinate and collateral political departments invested with limited powers instead of that absolute power, so highly pernicious in the hands of any one of the three ancient principles, and so far from being made harmless by their mixture. Thus we constituted a wide difference between our policy and that of the English ; in its origin ; in expelling from it two of their principles entirely ; in rejecting the balances for the better security of co-ordinate departments ; and in with-holding from these departments, either singly or united, the rights of sovereignty, as exercised by the English government. The first division of power we have established according to this new policy, consists of the limited rights delegated by the people to their governments or trustees; and of all the residue of the attributes of sovereignty, retained, as not having been delegated by the people. Under the English form of government, this division, with its concomitant limitations, is utterly unknown.

Our second division of power, also unknown to the English system, is that between the governments of the states, and the government of the union. Previously to our revolutionary war, the colonies had been thoroughly lectured upon the subjects of sovereignty, supremacy, and a division of powers. The English parliament contended, that its sovereignty or supremacy included all means necessary or convenient, in its own opinion, to effect its ends. The colonies admitted its supremacy in making war and peace, and in regulating commerce; but denied that this admission included a concession of means, subversive of their own right of internal or local government; as to which they claimed a supremacy for themselves. The parliament contended, that the right of making war, conceded by the colonies, implied a right of using all the means necessary for obtaining success; such as raising a revenue, appointing collectors, raising troops, quartering them upon the colonies, and many other internal laws; and that the right of regulating commerce, also involved a right of imposing duties, and establishing custom houses for their collection; arguing, that it would be absurd to allow powers, and with-hold any means necessary or proper to carry them into execution. The colonies replied, that it would be more absurd to limit powers, and yet concede unlimited means for their execution, by which the internal supremacy, upon which their liberty and happiness depended, though nominally allowed, would be effectually destroyed : That the terms " sovereignty or supremacy," however applicable to the parliament, were applicable also to the colonial governments, as to internal powers : That the necessity of controuling supreme, sovereign or absolute power, in governments, had been proved by experience, particularly in England ; where magna charta, the petition of right, and many declaratory laws, had limited its means to a great extent: and that however the means contended for by the parliament, might be useful for carrying on war or regulating commerce; yet, that a restriction of those means would be still more useful, because it was necessary for the preservation of their liberties. The parliament closed the debate, by declaring that it had a right to legislate over the colonies in all cases whatsoever; and denying the distinction between internal and external legislation, imposed some trifling taxes of the former character, as an entering wedge into the colonial claim of local supremacy, to be gradually driven up to the head. In that on tea, the ingenuity was used of attempting to establish a ruinous precedent, by conferring a pecuniary favour, in diminishing the price of the article in favour of the colonies. But the colonies, too wary to be caught by a gilded hook, detected, resisted and defeated the artifice.

The controversy lasted for many years. It drew forth the talents of the ablest writers on both sides the question; and those of the great Doctor Johnson were exerted to the utmost, in favour of the passive obedience due to sovereignty or supremacy. All the treasures of wisdom, and all the sensibilities of interest, united to attract the attention of both countries to the subject. There never was one more ably discussed, or better understood. And no national interpretation of the terms used in the debate could possibly be more complete. Their right to local supremacy and internal legislation, was asserted by every colony, ably defended by many individuals, and conclusively proved by our early congresses composed of a rare body of men. This thorough investigation produced a conviction, never I hope to be eradicated, which dictated our political system, prescribed the terms both of the first and second union, and defined the nature of the division of powers between the state governments, and the government of the union.

I have never met with but one respectable authority among our own writers, by which the correctness of the colonial principles has been questioned; and this is only comprised in a relation of facts, without being stampt by the concurrence of the author. In Marshall's life of Washington, vol. ii. 71 and 72, it is said, " that many of the best informed men in Massa-" chusetts, had perhaps adopted the opinion of the parliamen-" tary right of internal government over the colonies, that the " English statute book furnishes many instances of its exercise;

" that in no case recollected was their authority openly contro-
" verted ; and that the general court of Massachusetts on a late
" occasion, explicitly recognized the same principle." These
historical facts are undoubtedly designed to warn us of the
stealth with which oppression approaches, and the enormities
towards which precedents travel ; that they ought not to be sanctified by time nor repetition ; and that the best informed men
may be led by them into the most obvious errors ; for the same
book abounds with eulogies upon those who denied this doctrine ;
and concurs, when the author expresses his own opinion, in the
propriety of resisting it. The essays of president Adams, written in 1774 and 1775, fully explain how it happened, that many
of the best informed men in Boston took a side, opposite to that
which was embraced by almost all the philosophers of Europe,
who annexed a degree of veneration to the characters of our
own patriots, in which even other nations participate. These
essays, lately published, are replete with profound observations
upon the principles we are considering.

It is sufficient however for my argument, if the people of the
colonies believed in the doctrines which they asserted, bled for
and established ; because the influence of opinions thus rivetted,
upon their political measures, will be weighed by impartiality
and admitted by candour. During, and soon after a war, firmly waged for eight years, to resist a right to legislate for them
locally and internally, inferred from parliamentary sovereignty
or supremacy, the colonies or states constructed two unions, and
established in both a division of power, bearing a strong similitude to that upon which they were willing to have continued
their union with England ; yielding to her the regulation of war,
peace and commerce, and retaining for themselves local and
internal legislation. The first " union between the United
States of America for *their common defence and general welfare*" begins where the second ends. The first " retains the
*sovereignty and rights to the states not delegated to the United
States.*" The second " *reserves to the states the powers not
delegated to the United States.*" The first confers upon congress, almost all the powers of importance bestowed by the
second, except that of regulating commerce ; and among them
the power of establishing a post office. The second only extends the means for executing the same powers, by bestowing

on congress a limited power of taxation; but these means were by neither intended to supersede nor defeat those ends retained or reserved by both. By the first, *unlimited requisitions* to meet " the charges of war and all other expenses for the *common defence and general welfare*" were to be made by congress upon the states. By the second, congress are empowered to lay taxes under certain restrictions "*to provide for the common defence and general welfare.*" But a sovereign and absolute right to dispose of these requisitions or taxes without any restriction is not given to congress by either. The general terms used in both are almost literally the same; and therefore they must have been used in both, under the same impression of their import and effect. By connecting in one view the controversy with England, the first, and the second union; the vindication of colonial, local and internal government by a long war, and innumerable publick acts; the retention of it by the first union; its reservation by the last; and the accommodation proposed with England on the terms of allowing to the parliament the powers of war, peace, and regulating commerce, given to congress; it is impossible not to discern a series of testimony, demonstrating a strict subserviency of each distinct item to the primary end, of establishing a division of power, by which an independent internal government should be secured, first to the colonies, and subsequently to the states. Nor can a better expositor of particular words and phrases, than this primary end, be discovered.

In fact, the question between England and the colonies was far more favourable to the former, than that which has arisen between congress and the states. The colonial governments were chartered bodies politick, and the acceptance of these charters was an acknowledgment of a supremacy in the grantor. As the English king in granting these charters acted as the agent of the English policy, he had no better right to dismember the parliamentary sovereignty by charters, than congress have to dismember the state sovereignty by the same instruments. Therefore these charters could not contract the parliamentary supremacy of legislation. But they contained no restriction of it, nor any reservations or donations to the colonies of *exclusive* internal legislation. Now, the state governments are not chartered by congress, and instead of a tacit acknowledgment of a

supremacy in that body, or in any other department of the government of the union, the states have expressly asserted and
retained their *respective* internal sovereignties. The case is
yet stronger against the claim on behalf of congress. The government of the union is chartered by the states. Had the
colonies, under their charters from the king of England, claimed
a supremacy over the parliament, their pretension would have
been equivalent to a claim of supremacy by the government of
the union over the states. The grant of a charter implies a
retention of every power not granted, just as a deed of gift or
sale for a portion of an estate leaves unimpaired the title of the
owner to the portion he does not convey away. A conveyance
of part does not entitle the grantee to take more, or the whole
of the residue if he pleases. The people were the true owners
of a great fee simple estate. They have granted one portion of
it to the state governments, another to the government of the
union, and retained the residue for themselves. The grants
were in trust for their benefit; and created the division of power
between the government of the union, and the state governments, which we are contemplating. Now, if one trustee can
by construction or by force, despoil the other of his portion, he
will become so rich, as to be able to betray his trust, and deprive the owner of the part of his own estate retained. To
allow, that a claim of sovereignty or supremacy in the government of the union, over the state governments, stood on as
strong ground, as the same claim of the English parliament
over the colonies, would be a concession more favourable than
the fact; and, if neither the opinions of several well informed
men in Massachusetts, nor the continued endeavours of the
parliament to sustain the more plausible pretension, could
suffice to obliterate the necessity of a division of power for the
preservation of liberty, between the English and colonial governments, able to resist the assaults of encroachment; neither
opinions nor precedents ought to unsettle the division of power
between the state and federal governments, dictated by the
same motive. Many of the arguments which convinced the
colonies of the necessity for such a division in relation to England, apply forcibly to the government of the union; and a
supremacy at London or at Washington, however more direful
to liberty at one place, would not be divested of terrors at the

other. The objections arising from distance, though the colonies should be represented in the parliament, were forcibly urged; and the experience of Ireland has subsequently furnished a proof of their propriety. From the same source, a number of weighty arguments may be drawn by the reader, sufficient to prove, that the great extent of the United States will not admit both of a central supremacy, and of a free form of government; and that the preservation of liberty must depend on the division of power between the state and federal governments; or an accurate distinction between the powers bestowed and reserved.

Our system of civil policy, having established two divisions of power; that between the people and their governments, and that between the state governments and the government of the union; proceeds to avail itself of all the advantages which could be extracted from the English form of government. Had it set out from this point, I do not deny that it might have given some countenance to sundry constructions to which it has been exposed; but, if I am right in ascribing to it the two previous principles for which I have contended, they seem to be insurmountable obstacles to such inferences as the British system, controuled by no such obstacles, might supply. But though it has derived an intimation from this system, that the principle of dividing power is a good one, it is far from copying its checks and balances; and after having established the two great and operative divisions we have passed over, it proceeds to those of an inferior character, and continues to enforce the principle of division in a mode wholly new and entirely intrinsick. It rejects two of the English balances or divisions, and substitutes for them, an elective president and senate. It substitutes for the unsettled idea of the balances, a co-ordination of departments, a definition of the powers of each, and a subserviency of all to the power of the people. And it advances judicial power to an equivalency of independence, by an allotment of powers and duties conferred by the same constitutions, which prescribed the powers and duties of the other departments.

Our political philosophers surveyed the world of governments, not for the purpose of a servile imitation, but to collect, to compare and to weigh facts, in order to enrich their own by improvements; and by a more refined organization, to reap the benefits, unalloyed by the calamities of the models which they contemplated. Far from believing that man, whilst constantly advancing in his other attainments, had gotten to the end of his capacity in the science of government, and ought still to expect liberty in the lethargick lap of a political vis inertiæ; they saw that an extraordinary shock had aroused his faculties, and wisely seized upon a series of happy dispensations, to gather the moral blessings, which Providence seemed to have revealed.

The divisions, balances or limitations of power, in Greece, Italy, and England, had all been the result of civil wars, personal ambition, or domestick commotions; and therefore none had provided any visible restrictions for preventing, assuaging or deciding the hostilities which must forever ensue, between political departments invested with the right of controuling each other. Such hostilities between the people and senate of Rome, and among the king, lords and commons of England, had produced consequences which inculcated two truths; one, that a division of power so imperfectly delineated as to cause perpetual and violent collisions, was nevertheless greatly preferable to any form of government, founded in the most perfect series of subordination; the other, that these violent collisions were serious calamities, and seeds of frequent revolutions or settled despotisms. The object of our wise and good patriots, was to reap the benefits and avoid the evils arising from a division of power. By the declaration of independence, they solemnly stationed our social institutions upon solid ground, for the purpose of effecting both ends. It proclaims it to be " the right " of the *people* to alter, abolish and institute governments, as to " them shall seem most likely to effect their safety and happi- " ness." This right had been previously exercised by balanced orders. Their usurpation was thus subverted. A powerful supervisor and arbitrator, for moderating and deciding the controversies of political departments, was formed and recognized in the people; and a great defect of the old theory of the balances, in supposing there was none, removed. The same source of civil society furnished a specification of the rights and duties of each co-ordinate political or civil department, to which the theory of the balances was inadequate, as neither member of this theory could submit to another to ascertain its rights and powers, without being reduced to insignificance; and therefore the rights and powers under the balancing theory, were left to be distributed by perpetual contentions, secret frauds or open violence. But when this genuine authority for defining and limiting the rights and powers of political departments was found, the contentions between regal, aristocratical and demo-cratical orders ceased; and a new species of political subordi-nation, more perfect than any subsisting under the theory of balanced orders, succeeded. I ask the reader's attentive con-sideration of the doctrine I am about to advance, as the truth or error of many subsequent observations will depend upon it. Between balanced orders there is no supremacy and no subor-dination. The supremacy they possess is over the nation, and the subordination they inflict, is not upon each other, but upon the nation, and upon the inferior officers of government. Are our political departments, balanced orders; if so, one depart-ment cannot be subordinate to another, according to the English system. Indeed a supremacy of one check or balance, over that check or balance intended as a controul or abridgment of this one's power, would obviously defeat the check or balance designed to be substantial. By the authority of the right of self-government, we have with great deliberation established divi-sions of power, created political departments subordinate to the people, defined the functions of each, and prescribed to in-dividuals and the inferior officers of each, the obedience respec-tively due to these departments. The only supremacy bestowed on these departments, is over the persons and things specifi-cally subjected to the limited power of each; and the only su-bordination due to them, is from such persons and things. No supremacy is given to one department over another; and the sovereignty and its relative, subordination, contended for and admitted, as an indissoluble attribute to civil government, is established between the people and these departments; whilst good order is secured by the subordination of individuals and inferior officers, to the political departments to which they are severally subjected. Of this improved system for dividing and limiting power, we took the hint from the balances between monarchy, aristocracy and democracy, as established, not by a deliberative choice, but by violence; but whilst we adhered to the principle practised by this triumvirate for self-preservation, we applied it to the preservation of the general liberty, by creating co-ordinate and collateral political departments, with distinct powers, for the special design of making them mutual checks upon each other. For this end we have divided power between the people of each state and their governments; between the legislature, executive and judicature of the state governments; between the people of the United States and the government of the union; between the legislature, executive and judicature of the government of the union; and between the state governments and the government of the union. These divisions are surely as natural and practicable, as that between monarchy, democracy, and aristocracy. If a subordination of the king to the house of lords, or of the lords to the king, would destroy the intention of that division of power; a subordination of the government of the union to the governments of the states, or of the governments of the states to the government of the union, would also destroy the intention of this. The same idea applies with equal force to our other divisions of power, and proves, that an exchange of their mutual independency of each other, for a dependency and subordination upon one, would be contrary to the only principle, for which the balances and checks of kings, lords, and commons have been so much applauded. If two of these co-ordinate divisions of power were subordinate to the third, that system would be destroyed, because its essence, the checks and balances, would be no more. Should either of our co-ordinate divisions of power acquire a supremacy over another, the effect would be the same. Less than two centuries ago, the identical question we are now considering was debated with great pertinacity by the ablest writers in England, and was finally settled by a civil war. Filmer and Sydney espoused opposite sides. The former, with his co-adjutors, asserted the supremacy of the regal balance, and taught the Stuarts this principle, which lost the throne, and rendered their names detestable to posterity. Sydney became a martyr to the contrary faith. All the eulogies to the English system have been paid to their checks and balances; and all the liberty of the English nation, has been ascribed to the principle of dividing power. If, having more studiously laboured to avail ourselves of this principle, considered even in England as indispensable for the preservation of liberty, than any nation ever did; we have yet stupidly annihilated it, by investing one check or one balance with a supremacy over the rest, we had better go back to the English system, where it imperfectly exists, but in a degree to do some good, than to surrender it entirely. But if we construe our system of government as the English do theirs; that is, with an eye to the preservation of our checks and balances, as the only securities for a free government; its superior theory will secure to us more beneficial consequences, than they have ever experienced. A great defect of the English system is, that although in theory it professes to have created three co-ordinate departments of power, it has neglected to specify the rights of each with any precision; wherefore the triumvirate have had many violent contests to settle them; and these contests have only subsided in one mighty chaldron of corruption. But by ours, the powers of the several co-ordinate or balancing departments, far from having been left undefined to be scrambled for, are specified with such deliberative exactness, that each may very easily descry its own, unless it be blinded by avarice and ambition. Collisions are therefore likely to be more rare. But should they occur, our system has provided a safe referee and impartial judge, sufficient to prevent them from producing the aggravated consequences, which have been so often experienced in England for want of this powerful moderator. After having thus given practical effect, to the great principle of checking power by division, recommended by all sound politicians; constituting the boast of England and the envy of all other European nations; with an ingenuity and success, hitherto unexampled ; shall we imitate some whimsical artists, who after having invented a beautiful machine, throw it away?

Let us go back to the quotation from the declaration of independence, for the sake of remarking, that its assertion of the " right of the *people* to alter, abolish and institute governments" could only have a reference to the conventional or collective beings, under that denomination, then existing. These were a people of each state. Accordingly the people of each state executed the vindicated right, and no body thought of any other people. By virtue of this right, the people of each state established certain co-ordinate divisions of power, without investing one with a supremacy over the others; and by virtue of the same right, solemnly asserted in that sacred instrument, the same people uniting with each other, established other co-ordinate divisions of power, still excluding an investiture of one, with a supremacy over the others. If this last act, so similar to the first, left an unexpressed supremacy to be found by construction; the first is exposed to the same species of ingenuity for abolishing from our entire political system, every thing analogous to checks and balances : For, legislative, executive and judicial mutual independence, cannot in my view, be placed upon stronger ground, than the independence of the governments of the states and of the union upon each other.

Lest however some future Filmer may undertake to prove, that one of these departments may constitutionally assume a supremacy over the other, by the instrumentality of means to effect good ends ; as Charles the first did over the lords and commons, by resorting to ship money, as a convenient or necessary means, to effect an end highly beneficial to the English nation ; I shall, on account of my own deficiency in authority, conclude this section with a few quotations, leaving their application to the reader. Ramsay's history of the United States vol. ii. p. 167. " The rejection of British *sovereignty* therefore drew after it the necessity of fixing on some *other principle* of government."

P. 172. " The far-famed social compact between the people and their rulers, did not apply to the United States. The sovereignty was in the people. In their *sovereign capacity*, by their representatives, they agreed to forms of government for their own security, and deputed certain individuals as their agents, to serve them in publick stations, *agreeably to constitutions which they prescribed for their conduct.*"

P. 173. " It is hoped for the honour of human nature, that the result will prove the fallacy of those theories, which suppose that mankind are incapable of self-government."

P. 174. " Political evil will at least be prevented or restrained with as much certainty, by a proper *separation or combination* of power, as natural evil is lessened or prevented, by the application of the knowledge or ingenuity of man to domestick purposes.

" From history the citizens of the United States had been taught that the maxims, adopted by the rulers of the earth, that society was instituted for the sake of the governors, and that the interest of the many was to be postponed to the convenience of the privileged few, had filled the world with bloodshed and wickedness; while experience had proved, that it is the *invariable natural character of power, whether entrusted or assumed, to exceed the proper limits, and, if unrestrained, to divide the world into masters and slaves.* They therefore began upon the opposite maxims; that society was instituted, not for the governors but governed; that the interest of the few should in all cases give way to the interest of the many; and that *exclusive* and hereditary privileges were *useless and dangerous* institutions in society. With them the sovereignty of the people was more than a mere theory. The characteristick of that sovereignty was displayed by their authority in written constitutions."

P. 175. " It therefore became necessary to run the line of distinction between the *local legislatures,* and the assembly of the *States* in congress."

Federalist. p. 81. H. " The general government can have no temptation to *absorb the local authorities left with the states.* Commerce, finance, negociation and war, comprise all the objects of a love of power. All those things which are proper to be provided for by local legislation, can never be desirable cares of general jurisdiction. It is therefore improbable, that there should exist a disposition in the federal councils, *to usurp the powers with which they are connected.* But let it be admitted, for argument sake, that mere wantonness, and lust of domination, would be sufficient to beget that disposition; still it may be safely affirmed, that the sense of *the people of the several states would controul the indulgence of so extravagant an appetite.*"

P. 254. M. " The federal and state governments are in fact *but different agents and trustees of the people, instituted with different powers, and designed for different purposes.*"

P. 282. H. " In the compound republick of America, *the power surrendered by the people,* is first divided between two *distinct governments,* and the portion allotted to each subdivided among *distinct and separate departments.* Hence a double security arises to the rights of the people. The *different governments will controul each other,* at the same time that each will be controuled by itself."

P. 288. H. " The federal legislature will not only be restrained by its dependance on the people, but it will be moreover watched and *controuled* by the several *collateral* legislatures."

P. 302. H. " I am unable to conceive, that the state legislatures, which must feel so many motives to watch, and which possess so many means of counteracting the federal legislature, would fail either to detect or to defeat a conspiracy of the latter against the liberties of their constituents."

SECTION 6.

PROPERTY.

Blackstone has treated of "The rights of persons, and the rights of things;" but the rights of man include life, liberty and property, according to the prevalent fashion of thinking in the United States. The last right is the chief hinge upon which social happiness depends. It is therefore extremely important to ascertain, whether it is secured by the same principle with our other rights; and whether the security, if the same, ought to be equivalently efficacious; before we proceed to the contemplated examination of several constructions of our constitutions. The rights to life, liberty and property, are so intimately blended together, that neither can be lost in a state of society without all; or at least, neither can be impaired without wounding the others. Being indissolubly united, a principle which embraces either must embrace all; and by allowing it to constitute the only solid security for one, we admit it to be the only solid security of the rest. A sovereignty in governments, of every form, has universally claimed and exercised a despotick power over life, liberty and property. Whether enjoyed by a monarchy, aristocracy, democracy, or by a mixture of the three, it acknowledges no controul, and submits to no limitations. In England, this sovereignty has in many instances legislated death, banishment, and confiscation; and in many more, exercised a despotick power over property, by giving away the national wealth, not for the national benefit, but according to its own will, or to purchase adherents to sustain its own power. All this is a correct and legitimate consequence of the principle of a sovereignty in governments. Every thing within the scope of a sovereignty belongs to it; therefore the sovereignty of king, lords and commons in England, exercises an unlimited power over every thing, not only in the direct modes of cutting off heads, confiscating

property, and lavishing the national money upon themselves and
their dependants; but by the indirect modes of exclusive and
corporate privileges, for enabling some individuals to obtain the
property of others. To avoid such calamities, we have adopted
the policy of transferring this illimitable power called sovereignty, from the government to the people; and the present question
is, whether the transfer is partial or complete; whether our
governments still possess a sovereign power over our property,
like the English government; or whether they are only trustees
in respect to that, as they are in respect to our lives and liberties.

In deciding this question, our suffrages are solicited by two
distinct and opposite principles; the principle of a sovereignty in governments, with its boundless appendages; and the principle of divided, defined and limited powers, under the supervision and controul of the people. If we waver between them,
we cannot guide our policy by any fixed rules, nor pursue any
steady ends. If our accomplished men should halt between the
two opinions, sometimes leaning towards one, and then towards
the other; the people must rove in conjecture for representatives, be deprived of the means of judging as they wish by the
distractions of complicated professions, and may often catch a
tartar instead of a friend. If, like an archbishop Laud, leaning
sometimes towards the church of Rome, and at others towards
the church of England, politicians of high standing should
endeavour to find a medium between these two principles, infinitely more remote from each other than the two churches;
they may generate evils more calamitous than he did; and
prepare the nation for a revolution, by weakening its affection
for our present form of government. For my part, when I
contemplate on one hand, the justice, the mildness, the restraints upon arbitrary power, the subordination of individuals,
the security of property, and the social harmony, flowing from
the sovereignty of the people, and the division and limitation
of power by their authority; and on the other, the endless
catalogue of overwhelming evils which have flowed from a
sovereignty in governments; veneration and abhorrence seem
as instinctively to rush into my mind, as in viewing the most
lovely or the most hateful objects. Under such impressions,
my reason is wholly unable to conceive what advantage can

arise to mankind, from leaving property in bondage to governments; after other human rights have been released from the
same species of thraldom, by transferring sovereignty to nations,
and reducing governors to trustees. A constitution which
should secure life and liberty, but invest the government with
an absolute power over property, would only have the merit
of forming a society of naked people, divested of those appen·
dages upon which social happiness depends.

Pecuniary patronage, and the creation of corporations to
transfer property, are among the appendages of sovereignty,
because its power over property is unlimited and absolute ;
and mankind have undoubtedly suffered more injustice and
oppression, from the exercise of these two sovereign rights,
when sovereignty is lodged in governments, than from all the
rest. In the civilized world, property is the franklin for conducting the electrical stream, either of liberty or of slavery,
to invigorate or to degrade mankind. If therefore in exercising the right of self-government, and vindicating the sovereignty of the people, we have left a sovereign power over
property, in the hands either of the state governments or the
government of the union, all our work will be fruitless; because we shall have placed in the hands of power the precise
instrument, with which it can root out any restriction however
carefully planted. This error is the rock, upon which most
republican governments have split. Possessing a sovereign
power, that power included a right of disposing of and regulating both national and private property, by the will of the government; and the greater the number of individuals who
participate of this sovereign right, the more people there will
be whose avarice must be gratified at the public expense, and
by private oppression. It has been owing to this uniform consequence of investing republican governments with a sovereign
power over property, that nations have been constantly driven
to take refuge from a host of sovereigns, under one, as the
lesser evil of the two. The history of Athens furnishes us
with many instances of the great wealth amassed by these
republican sovereigns ; and that of Rome exhibits the frauds
and tyranny produced by a republican sovereignty over property, to an extent which would have been incredible, except
that the enormous wealth of the few, the great poverty of the

many, the perpetual struggles between these two parties for riveting or subverting the abuse, and its exchange for the sovereignty of one man, testify to their truth. These consequences of a sovereignty over property in a republican form of government, demonstrate the importance of the enquiry to ourselves, whether our governments do, or do not possess it.

The sovereignty over property, always claimed and often exercised by governments, regal, aristocratical, or republican, is a subject for historical research, which neither my capacity nor the limits of this work, will allow me to attempt. Such a history would detail the different forms it has assumed, the struggles it has produced, and the evils it has inflicted. It would prove that the notion of a sovereignty over private property was derived in England from the feudal system, and borrowed by us from England. Kings bestowed and resumed seigniories, and barons sub-divided them; both giving and taking away property at their will, and placing it in a state of vassalage to sovereignty. Out of the vassalage of property gained by conquest, grew the vassalage of property gained by industry. Under the impression of this habitual way of thinking in England, our revolutionary struggles commenced; and before we had transferred sovereignty from the government to the people, we yielded to its force, by only contending for representation as the solitary protector of private property. In the ardour of asserting that representation and taxation ought to be indissoluble, and from the forbearance of our government for a long time to assert a sovereignty over private property, the other securities it derives from our constitutional principles, have been too much neglected. In contending that our property could not be taken from us without our consent by our representatives, it was admitted, whilst we spoke in reference to the English system of government, that it might be both taken and expended by our representatives, without restriction; because, an unlimited power over property was an attribute of the English sovereignty. But when we separated from that government, this admission, suggested by the wish for a compromise, was renounced by the adoption of forms of governments founded in the principles, that sovereignty resided in the people, and that these governments were their trustees. Far from acknowledging that representation was the sovereign and solitary guardian of the rights of persons or of property, according to the English system, we abandoned that doctrine by sedulously inventing and prescribing sundry additional securities for both, as I shall presently shew. We resorted to election and representation, not to liberate our representatives from the principles and restrictions of our constitutions ; nor to invest them with an absolute power over either persons or property ; but as modes of carrying those principles into practical effect. Election is one security against their infringement, and cannot therefore be a good argument for justifying it. Such arguments are synonymous to that urged by criminals to excuse violations of civil laws. They teach their consciences to believe, that a risque of punishment balances every crime, as an exposure to the judgment of election is pleaded as an absolution from conforming to political law. In both cases, the remedy is enlisted as an ally of the misdeed, and converted into an incentive to commit that which it was intended to prevent.

The first, the most obvious and the most conclusive argument to prove, that our governments including those of the states, do not possess an absolute or sovereign power over the national property, arises from the admission, that they are the trustees of the people. The relation between principal and trustee is sufficiently understood to induce the reader to accord in the conclusion, that the trustee, so far from possessing an unlimited power over the property of his principal, is limited to the exercise of his authority and the execution of his trust, by the intention with which it was conferred. It has often been imagined that the state governments have been absolved from an obligation so obvious ; and their absolute sovereignty has been frequently asserted, without considering that the doctrine would subvert the great principle (the sovereignty of the people) upon which our political superstructure is founded. But, if that principle is held sacred, then it follows, that the powers not delegated by the people to the state governments, are as undoubtedly reserved to them, as the powers not delegated to the government of the United States ; and that the exercise of any undelegated power by either, under a belief that it will advance the publick good, is unconstitutional in both cases ; because a right to seek for the publick good, without our constitutional limits, involves a power of finding publick harm. No reservation of powers not bestowed can be necessary ; nor can this superfluous precaution in the constitution of the United States invest the state governments with a sovereignty over property, and only leave to the people the franchise of election for its security ; so as to slide it back upon the scates of modern construction and old prejudices, under the same bondage which exists in England. This would be to repass the Rubicon, after we had gotten safely over it.

If the state governments are not sovereigns and only trustees, then their powers are restricted by the intention of their institution, and when this intention is ascertained, the restriction is also discovered. Were they invested with an unlimited power of taxation for the purposes of sustaining civil governments, and meeting national exigencies ; or for those of transferring property from one man to another, or of gratifying personal friendship, charity or a love of fame, at the expense of their constituents ? A sovereign has a right to exercise his caprice, his partiality or his benevolence at the expense of his subjects, because both their persons and property are his, and his power over both is uncontrouled. But, as mankind advanced in knowledge, the tyranny and falsehood of this doctrine were gradually detected ; and therefore in many civilized nations it has ceased to be openly avowed, whilst it is yet indirectly practised ; to avoid the effects of an overwhelming popular indignation, which the unconcealed despotism would inspire. In the greater portion of Europe, regal sovereignty at this day exercises an uncontrouled power over property by taxation, by an unfettered appropriation of taxes, by exclusive privileges, by corporate bodies, and by an unrestrained patronage. Thus the pretext of publick good is made into a mask with which to hide publick oppression. To this pretext, in England, and at length in France, has been added election ; not to subvert the false principle from which the evil has arisen, but to render the sovereignty of the government over property still stronger ; and harder to transmute from being an instrument for inflicting private misery, into one for securing national happiness. Accordingly, the sovereignty over property, claimed by the English government, has been more grievously exercised, than in neighbouring countries, where election has not been used to betray, that which it was designed to preserve. Yet the English government does not derive its absolute power over property from the partial franchise of election, but claims it as being one of the appendages belonging to the illimitable power called sovereignty; and indeed, two of the branches of that government have no pretensions to an accession of rights from the former source. If then this absolute power over property flows from sovereignty, and not from election; and if the people of the United States, and not their governments, possess the sovereignty; it follows, that the source of that stream of despotism, called a sovereignty over property, which has flowed over mankind immemorially, being dried up here, our system of government ought not to be poisoned by its effluvium. A sovereignty in the government is the proposition, from which an absolute power over property is inferred; but if the proposition be false, the inference fails.

Having established a principle so distinct, let us proceed to enquire, whether the state and federal constitutions recognize or explode it. To avoid prolixity, the reasoning must be often generalised. In some of the state constitutions, exclusive privileges are prohibited, because they operated fraudulently upon private property. In all, great attention is bestowed upon the publick treasury, to ensure the proper application of the publick property. And for both objects, divisions of power, distinct departments, specifications of rights and duties, and special assignments of patronage, were instituted. These unite to indicate an anxiety in the people to preserve their property, and to withhold an absolute power over it from the government. Suppose a state legislature should, as sovereigns have often done, directly take by law the property of one man and bestow it upon another. Would the judges sustain an act so despotick? And upon what ground could they annul it, except that the legislature were trustees only and not sovereigns? Is there any difference between offending against the same principle, directly or circuitously?

One of the chief motives for amending the union, was the sovereign power, unwisely assumed, and imprudently exercised by the state governments. To correct an usurpation in theory, and an evil in practice, the constitution of the United States prohibits the state governments from passing " any bill of attainder or expost facto law, or any law impairing the obligation of contracts," and empowers congress " to coin money and fix the standard of weights and measures." These precautions for defending property against modes for assailing it, are examples for establishing its substantial rights, and precedents against a recourse to other modes, infringing the principle upon which these prohibitions are imposed. And a specified permission to congress, by which they may establish modes of measuring property for the whole union, would have been unnecessary, had that body possessed any species of sovereignty over property itself; because such modes would have been included among its appendages. No power is given to congress to do that which the state governments are thus prohibited from doing; and if some species of sovereignty can extend the power of congress to ends not delegated, it can also extend the powers of the state governments to ends prohibited; and effectually undermine our system of government, made up of delegation and prohibition. The power to " coin money and regulate foreign coin" is limited by the terms " coin and foreign" to the precious metals, because it could not extend to native paper currency, without including foreign; and a standard of weights, respecting money, refers to money capable of being weighed. The states are prohibited " from coining money, emitting bills of credit, or making any thing but gold and silver a tender in payment of debts." The distinction between specie and paper currency is in this clause established. A power, prohibited to the states and not delegated to congress, can be exercised by neither. A power, the direct exercise of which is prohibited, ought not to be indirectly exercised. A power, prohibited or not delegated to the principal, cannot be delegated by that principal to another. Bills of credit are distinguished from other objects of tender laws, which had been numerous among the states, and are prohibited absolutely, whether the quality of being made a tender for debts was annexed to them or not. Otherwise, it would have been unnecessary to mention them at all. The powers of " coining money, emitting bills of credit, and making any thing but gold and silver coin a tender in payment for debts," being prohibited to the states; and the first power only being delegated to congress; it follows that the other two are prohibited and not delegated. And it seems to me, that it may be as speciously contended, according to the late fashion of construction, that the states may make *any thing*, but gold and silver, a tender; as that either congress or the states can delegate to individuals or corporations a power to emit bills of credit; or impair contracts by suspensions of payments in favour of their own creatures, or of unlucky speculators. Either would be a usurpation of a sovereign power over property, not delegated to one department, and expressly prohibited to the other. It may be also remarked, that the power given to congress " to provide for the punishment of counterfeiting the securities and current coin of the United States" by omitting bills of credit, recognizes their exclusion, and does not include bills of credit emitted by corporations.

From these efforts to protect the rights of private property, or rather the right of individuals to what belongs to them, let us pass on to those for securing the national property, collectively. Here the question is, whether congress derive from the power of taxation, a sovereign power to expend the money thus raised, according to its own will and pleasure, like an English parliament or a Russian emperor. If congress possessed an unlimited power to appropriate the publick money raised by taxes, there was no occasion to specify the objects to which it might be applied, such as to raise and *support* armies, to provide and *maintain* a navy. Among these objects, all the powers granted, requiring an expense, are enumerated ; and this enumeration proves, that no object of expense, not included within the delegated powers, can be constitutionally adopted by congress. For where was the necessity of any enumeration at all of the objects of expense, if congress were not subject to any restriction in the appropriation of the publick money ? The widest scope for appropriation is included in the words " to pay the debts and provide for the common defence and general welfare of the United States." The defence and welfare of the United States, without any explanatory words, would of themselves refer to the affairs of the union, and exclude those of the states ; but the words *general and common,* are used in contrast to *local and individual,* for the purpose of more explicitly excluding congress, in the appropriation of the money raised to be applied to the benefit of the United States, from indulging a sovereign legislative patronage in favour of local, private or individual interests.

Let us suppose, that a reconciliation had taken place between Great Britain and the colonies, by which precisely the same powers of taxation for the common defence and general welfare had been conceded to the British parliament, the same objects of expense specified, and the same reservations of local and internal government to the colonies made, as are contained in the constitution of the United States. Is it not obvious, that an assumption (under a compact intended to provide for the common, and not for the separate interests of these parties,) of a power to appropriate the common ; urse to local or personal interests, would have infringed its intention, and would gradually have swallowed up the rights reserved? The same chastity of construction may possibly be necessary to preserve our union, which would certainly have been indispensable for the preservation of such a reconciliation.

It is true that the doctrine of absolute sovereignty, with its indefinite catalogue of appendages, can adduce in its defence many plausible arguments, and enumerate sundry conveniences which might result, from its unlimited capacity to devote both persons and property to whatever purposes it may think proper. What conveniences may arise from the absolute subordination appertaining to it, in war ! How wonderful are its energies, in punishing crimes which will for ever elude established laws ! How inexhaustible are its resources for rewarding merit, fostering the arts, and rearing pyramids ! Limited powers and co-ordinate departments, occupied by dependant trustees, are often incompetent to effect ends really good, and never able to perform exploits, which historians have called magnificent; whilst sovereignty can enshrine itself in splendour, and dazzle the quietism with which it is able to encircle its throne. Such indeed are the advantages arising from a sovereignty in governments ; but, to decide whether it is preferable to our system of self-government and a division of power, a strict comparison between the whole mass of good and evil resulting from both forms, ought to be made. As imperfection is an attribute of every human contrivance, comparison is the only resource for a judicious preference. In the particular case of property, if we were to confine it to the good and evil derived by nations from a sovereign or limited power in governments over the publick purse, a dismal balance of evil would render the first principle even hideous ; and inspire a horror, sufficient to make the latter, with all its imperfections, appear beautiful. Evil is indissolubly attached to good ; and therefore the inconveniences, arising from the sovereignty of the people and a limited power in governments over persons and property, are by no means sufficient to establish the expediency of undermining these principles. Many wise and good men, however, alarmed by the illusions of Rousseau and Godwin, and the atrocities of the French revolution, honestly believe that these principles have teeth and claws, which it is expedient to draw and pare, however constitutional they may be; without considering that such an operation will subject the generous lion to the wily fox ; or to speak without a metaphor, that it will subject liberty and property to tyranny and fraud. In short, that if our new principle of a sovereignty in the people can be disarmed of its property, by transferring to the government an unlimited power over it ; the old English principle must inevitably swallow it up, with all its appurtenances.

The reader perceives, that the freedom of property is the chief principle, which distinguishes governments founded in the rights of nature, from those founded in some arbitrary act. Our societies were instituted by a resignation of such natural rights, as was necessary for the preservation of those retained. Property was only made a common stock, so far as the social safety and happiness required ; but social safety and happiness, far from requiring that governments should possess a power of dooming one portion of the people to indigence and ignorance, and another to opulence and insolence, by supplanting industry, and substituting law, as the dispenser of private property, require a system precisely the reverse. Modern philosophers, without discerning, or if it was discerned, without assailing the usurpation of an absolute and despotick power over private property, have yet strenuously contended for a system of policy, founded upon the opposite principle ; which they have called the economical system ; and have agreed almost unanimously, that there is little hope of free governments, until it is better understood, and more actively enforced. The difference between judicatures to secure, and corporations to defraud private property, concisely displays both the power delegated, and the right reserved under our system of government ; and the possibility of reaping a social blessing by a limited power, without the alloy of a social curse, by an unlimited power over private property. Common interest is the object of a restricted power, and therefore it dispenses general prosperity; an accumulation of individual honours or wealth comprises all the business in which an absolute power over property can engage; and therefore it dispenses comparative disgrace and poverty upon the mass of society. The freedom of property from the indefinite despotism of sovereignty, is the best security to be found against those unjust laws by which social liberty is so often injured; and against that despotism of majorities, by which it has been so often destroyed. This wise and just principle even denies to the sovereignty of the people, a right to the private property of individuals, because the conventional act by which that species of sovereignty was created, conceded a right to tax for social purposes only, and withheld a right to tax for individual aggrandizement. I conclude therefore, that neither the state governments nor congress have a sovereign power over property; that neither of them has any right at all to create modes for transferring it artificially from one man or one interest to another; that the right of taxation, with which they are invested, is limited to the attainment of social ends or specified objects; and that the right of appropriation, being merely an appendage of the right of taxation, is restrained to the same ends or objects.

But, admitting the truth of this conclusion, though much will be gained, the difficulty of distinguishing between spurious and genuine ends or objects will still remain; and the impossibility of conceiving a complete catalogue of either leaves no remedy but a watchful attention to current measures, and a fair investigation of the principles by which they ought to be justified or condemned. Yes, there is another. If the honourable, just and patriotick men, who abound in our legislative bodies, should consider the subject and concur in the conclusion, they will, in obedience to an essential social principle, through affection for their country, and from a zeal for its glory, forbear to impair the foundation upon which it has been erected. They will not approach towards the rival principle arrayed in calamities to mankind "that governments possess a sovereignty over property," without a sensation of horror, and shrinking from its contamination. The right to property or labour is involved with our whole subject, and as it must consequently be often adverted to, its consideration is not here concluded.

SECTION 7.

THE BANK DECISION.—CORPORATION.

The previous pages have been devoted to the establishment of several important principles, from an opinion, that they are better expounders of our constitutions, and sounder arbiters of construction, than dictionaries. The philosopher, who is led astray from things by signs, resembles a botanist whose taste leads him to wander in a wilderness of flowers, and to contemplate their hues, without caring whether their fruit is noxious or wholesome. Principles are the fruit of words; and as no man in his senses would swallow poison, because it grew from the beautiful flower of the poppy; so bad principles ought not to be recommended nor good ones defeated, by a verbal Mosaick, however ingenious. By the standard of principles, I shall therefore proceed to examine several measures and opinions; and beginning with the most recent, select a few others, without regard to chronological order, as opposite to such as I believe to be constitutional.

An examination of the opinion of the court of appeals, against the right of the state governments to tax the bank of the United States, not with arrogance, but with humility; not with confidence, but with distrust; will I hope be pardonable. Against the talents and integrity of that respectable body of men, I have no counterpoise but my creed; against the acute argument by which their decision is defended, I have no offset, but an artless course of reasoning. An unknown writer is but a feather, weighed against acknowledged uprightness, erudition, and well merited publick confidence; yet under all these disadvantages, as wisdom and virtue are sometimes liable to error; as the battle is not always to the strong, nor the race to the swift; and as enquiry is the road to truth; I shall endeavour to reconcile my respect for the court, with my right, perhaps my duty, as a citizen of our happy commonwealth.

Before I proceed, as some defence of this presumption, I quote a judicial precedent. The decision of a bad or a corrupt judge would not apply; but one rendered by the great, the good, the wise Sir Matthew Hale, so late too as the seventeenth century, is quite in point. This judge, of superior talents and spotless integrity, condemned and put to death two poor old women as witches; and the correctness of his judgment was not questioned. Behold in this case, confidence yoked to fallibility. Perhaps the time may arrive, when it would be as absurd to contend for the witchcraft said to be lurking under the words sovereignty, supremacy, necessary and convenient, as it would be to prove now, that it does not lurk under a wrinkled visage; and when it would be thought as superfluous to prove, that our constitutions ought not to be destroyed by one species of witchcraft, as that old women ought not to be burnt out of compliment to the respectable Judge Hale's decision establishing the other.

The following quotation from the opinion of the court is copious, from an apprehension of omitting any thing material towards a thorough knowledge of the question.

" Banking was introduced at a very early period of our his-
" tory, has been recognized by many successive legislatures,
" and has been acted upon by the judicial department in cases
" of peculiar delicacy, as a law of undoubted obligation."

" It has been said, that the people had already surrendered
" all their powers to the state sovereignties, and had nothing
" more to give."

" If any proposition could command the universal assent of
" mankind, we might expect it would be this; that the govern-
" ment of the union, though limited in its powers, is supreme
" in its sphere of action. This would seem to result necessa-
" rily from its sphere of action. It is the government of all;
" its powers are delegated by all, it represents all, and acts
" for all. The people have said ' This constitution and the
" laws of the United States, which shall be made in pursuance
" thereof shall be the supreme law of the land, any thing in
" the constitution or laws of any state notwithstanding."

" There is no phrase in the constitution which excludes
" incidental or implied powers." " Its nature requires that
" only its great outlines should be marked." " We find in

" it the great powers to lay and collect taxes, to borrow money,
" to regulate commerce, to declare and conduct war, and to
" raise and support armies and navies. Can we adopt that
" construction, unless the words imperiously require it, which
" would impute to the framers of the instrument, when grant-
" ing these powers for the publick good, the intention of impe-
" ding their exercise by withholding a choice of means? The
" instrument does not profess to enumerate the means by which
" the powers it confers may be executed, nor does it prohibit
" the creation of a corporation, if the existence of such a thing
" be essential to the beneficial exercise of those powers. The
" creation of a corporation appertains to sovereignty."

" The powers of sovereignty are divided between the govern-
" ment of the union and those of the states. They are each
" sovereign with respect to the objects committed to it, and nei-
" ther sovereign with respect to the objects committed to the
" other."

" Congress shall have power to make all laws necessary and
" proper to carry into execution the powers of the government."

" Let the end be legitimate, let it be within the scope of the
" constitution, and all means which are appropriate, which are
" plainly adapted to that end, which are not prohibited, but
" consist with the letter and spirit of the constitution, are con-
" stitutional."

" That banking is a convenient, a useful, and essential in-
" strument in the prosecution of fiscal operations, is not now
" a subject of controversy."

" The power of taxation by the states is not abridged by the
" grant of a similar power to the government of the union; it
" is to be concurrently exercised by the two governments. The
" states are forbidden to lay duties on exports or imports. If
" the obligation of this prohibition must be conceded; if it
" may restrain a state from the exercise of its taxing power on
" imports and exports, the same paramount character would
" seem to restrain as it certainly may restrain, a state from
" such other exercise of this power, as is in its nature incom-
" patible with and repugnant to the constitutional laws of the
" union."

" All subjects over which the sovereign power of the state
" extends, are objects of taxation; but those over which it does

" not extend, are upon the soundest principles exempt from
" taxation. The sovereignty of a state extends to every thing
" which exists by its own authority, or is introduced by its per-
" mission, but does not extend to the means employed by con-
" gress to carry into execution, powers conferred on that body
" by the people of the United States."

" Such is the character of human language, that no word
" conveys to the mind, in all situations, one single definite idea.
" It is essential to just construction, that many words which
" imply something excessive, should be understood in a more
" mitigated sense."

" We find, on just theory, a total failure of the original right
" to tax the means employed by the general government of the
" union for the execution of its powers."

" That the power to tax involves the power to destroy ; that
" the power to destroy may defeat and render useless the pow-
" er to create ; that there is a plain repugnance in conferring on
" one government a power to controul the constitutional mea-
" sures of another, which other, with respect to those very
" measures, is declared to be supreme over that which exerts
" the controul, are propositions not to be denied."

" The legislature of the union can be trusted by the people
" with the power of controuling measures which concern all,
" with the confidence that it will not be abused."

" The principle, for which the state of Maryland contends,
" is capable of arresting all the measures of the general govern-
" ment, and of prostrating it at the foot of the states."

" It is a question of supremacy." " It is of the very essence
" of supremacy to remove all obstacles to its action within its
" own sphere, and so to modify every power vested in subordi-
" nate governments, as to exempt its own operations from their
" influence."

" The result is a conviction, that the states have no power by
" taxation or otherwise to retard, impede, burden, or in any
" manner controul the operation of the constitutional laws en-
" acted by congress to carry into execution the powers vested
" in congress. This we think the unavoidable consequence of
" the supremacy, which the constitution has declared."

The essential conclusion of this opinion is, that an absolute
sovereignty as to means does exist, where there is no sovereignty

at all as to ends. This doctrine seems to me, to be evidently inconsistent with the principle of dividing, limiting, balancing and restraining political powers, to which all our constitutions have unequivocally resorted, as the only resource for the preservation of a free form of government. If the means to which the government of the union may resort for executing the powers confided to it, are unlimited, it may easily select such as will impair or destroy the powers confided to the state governments. If a delegation of powers implies a delegation of an unrestrained choice of means for the execution of those powers, then this unrestrained choice of means was bestowed by the people on the state governments, by the double act of delegation and reservation, and is attached to their powers ; and the same principle, by which it is contended that the government of the union may impair or destroy the powers of the state governments, entitles the state governments to impair or destroy those of the government of the union. It will be admitted, that the powers delegated and reserved to the state governments, are positive limitations of the powers delegated to the government of the union; and that the powers delegated to the union, are limitations of those delegated and reserved to the state governments; and from this assignment of powers, made by the same authority, it arises, that both are limited governments. The ends with which these governments are respectively entrusted, are allowed to have been exclusively bestowed, and neither could constitutionally use its legitimate ends, to defeat or absorb the legitimate ends assigned to the other. So far the array of ends against ends appears to have been placed by the constitution on equal ground, and this equality justifies the inference, that a mutual check upon the exercise of political power by each government was intended. In dividing these ends, the constitution of the union is positive and explicit; but, it is quite silent as to the means to be employed by the state governments for effecting the ends committed to them by the people; and also as to the means to be employed by the government of the union, in some degree. And this silence is attempted to be exclusively appropriated to the government of the union, so that by the instrumentality of a monopoly of means, it may supplant and destroy the equality of ends plainly established by the constitution, subdue the state ends by the appendages of the union ends, though neither catalogue of these ends would be allowed openly to batter down the other; and thus effectually overturn by implied means, our whole positive division of ends, made for the purpose of limiting, checking and moderating power. As ends may be made to beget means, so means may be made to beget ends, until the co-habitation shall rear a progeny of unconstitutional bastards, which were not begotten by the people; and their rights being no longer secured by fixed principles, will be hazarded upon a game at shuttlecock with ends and means, between the general and state governments. To prevent this, means as well as ends are subjected by our constitutions to a double restraint. The first is special. In many instances, the means for executing the powers bestowed, are defined, and by that definition, limited. The other is general, and arises necessarily from the division of powers ; as it was never intended that powers given to one department, or one government, should be impaired or destroyed, by the means used for the execution of powers given to another. Otherwise, the indefinite word " means" might defeat all the labour expended upon definition by our constitutions. Numberless illustrations might be adduced in support of this reasoning, but those which have appeared, are preferable to such as are conjectural. The constitution of the United States contains many positive restrictions of the means for executing the powers bestowed. It bestows on congress the power of declaring war. But it restricts the means of executing this power, by limiting the right of taxation ; by withholding the right of ordering the militia without the United States ; by withholding the right of impressing seamen or landmen ; by confining appropriations for an army to two years, and by excluding the government of the union from the appointment of militia officers. This last power, positively reserved to the state governments, is evidently intended as a check upon the power of the sword, by dividing it between the two governments ; and a volunteer militia, officered by the president, or a general, is a mean, both convenient for the end of war, and also for impairing or defeating the end designed to be accomplished by the constitution. Is this inferred convenience, a fair abrogation of the specified end? Again; a sudden inroad under the authority of the president into a country at peace

with us, might be a beneficial and convenient mode of beginning
a war, and a mean towards ultimate success; but the right of
involving us in war, is exclusively limited to congress for ends
infinitely more beneficial to the nation. Ought these more valuable ends to be sacrificed, for the sake of one less valuable?
So congress is empowered to borrow, and to coin money; and
as one mean for the execution of this power, to provide for
the punishment of counterfeiting the securities and current coin
of the United States. Ought this restraint of a power to create
or punish crimes, to be extended by construction, to a power
of punishing counterfeiters of corporation or individual paper?
Such a power was not given, because a paper currency was not
recognized. To secure a fair exercise of the legislative power
of congress, two means are resorted to. One, that no legislator
shall receive an office created, or the emoluments of which
shall have been increased, during the time for which he was
elected ; the other, that no person holding an office under the
United States, shall be a legislator. If corporations are used
to enable members of congress to be both legislators, office-
holders, and emolument-receivers under their own laws, the
means for effecting this triple violation of the constitution
ought surely to be compared, if the word "beneficial" is to
decide the preference, with the means for preventing it. The
judicial power is invested with the right of deciding controversies between private persons, and between individuals and
our governments, and even between states, to prevent the mischiefs of legislative patronage and adjudication. A legislative
judicature is both excessively imperfect and expensive, and
also defeats one of the most beneficial means, for attaining the
great social ends of fair trials and impartial decisions.

A specification of some means for the attainment of ends,
is a proof that means were not intended to be unlimited ; but
as it was impossible to specify all which might be constitutionally used, for the execution of the powers delegated to the government of the union, or reserved to the states, those not
specified were unavoidably left to be controuled by the division
of powers and rights, which was specified. This controul is
indispensably necessary for giving the intended effect, to all
the minor divisions of power in the state constitutions, and
also to the major division of power, between the state govern-

ments and the government of the union, as well as to the inferior divisions of the latter. By rejecting this controul, our whole system of social policy would be rent to pieces from top to bottom. If the unspecified means of the states for executing the powers reserved to them, were not limited by the powers delegated to congress, the state governments might defeat the latter powers, by the instrumentality of means. But, if the unspecified means which the states may use to effect the ends committed to their care, are limited by the powers delegated to the government of the union, it follows, as being the same principle, that the unspecified means which congress may use to effect the ends committed to the care of the government of the union, are also limited by the powers delegated and reserved to the states. Neither government can, under cover of such words as " sovereign, convenient, necessary and supreme," legitimately resort to means which would impair their co-ordinacy of origin, or the distribution of ends made by the people for their own security ; and both or neither must be restrained by a principle, exactly common to both. Otherwise, the words " sovereign, convenient, necessary and supreme" will enable the same parties, factions and exclusive interests, which have been changing and modelling the English form of government from time immemorial, gradually to work up ours into a similar compound of exclusive privileges and emoluments, legislative corruption and venality, excessive taxation, and stock aristocracy. Our civil revolution will then have eventuated, precisely like the religious revolution in England under Henry the 8th. The pope was gotten rid of, but the tithes and the episcopal aristocracy remained.

But, the wise men who framed our form of government never intended, that its great principles and great ends should be altered and modelled from time to time, by the means and ends of factions, parties or individuals ; to render it quite unsteady, liable to important innovations without any real reference to the people, or to the right of self-government ; and to carry it back to the same unfixed principle or no principle of the English form of government ; in which, change has been so constant, and constitution so changeable, that it is said in a late Edinburgh Review, that the old English reporters do not contain a single precedent which is now law; and in England, law is constitution.

On the contrary, they intended to erect a political fabrick, with separate compartments, each watered by distinct streams of power; and not, whilst apparently perfecting a work so glorious, to invent covertly a machine, then nameless but now called the "supremacy of means," for diverting the streams assigned to some departments into others, so as to famish some occupiers and poison others by a plethora. Though the outside walls of the fabrick may still stand after the operations of this machine, like those of an old Gothick castle, and occasionally attract the admiration of future connoisseurs; yet they will no longer be capable of sheltering liberty against the blasts of ambition or the reptiles of venality, after the apartments cease to be habitable.

Having thus opened the way for a more particular consideration of the opinion of the court, I shall proceed to exhibit to the reader extracts from the quotation, arranged with a view to the perspicuity of the argument.

" The creation of a corporation appertains to sovereignty." This position, the fountain from whence the court draws all its arguments, is assented to ; but I shall endeavour to prove, that if their proposition be true, their inferences are false.

There are some words innately despotick, and others innately liberal. Among those of the former character, corporation and hierarchy bear the most exact analogy to each other, the first being used to destroy civil, and the second to destroy religious liberty. Both are appurtenances of sovereignty, and sovereignty being despotick because it is indefinite, both are appurtenances of despotism. The fruit uniformly produces a tree like that on which it grew. The English sovereignty has availed itself of these two appurtenances to a great extent. Kings and towns conspired in the use of corporations ; Kings to purchase partisans, reduce the barons, and increase their own power ; towns to obtain more liberty than the rest of the people. Kings soon discovered, that the sovereign right of granting exclusive privileges was much better adapted for getting money, corrupting factions, and gratifying minions, than for diffusing liberty ; and they substituted this new appurtenance of sovereignty for its old prerogatives, with the advantage which a plausible novelty possesses over a detected oppression. Commercial monopolies, commercial companies, local immunities and personal privileges, fully compensated their ambition and avarice for the loss of prerogatives, and the word " corporation" has furnished history with a list of grievances, often resisted, occasionally redressed, again revived in new forms, and terminating in taxation and pauperism, both so excessive, that England is as ripe for reformation, as it was under royal prerogative in its most aggravated form. The word was adopted into English jurisprudence, and endowed with a character both sacred and indefinite, by regal " during pleasure" judges, to enlarge regal power, to obtain regal favour, and to avoid regal displeasure. It was thrust into the English law books by sheep, clothed in ermine by lions, and sanctified by precedents bottomed upon fear, hope and flattery. From these receptacles, wherein it hides the heart of a prostitute under the habiliments of a virgin, it has found its way into the heads of lawyers, seduced by the habits of intercourse, or deceived by a primness of feature, adjusted to conceal imposture, and to impose upon credulity. But it did not get into our constitutions, and the question is, whether its congeniality with their principles is sufficiently apparent, to justify our judges in supplying the oversight of the people. Regal sovereignty was its father, and regal prerogative (a respectable matron in England, though not much beloved here,) its mother.

The English dictionaries, in accordance with their intention and effects, define corporations to be " bodies politick." Sovereignty alone could create bodies politick, and therefore it exclusively granted the charters or enacted the laws by which they were created in England. The English law books themselves do not recognize a right in some bodies politick to create other bodies politick. Whether our governments are sovereigns, or only bodies politick created by the charters of the only sovereignty we acknowledge, is a question, involving in my view the existence of our form of government. If they are sovereigns, it must be admitted, that according to the English precedents, they have a right to prop and secure themselves by all bodies politick, capable of defending an absolute, unquestionable, and indefinite power, the attribute of sovereignty ; but if they are not sovereigns, they can only be bodies politick, created by the charters, called constitutions, and as such, according to the incorporating principles of the English law books, they have no right to create other bodies politick. If we are to be bound by the laws of England, those laws ought surely to be correctly construed. Do these allow bodies politick created by the sovereignty of that country, to create other bodies politick, without the assent of its sovereign power? Is it less necessary for the safety of the sovereignty of the people, to attain its appurtenant power of creating bodies politick, than for the sovereignty of a king or a government? It is undoubtedly a power, which cannot be surrendered by any species of sovereignty, without ultimately losing the sovereignty; because, after its attributes are gone, an empty shell only remains. If therefore it be true, as the English anthorities assert, that the opinion of the court admits " that the creation of corporations appertains to sovereignty," and if sovereignty among us appertains to the people, it follows that the creation of corporations does not appertain to either of our governments, or to either of their departments.

There is no political influence capable of producing greater impressions upon the sovereignty of the people, or their forms of government, than a system of legislative patronage, or of shedding wealth upon corporations, and lustre upon ambition. By incorporations, great bodies politick, whole parties, and entire states, may be degraded into clientage, and bribed to obedience; and legislators themselves may participate in every bonus they bestow. Among these, an exemption from taxation extended to a great mass of incorporated wealth, is an exclusive privilege, of a value sufficient to purchase the most abject submission to political projects, the expense of which is imposed upon other classes of society. This mode of purchasing the adherence of priests and nobles was universally resorted to by European kings, and is still practised by all European governments. And although our system of election and representation, is often urged as a complete security against this palpable injustice to the rest of society, yet it must be admitted, that the additional securities we have provided against an evil so general, by divisions and restrictions of power; that the experience of the whole world; that the example of England in particular; that the concurrence of all political writers ; unite in concluding, that election, alone, is insufficient, and requires many auxiliaries. Why should these auxiliaries be renounced, if the consequence is acknowledged, under the pretext, that election, unaided by divisions and limitations of power, has universally failed to prevent the evil ?

Congress is prohibited from legislating respecting the *establishment* of religion. But, if it possesses a sovereign power to create corporations, it may nevertheless incorporate a sect, without establishing a religion, invest that sect with a right to acquire wealth ; and protect that wealth against taxation, under the doctrine contended for in the case of banking corporations. The states might exercise the same power. And thus, a positive principle of our constitutions might be evaded by the sovereign incorporating privilege, which has every where sufficed to beget the most enormous oppression. But supposing that this species of incorporation is prohibited by our constitutions ; yet, allowing that it would have sufficed to destroy religious liberty, had it not been prohibited, it follows, that a sovereign power to create civil corporations would also suffice to destroy civil liberty. The wise men who prepared the constitution of the United States, conceived, that as no power was delegated to congress to create religious corporations, its exercise was sufficiently prohibited ; and such was the construction of the instrument before its adoption. Hence it follows, that this patriotick convention was of opinion, that the same absence of any power to create civil corporations, also prohibited its exercise. And though the object of adopting the constitution suggested the amendment referred to, for quieting unfounded apprehensions, yet the weight of this respectable contemporaneous opinion remains unshaken. If the convention was mistaken, and really conferred upon congress an unlimited incorporating power, though it intended to do no such thing, then congress may create an East India corporation, settle it upon the Pacifick ocean, and under the power to dispose of the lands of the United States, endow it with a western territory ; or it may create commercial corporations ; or it may incorporate towns ; and shield all against taxation. I need not remind the reader of the political consequences which would flow from such measures.

A power of excusing either personal or real property from taxation, is so far from being found in the constitution of the United States, that it contains positive prohibitions against it, in the modes prescribed for taxing both. Congress is prohibited from exempting the whole personal or real property of a state from taxation by these prescribed modes, and not invested with a power of granting partial exemptions to any portion of either, even in the imposition of taxes for the benefit of the union ; but, if it may assume the latter power, it may in detail defeat the actual prohibition. If however it cannot exercise this partiality even in taxing for the benefit of the union, the construction, which supposes that it may partially exempt real or personal property in particular states from state taxation, as still more violent, cannot be admitted.

A power to exempt, is equivalent to a power of imposing ; since the deficit it creates, must produce a relative accumulation upon property not exempted. The whole field of taxation not delegated to congress, is reserved to the states. A construction which imposes a restriction upon the states, where there is none ; and destroys the restrictions to prevent partialities actually imposed upon congress, is doubly at war with a construction, drawn from positive rules. There is no distinction in the right of taxation reserved to the states, between real and personal property. Their original right to tax both is reserved to them as it stood, and a right to tax both in specified modes only is delegated to congress. If congress can exempt personal property from taxation by the instrumentality of corporations, it may exempt real, as the stock of banks as well as of other corporations, may as easily be composed of lands as of money ; and thus accumulate direct taxation upon lands not exempted.

But it may be said, that though congress possess a dispensing power of exempting both real and personal property from state taxation, by first inferring from a gratuitous sovereignty, never created, a right to create corporations, and then inferring from this inference, a right to exempt the property of these corporations from taxation ; and though these same inferences from the gratuitous sovereignty allowed also to the state governments, are rejected ; yet, that congress may tax the property of these corporations, and observe in so doing, some degree of

uniformity. But suppose their stock is made to consist of land.
Is this land to be taxed by the rule of population? If so, a thousand acres of landed corporate stock, in a state having fifty
thousand people, will only pay one-twentieth of the amount to
be paid by a thousand acres in a state having half a million;
and states having no land stock, would pay no part of this
direct tax. The same inequalities would ensue from the taxation of personal stock by congress. This power of exemption
claimed on behalf of congress, (for congress has never claimed
it for itself, and I believe never will,) must have the effects of
rendering state taxation unequal and unjust, by shielding
masses of state property, real or personal, from contribution;
and also of rendering union taxation unequal and unjust, or of
placing corporation property beyond its reach: thus it is in
fact already exempted from taxation, great as it is, and greater
as it may become; and exactly occupies the privilege of the
clergy and nobility of France, which caused the revolution of
that country. By taxing state banks, congress has acknowledged the injustice of exempting corporate property from taxation.

There is no idea expressed in the constitution, of any object
of internal taxation, or any species of internal property, within
the reach of congress, and without the reach of the state governments. Their power, as to all such objects, is evidently
considered as concurrent, except where the taxing power of the
state governments extends farther than the taxing power of
congress. Whatever internal property congress may tax, the
state governments may tax, and therefore corporation property
must be exposed to state taxation, or it must be entitled to an
absolute exemption from paying taxes, both to the state governments, and the government of the union. Thus, the power of
exemption claimed will defeat the concurrent power of taxation,
bestowed for the mutual security of both governments; and
also introduce either an inequality of taxation, or a complete
exemption from it, both of which are inconsistent with a fair
and free government, and neither of which was intended to be
introduced by the general or state constitutions. Both partial
exemptions and partial douceurs have the same effect, as if
congress should tax in accordance with the formalities prescribed by the constitution, and then restore their proportional

contributions to states or individuals, instead of applying them to publick use. A shield against unequal taxation, which can be pierced by any of these contrivances, is no shield at all.

Let us suppose, that the state governments could diminish the objects of the concurrent right of taxation, on the part of congress. The gratuitous sovereignty conceded to both, carries with it the mutual right, it is supposed, of establishing corporations. So far the doctrine of the court, though erroneous, is consistent. But at this point it becomes eccentrick. Having created mutual sovereignties, and having endowed them with a mutual right of creating corporations, it becomes suddenly disloyal to the sovereignty bestowed upon the states, and denies to it the same appurtenance, claimed for the sovereignty bestowed upon congress; although these sovereignties must be co-ordinate, whether they are bestowed by the people or the judges. But, consistency required an acknowledgment, that if the state governments cannot controul or defeat the sovereignty of congress, so neither can congress controul or defeat the sovereignty of the state governments, as to incorporations; these being included within the spheres of both governments. Now, if the state governments could diminish by corporations, the concurrent objects of taxation on the part of congress, it is very evident that by multiplying them they might weaken and endanger the government of the union. This danger both congress and the court have distinctly discovered. Congress have warily resisted it, by the precedent of a slight tax on state banks; and the judges have wisely sacrificed consistency to prevent it. But then this foresight, both of congress and the court, as to the danger to the government of the union, from a power in the state governments to diminish the objects of a concurrent right of taxation on the part of congress, ought not to make the governments and courts of the states blind, as to their danger from a power in congress, to diminish the objects of the concurrent right of taxation on the part of the states.

There is no view, in which a power to create bodies politick with pecuniary privileges and exemptions, is more manifestly unconstitutional, than in its capacity to subvert the distinct division of powers between the general and state governments. It has been remarked, that the opinion of a state right to local and internal regulation, was derived from the principles of our revolution ; and that the idea of a union was derived from general relations, and not from local considerations. To these sources, both the special powers given to congress, and the residuary powers reserved to the states, must be referred. The creation of bodies politick by the states or by congress, endowed with privileges inconsistent in any degree, with the ends and duties expected from either, is substantially unconstitutional ; and substance is the best lexicographer for ascertaining both political rights and wrongs. There are two principles pre-eminently unfavourable to a free government ; an absence of checks and balances, and a partiality in taxation. The judgment of the court subverts our best counterpoise of power by power, and admits of an exemption from taxation in favour of wealth.

The admission, that our primary divisions of power were coordinate, was liberal, if the general government was created by a union between states politically existing ; because a claim of superiority rather appertains to the creator, than to the created ; and because this co-ordinacy is the highest ground, upon which the created power can be placed, and is precisely its guardian angel ; since a superiority in one and a subordination in the other, would certainly cause the destruction of both. Usurpation may be an appendage of spherical sovereignty, unnoticed by the court, and revolution is its sequel. These consequences can only be prevented, by considering our governments as the creatures of the people, invested with expressed, and prohibited from implied powers, derived from the idea that they are sovereigns.

An indiscriminate use of the term " corporation" has introduced a loose idea of its meaning, which appears to me to be incorrect ; but if correct, as militating against the opinion of the court. It is applied to towns, counties, and other sectional divisions, necessary for civil government, for the administration of justice, the prevention or punishment of crimes, the care of the poor, the removal of nuisances, and the preservation of roads, streets and bridges; all objects of a social rather than a political nature; meaning by the first term, modes of civil government, and by the second, modes of changing that civil government. There is an evident distinction, between provisions for executing a government, and means for changing its first principles; between municipal and political ends. And, if there is, it is incorrect to infer from the application of the word " corporation" to a constitutional class of ends, an extension of the power of government to an unconstitutional class of ends, from the mere accident of both being called by one name, arising from the want of different words to express every different thing; just as it would be incorrect to suppose, that two men had the same rights and qualities, because they were called by one name. Though the same word may have been applied to sectional divisions for sustaining civil government, and also to " bodies politick" for altering civil government, it does not confound things so different in their nature, and only proves that our language, participating in some degree of the hieroglyphical defects of the Chinese, has often but one word to convey ideas, extremely distinct. Besides, it will appear from a careful perusal, that the state constitutions, literally, virtually or impliedly, recognize the class of municipal sections for executing civil government, never recognize the class of corporate exclusive privileges or bodies politick for altering its principles, and sometimes express an abhorrence of them.

But, if the term " corporation" is to be so loosely construed as to convey these distinct powers, the claim of congress to its instrumentality must become still more remote, unless it can be proved, that this body can incorporate towns, divide counties, and create the whole genus, comprehending both the municipal and political species. To exclude congress from the former class, although it is a legitimate appurtenance of a limited government, and to invest it with the latter, although it is an illegitimate attribute of a limited government, would be a strange perversion of the science of construction. As therefore the state governments are either invested with, or not prohibited from, the power of creating municipal sections for local state governments ; and as congress is not invested with, but prohibited from, the power of creating municipal local sections for internal government, this word must be considered as exclusively appertaining to the state vocabulary. It is neither literally nor virtually applied by the constitution of the United States, to " the common defence and general welfare." On the contrary, this common defence and general welfare had for its chief object the common security of the state governments.

And the union, far from intending to defeat, was entered into, for the purpose of attaining this object. The use of the word "corporation" must either be disallowed to the government of the union, or the union must be considered as intended to absorb and abolish the powers reserved to the states, and to create an absolute general sovereignty, which it was instituted to prevent. If however this word may be used by the state governments, to contaminate their own principles, (which I deny,) some consolation exists in the consideration, that a weapon so dangerous will be local; and that they are prevented by the federal constitution from extending its malignancy to the government of the United States.

Political words of all others are the most indefinite, on account of the constant struggle of power to enlarge itself, by selecting terms not likely to alarm, but yet capable of being tortured by construction to produce effects generally execrated. In the catalogue of examples testifying to the truth of this observation, the words "sovereignty and corporation" occupy the most prominent place. If "despotism" were substituted for "sovereignty," the mask would be torn from the latter, and its deformity would be exposed to the weakest minds; and if "exclusive privileges" were substituted for "corporation," the position "that exclusive privileges are general grievances" so generally assented to, would detect that.

An unlimited right of taxation was possessed by the states, previous to the union. The solitary exception to this right is contained in the prohibition to tax imports and exports. A concurrent right of taxation under some limitations, is given to congress; but one concurrent right is no restriction upon the other, and both reach every object of taxation to which either extends. Therefore, congress in virtue of this concurrent right, can inflict no tax, to which the same right in the states does not extend. Hence it irresistibly follows, either that the states can tax corporate wealth under their original power of taxation, not prohibited, but reserved by the constitution; or that congress cannot tax the corporate wealth of their own creation, because no such exclusive right of taxation is given to them, and therefore it must either be a concurrent right or no right at all; and in the concurrent right of taxation, the states participate. Can congress exempt any species of wealth from taxation, and how would the consequences of a power so fatal to civil liberty terminate?

I shall conclude this section with a few quotations, still leaving to the reader their application.

Fed. p. 163. H. " I affirm that (with the *sole exception* of " duties on imports and exports) the individual states retain an " *independent and uncontroulable* authority to raise their own " revenue, in the most *absolute and unqualified* sense, and that " an *attempt on the part of the national government* to abridge " them in the exercise of it, would be a *violent assumption* of " power, *unwarranted by any article or clause of the consti-* " *tution.*"

Fed. p. 168. H. " Suppose that the federal legislature, by " some *forced construction* of its authority (which indeed cannot " easily be imagined) upon the *pretence of an interference* with " its revenues, should undertake to abrogate a land tax, imposed " by the authority of a state, would it not be evident that it " was an *invasion of that concurrent jurisdiction* in respect to " this species of tax, which the constitution plainly supposes to " exist in the state governments."

Fed. p. 169. H. " Though a law, therefore, laying a tax for " the use of the United States would be supreme in its nature, " and could not legally be opposed or controuled, yet a law " abrogating or *preventing* the collection of a tax laid by the " authority of a state (unless upon imports or exports) *would* " *not be the supreme law of the land, but an usurpation of* " *power not granted by the constitution.*" " The inference " from the whole is, that the individual states would, under the " proposed constitution, retain an *independent and uncontroul-* " *able* authority to raise revenue to any extent of which they " may stand in need, *by every kind of taxation,* except duties " on imports and exports."

Fed. p. 175. H. " The convention thought the *concurrent* " jurisdiction in the case of taxation, preferable to *subordi-* " *nation.*"

We shall meet with many other disagreements in construction, between avarice and great statesmen.

SECTION 8.

THE BANK DECISION.—SOVEREIGNTY OF SPHERES,

" If any one proposition could command the universal assent of
" mankind, we might expect it would be this; that the govern-
" ment of the union, though limited in its powers, *is supreme*
" *in its sphere of action.* This would seem necessarily to result
" from its sphere of action. *It is the government of all; its*
" *powers are delegated by all, it represents all, and it acts for*
" *all.*" " The powers of sovereignty are divided between the
" government of the union and those of the states. *They are*
" *each sovereign with respect to the objects committed to it, and*
" *neither sovereign, with respect to the objects committed to the*
" *other.*"

The word "sphere" conveys an idea of something limited,
in which sense it is correctly applied to our governments by the
Federalist, and may be easily undersood; but I confess myself extremely puzzled to discern, how this word, being a substantive circumscribed, can be converted into a substantive un-
circumscribed, by the help of the adjective " sovereign." And
I think it almost as difficult to see what is meant by the sovereignty of the spheres, as it is to hear the musick of the spheres.
But, as some change of the nature of a sphere must be effected
by an incongruous epithet, to sustain the opinion of the court,
the experiment deserves a very serious and respectful consideration.

The word " sphere" was very happily used in the Federalist,
and conveyed an idea of our system of government, both just
and beautiful. It refers to the structure of the universe, as
the model of our political system; and in the allusion, tacitly
suggests, and forcibly illustrates the sovereignty of the people
over the spheres they have created. The beauty of the similitude consists in the regularity produced by a strict confinement
of these spheres within their respective orbits; and it contains
a fine admonition, in extending our ideas to the consequences

which would ensue to the universe, should one of its spheres leave its own and travel into other orbits; to forewarn us of the consequences which would ensue to our political system from a similar aberration. But the similitude is utterly spoilt, by the idea that one of our spheres may annex to itself a long tail of means, reaching into the orbits of other spheres, so as to defeat the sublime allusion, and leave us only a regret for having neglected its admonition.

If the sovereignty of the spheres means any sovereignty at all, it supersedes the sovereignty of the people, since they can no longer possess that, which they have divided among spheres. But, if these spherical sovereignties are restrained by their orbits, called " spheres of action," then this new phrase means nothing at all, because a change in the description, does not alter the nature of the thing described; and if our divisions of power will still remain the same, whether they are called spherical sovereignties, spheres of action, limited powers, balances, checks or trusts (as the moon did under the several names of Phœbe, Cynthia, Diana, Dictynna, Hecate and Luna,) no sound argument can be deduced from using one appellation in preference to another. " The limited monarchy of spheres" would have been more appropriate to the apparent meaning of the court in this extract, as clearly conveying the idea of spherical limitation, and clearly excluding that of a spherical extension of power lurking in the word sovereignty. We see a sovereignty of spheres in England, to justify the language adopted by the court, and we know that the sphere of action of each is limited and restrained by the spheres of action of the other two. By calling each " sovereign with respect to the objects committed to it, and neither sovereign with respect to the objects committed to the other," I cannot see that the powers of the king, of the lords, or of the commons, would be enlarged in the least degree; or that a choice of means would be bestowed upon either, by which it could encroach upon the others. To our imitation of this model in the arrangement of legislative and executive power, we have, besides others, subjoined two improvements, by a judicial sphere possessing a great political power; and by the important spheres called state and federal governments. Now, if a spherical sovereignty exists here as it does in England, it would be as certainly destroyed, as it has often been there, if either sphere possessed an exclusive or an uncontrouled choice of means, in the exercise of a species of sovereignty separately from the rest. Encroachments of sphere upon sphere can only be made by means; and it is yielding nothing to admit that the spheres are circumscribed, but to insist, that their choice of means, by which encroachments are made, is unlimited; because a political sphere of action, cannot possibly be created in any other way, than that of withholding from it many means for effecting the ends, even the legitimate ends it may have in view. Even in bringing a murderer to justice, the means, as well as the sphere of action in the court, are all limited. If it was otherwise, confusions, usurpations, and oppressions would ensue on all sides; because power never finds any difficulty in choosing means calculated for its own enlargement. In fact, we know that the English political history is only a compilation of insidious and specious means, occasionally resorted to by each of the spheres, for the purposes of deluding the people, and encroaching upon the others. At length these spheres having harrassed each other for many centuries, by each having chosen means for encroaching on the others, came to a compromise; and compounded among themselves a sovereignty of spheres; and this precedent justifies the court, however puzzled I may be to understand it upon American ground, in using that phrase. But in quoting it, especially if I do not dispute its authority, I hope I may be allowed to contend, that it cannot prove the same thing to be wrong in England and right here. It proves that political spheres, by uniting, may acquire, not an individual but a collective sovereignty. It thence follows, if the sovereignty has passed in the United States from the people to political spheres, either by delegation, or by the usurpation of those spheres, that it can only be executed legitimately by the collective or united consent of all these spheres; unless it can be shewn, that a sort of interregnum or suspension of this spherical sovereignty, like those which often happened in England, has already happened here. The same precedent proves, that neither sphere ought to have any choice of means in the exercise of its own spherical powers, by which it may encroach upon its collateral spheres; for, though they were not co-ordinate, nor circumscribed to preserve the liberty of the people, yet they became balanced by mutual fear for mutual safety; and accordingly each sphere has been obliged, as the only chance for self-preservation, to be excessively jealous of the means resorted to by each to increase its own power. Now what does this English precedent teach us? That a spherical sovereignty can only be exercised by the mutual consent of the spheres: That one sphere can only be prevented by the watchfulness and resistance of the others, from using means to make itself the master of these others. That its success has always been considered as a usurpation, and has always introduced a tyranny: And that it was necessary to preserve the independence of the spheres of each other, to maintain even the semblance of a free government.

If then we are to adopt the English spherical sovereignty, we ought not to make it worse than it is, by subjoining to it vices, which it rejects, as utterly inconsistent with the spherical system, and certainly destructive of all the good it can produce. In that country, each sphere is a judge, independently of the others, of its own sphere of action, and of its own means; but both this sphere of action, and these means, are checked and restrained by the sphere of action and the choice of means, possessed by the other spheres. The same equivalency is necessary here to preserve a sovereignty of spheres, and prevent one from becoming the master of the others. The English system has made no specified provision to settle the collisions which will naturally arise, and have arisen in England from this equivalency of powers, " because power controuled or " abridged is almost always the rival and enemy of that power " by which it is controuled or abridged," as Mr. Hamilton justly observes in the Federalist, page 81; and this important office is loosely left to publick opinion, without establishing an orderly mode in which it might be expressed. Our system, foreseeing the probability of such collisions, both from the temper of human nature, and also from the occurrences in England, has provided a constitutional and orderly mode, by which publick opinion may exercise this supervising office. It would be a radical violation of the English policy of checks and balances, considered in that country, as the only safeguard of liberty, even without a specifick provision for reconciling collisions, were we to surrender the same safeguard, with specifick provisions for its exercise. By that, the sovereignty of the people is denied, and sovereignty is possessed by the three spheres, king, lords and commons ; this is the reason, why it contains no orderly mode by which a direct reference can be made to the people, for the settlement of collisions among these spheres ; yet the English system does not relinquish the essential principle of the co-ordinacy, independency and equality of the political spheres themselves, from an apprehension of their collisions. If we should relinquish this essential principle from the same apprehension, we should adopt the English spherical sovereignty, renounce the English security of a co-ordinacy or balance of spheres, and lose the sovereignty of the people. According to the English system, no sphere possesses the least degree of supremacy in the exercise of sovereign power, over the others, by the instrumentality of means, because it would enable the supreme sphere to swallow up these others ; and therefore to admit of such a supremacy in one of our spheres, would be contrary to the most valuable principle of theirs; and by adopting the sovereignty of the spheres, and also rejecting the only security against its abuse, namely the check and controul of these spheres upon each other, we should introduce here a worse government than the English, in an essential circumstance.

There is but one mode of getting over this reasoning, and to that mode the court has resorted. It asserts that " the " government of the union is delegated by all, represents all, " and acts for all." Do these assertions (the truth of which I shall presently examine) squint at consolidation, and ingeniously undermine the state spherical sovereignty admitted by the court ? Do they design to recognize the English spherical sovereignty of kings, lords and commons, as existing here in the president, senate and house of representatives ? Do they mean to insinuate that our system of government will be safe under the guardianship of these three departments, as the English system is safe under the guardianship of the king, lords and commons ? If these inferences were not intended, I cannot discern what was meant by these assertions; but admitting them to be true, I deny their sufficiency to justify such inferences. The people certainly had a right to create the union sphere to restrict the state spheres ; and to retain the state spheres, to restrict the union sphere. The court admit that they have exercised this right; therefore no inference from these assertions can be correct, by which this co-ordinacy of restriction would be abolished. Had the people of England created their co-ordinate spheres, they might have varied their form and their number from what they are; and surely the people of the United States might vary the form and the number of theirs from those of England, without defeating the principle of a co-ordinacy of spheres, and still retaining its application to whatever spheres they chose to create. The establishment of the union and state spheres, was not only a happy circumstance for extending the compass and capacity of republican government, but wisely comprised an advantage to which the English spherical system cannot pretend. Each of these spheres is invested with an independent legislative and judicial power within their respective orbits, so that collisions may be conducted and reconciled orderly and argumentatively, whilst those of the English spheres can only appeal to mobs or factions. Why therefore should these spheres, so much better supplied with the means of self-preservation and for mutual restriction, be considered as less estimable than those established in England by civil war, and the intrigues of faction? The ordinances of the people approved of by the best talents of the country ought at least to be as venerable, as the compromises of ambitious self-created orders.

Let us now calmly consider whether the prodigiously inclusive assertions, " That the government of the union is the " government of all; its powers are delegated by all, it repre- " sents all, and acts for all," are really true. Another assertion to confront it brings it to a fair test. The government of the union, in respect to the powers reserved to the states, is the government of none, is delegated by none, represents none, and can only act for all, by assuming a power, neither delegated nor representative. If one of these assertions be true and the other false, the reader will not hesitate in deciding to which a deficiency, in veracity, appertains. I admit, that the first may be made true by a restrictive qualification, similar to the qualification which makes the second assertion true, by adding to it the words, " in respect to the powers delegated to the general government." Both governments represent all in exer-

cising the powers committed to them respectively, and neither
represent any, with respect to the powers committed to the
other. Both may act for all, within their respective delegated
spheres; but neither can act for all within the spheres delegated to the other. " If any propositions could command the uni-
" versal consent of mankind, we might expect they would be
" these." And if these propositions are true, it follows, that
neither government can, under cover of a sovereignty of spheres,
or by the use of inferences, exceed its limitations, without vio-
lating the essential principles of delegation and representation.
If we were to admit the assertion of the court in all its latitude,
it would amount to the following position :—" A government
" representing all, may act for all." This position, unqualified,
applies more forcibly, (as I shall attempt to shew,) to the end of
unfettering the state governments, than to the end of unfettering the government of the union, because they actually represent all, which the latter government does not.

The principle of personal representation was violated to a
considerable extent, for the sake of compromise and accommodation, and because a spherical representation was necessary
to a union of states. The house of representatives only, of the
federal government, is elected with a view to the first principle,
whilst it is throughout applied to the state governments. The
senate of the United States is a representation of state sovereignties, not of numbers; and this fact circumscribes very
materially, the generality of the assertion made by the court,
or transfers its application to the state governments. It was
instituted to preserve that which it represents, and not as the
guardian of individuals whom it does not represent. The
union was established for the management of the general concerns of the states united, and not for the management of local or individual concerns; to which intention the construction
of the senate has a distinct relation. The present senate is
exactly analogous to the old congress, in which each state
had one vote, as each has two in the present senate; and the
present senate is no farther a representative of individuals,
than was that congress. Both were chosen by the state legislatures. Hence it appears that the government of the union
does not represent all, as the court assert, and of course, that
it has no right to act for all. The house of representatives is

elected by states; but that house is not the government of the union; and the mode of its election may be easily accounted for, exclusively of an intention by that mode, to extend the powers of the federal government. The want of a power in the old confederation to act upon individuals by taxation, had destroyed its efficacy, and this defect was the chief object to be removed in the formation of " a more perfect union." The concomitancy of representation and taxation, dictated the form of the house of representatives, and not an intention of extending the powers of the federal government, by the mode of representation established in that single branch. For, the president is also elected, in the first instance, upon indirect federal principles, and directly by states, in case of no election by electors. As two branches of the federal government are federally constructed, as only one participates of individual representation, and as the construction of this one was dictated by the limited power over persons bestowed for effecting federal, and not personal or local ends, the assertion of the court is exploded by fact, and the inferences from it subverted by a genuine construction of the federal constitution. It never intended to inflict upon state legislatures, elected by all, a responsibility to the federal senate, not elected by the people, and only the representatives of state sovereignties. Nor did it intend, by bestowing a limited power of taxation upon the federal government, for the special purpose of effecting federal ends, and by subjecting this power to the check of personal representation, to make this partial representation a pretext for assuming local or personal powers, and for exercising the unlimited power of "acting for all." If this reasoning be true, it applies conclusively to banks, corporations, roads, canals, and congressional patronage.

To sustain the assertions I have been combating, the court says, "There is no phrase in the constitution which *excludes* " *incidental or implied powers.*" " Its nature requires that " only its *great out-lines* should be marked." " We find in it " the *great powers* to lay and collect taxes, to borrow money, " to regulate commerce, to declare and conduct a war, and to " raise and support armies and navies. Can we adopt that " construction, unless the words *imperiously* require it, which " would impute to the framers of the instrument, when grant- " ing these powers for the *publick good*, the intention of *imped-*

" *ing* their exercise by withholding a choice of means? The
" instrument does not profess to *enumerate the means* by which
" the powers it confers may be executed, nor does it *prohibit*
" *the creation of a corporation, if the existence* of such a thing
" be *essential* to the beneficial exercise of those powers."

If the assertions we have just examined are true, they do not
need the various auxiliaries summoned to their assistance in
this extract; if they are false, these auxiliaries cannot make
them true; and as the assertions comprise the principles to be
vindicated, the auxiliaries brought forward in their defence are
of no use or weight, if the principles themselves should have
been exploded. The great weight of the authority of the court,
however, will justify their examination.

When the adoption of the federal constitution was under
discussion, its enemies expressed an alarm, on account of the
magnitude of the powers conferred on the federal government,
and its friends an apprehension of its feebleness, compared
with the powers reserved to the states; but neither party contended, that an amplification of the greater division of power,
and of course a diminution of the lesser, could constitutionally
be made by equipping the giant in all the panoply of means,
implication and inference, and compelling the dwarf to appear
naked in a combat with his antagonist. On the contrary, it
was successfully urged by the warmest friends to the constitution, and in particular by the authors of the Federalist, that the
supposed inequality of power between the state and federal
spheres did not exist; and that either division, especially the
state, was able to balance and controul the other. In this computation, the comparison was made between the federal sphere,
and the state sphere, comprising all the state governments;
and the equilibrium of power was deduced from the expectation,
that if the rights of one state were assailed by the federal government, the rest would not suffer their copartner to be over-
whelmed by the weight of power, and their own rights to be
destroyed by a victory, in a contest so unequal. To estimate
the magnitude of their relative powers, the state governments
ought to be considered as constituting one sphere, and the federal government another. Perhaps a cool philosopher may consider the security of private property, the protection of personal rights, the suppression of crimes, the care of good manners

and the catalogue of municipal regulations, as embracing a sphere of action, of greater moral extent, than the powers delegated to congress; and if the two spheres are to be geographically compared, the map demonstrates their equality. If these spheres are equal as to magnitude, one magnitude attracts undefined appurtenances as strongly as the other; and if the framers of the constitution designed to balance magnitude by magnitude, they could not also have designed to destroy the balance, by annexing to either an exclusive privilege of attracting undefined powers.

Be this as it may, I contend, that the federal constitution, so far from intending to make its political spheres morally unequal in powers, or to invest the *greatest* with any species of sovereignty over the least, intended the very reverse; and that the court have recognised the latter intention by avowing its right to declare an unconstitutional law, void. As the powers of congress must be confessed to transcend those of the court, much farther than they do those of the states, it follows, that if they cannot be constitutionally used to contract the powers of the court, they cannot be constitutionally used to contract the powers of the states. The reason why great spheres derive no authority from magnitude to transgress upon small spheres, is, that both are donations from the same source; and that the donor did not intend, that one donation should pilfer another, because it was smaller.

" Can we adopt that construction, unless the words impe-
" riously require it, which would impute to the framers of the
" instrument, when granting these powers for *publick good*,
" the intention of *impeding* their exercise by withholding a
" choice of means?" This question might be answered by another. Can we adopt that construction, unless the words imperiously require it, which would impute to the framers of the constitution, when granting powers for *publick good*, the intention of allowing one sphere by an unlimited choice of means, to *impede* the exercise of powers conferred upon others? It admits also of so many other answers, quite satisfactory, that a few only need be urged. There is no imperious, or rather positive power, requiring the judicial sphere to declare a law void; yet it claims this right, by which it may limit the means of legislative power, and *impede* its exercise. This can

only be justified by co-ordinacy and restrictions *imperiously* established, in the positive division of power, into limited political spheres. This division was intended to effect the precise end, for the *publick good*, here objected to; the end of controuling power by power. And if this controul does not extend to means, as power cannot be exercised nor usurpation become successful, except by means; all our divisions, restrictions and limitations of power, designed to prevent, for the *publick good*, the profligacy it has invariably displayed, when uncontrouled, must become nugatory and ineffectual. The words of the constitution arè literally *imperious* in reserving to the states, for the *publick good* also, a right of taxation subject only to a positive limitation. The means by which the states may provide for raising a revenue, being expressly bestowed by the people, are surely as sacred, and as constitutional, and as likely to advance the publick good, as any conjectural conflicting means, which can be imagined by congress.

" There is no phrase in the constitution, which excludes " *incidental* or implied powers. Its nature requires that only " its *great outlines* should be marked." A contrast between positions often elicits light. There is no phrase in the constitution which even insinuates, that the actual divisions of power should be altered or impaired by incidental or implied powers. A revolution in our system of government would be no longer anticipated, after supplanting the position " that actual powers controul implied powers," and planting in its place the dogma " that implied powers controul actual powers." A great one would be effected, if it could be established, that " incidental or implied powers not excluded" were not prohibited. Let it be remembered, that the *great outlines* of state governments are more slightly referred to by the constitution, than the outlines of the federal government; that the means for executing the powers delegated to the latter are frequently *marked*, whilst those for executing the powers reserved to the former, are left chiefly unlimited. And then let it be computed, which sphere may make the greatest use of the strange position " that means, or incidental, or implied powers not excluded, are not prohibited," however they may be at discord with the positive divisions of power. If this reasoning of the court be incorrect, the

conclusion it is used to establish " that the creation of a corpo-
" ration, if the existence of such a thing be essential to the
" beneficial exercise of the powers of congress, is *constitu-*
" *tional, because not prohibited*"—is incorrect also, if however
beneficial considered alone, it disorders or impairs actual powers bestowed upon political spheres, as in the case of limiting
the power of state taxation, farther than it is limited by the
constitution. The idea, that one limited sphere has an exclusive privilege of doing whatever it may conceive to " be *essential* to the *beneficial* exercise of its own powers" is still more
extravagant, more subversive of co-ordinate spheres, and utterly inconsistent, in every view, with our system of checking
power by power ; as well as with the English theory of balances.

Another argument urged by the court is, I think, less
ingenious than any of those we have previously considered. It
says " The power of taxation by the states is not *abridged* by
" the grant of a similar power to the government of the union ;
" it is to be concurrently exercised by the two governments.
" The states are forbidden to lay duties on exports or imports.
" If the obligation of this prohibition must be conceded ; if it
" may restrain a state from the exercise of its taxing powers on
" imports and exports, the *same paramount power* would seem
" to restrain, as it certainly *may restrain,* a state from *such other*
" exercise of this power as is in its nature *incompatible with*
" *and repugnant to the constitutional laws* of the union." The
artifice of acknowledging a constitutional principle, and distinctly admitting the powers actually bestowed on the federal
and state spheres of our government ; and then of immediately defeating these actual powers on one side, and extending
them on the other, is repeatedly resorted to in the opinion of
the court. But, this bold mode of reasoning is in every instance
completely overthrown by the principle, if it be a true one,
" that expressed powers and rights contract and limit implied
" powers and rights, and that implied powers and rights do not
" controul and limit expressed powers and rights." The assertion " that the same *paramount* power" (by which I understand
the constitution) " which restrained the states from taxing
" imports and exports, may restrain a state from such other
" exercise of their taxing power as is in its nature *incompatible*

"*with and repugnant to the constitutional laws* of the union," by blending a sequitur and a non sequitur together and confounding our ideas, endeavours to delude them into an erroneous conclusion. Stript of this ambiguity the argument stands thus : " The constitution might have further restrained, and therefore, " it has further restrained the taxing power of the states." Thus fairly stated, the conclusion does not follow. To use the prospective terms employed by the court, the argument would be this : " A constitution, *may*, and therefore has further re- " strained this power." This mode of anticipating innovation, renders the mode prescribed for amending the constitution quite superfluous. It unfolds to legislatures the entire cargo of powers not prohibited, but not given ; they are told that they may exercise any powers, which the constitution might have given them, and are very courteously invited to pick and choose. As a complete spherical sovereignty is conceded both to the federal and state governments, and as the constitution does not forbid to either this mode of extending their respective powers, it is open to both ; and the laws of neither, under this novel constitutional power, can be unconstitutional, because state laws made in virtue of its spherical sovereignty comprising' a right of construction, will be equally constitutional with federal laws, when both may defend themselves by a common principle. The clashings likely to arise between specified powers and rights will be nothing to those, which would be produced by a mutual power to assume implied rights and powers not prohibited. But I believe that I have misunderstood the court in supposing, that it meant " constitutional power" by the phrase " paramount character." It seems by the expression " constitutional laws of the union" as if it meant, not that the constitution, but that congress was the paramount power. The consideration of this idea is postponed to the next section; at present I shallonly observe that the laws both of the federal or state governments may be either conformable or repugnant to the constitution ; that one government is equally restrained with the other from passing laws repugnant to the constitution ; and that neither can be absolved by a claim of one to the title " paramount" bestowed upon neither, to defeat the laws of its co-ordinate sphere. The *paramount* power of the people, by prohibiting the states from taxing imports and exports, did not create a paramount power in congress, to extend the prohibition to internal objects of taxation. It is therefore obvious, that the restrictive expression "constitutional laws of the union" has no relation to the subject under discussion, as that relates entirely to unconstitutional laws; and that it is used merely to conceal, under the position "that the states have no right to pass unconstitu-"tional laws," which is true, the conclusion "that the federal "government possess a paramount and exclusive power of "deciding upon the constitutionality and unconstitutionality of "all laws, both state and federal," which is denied to be true.

Let us illustrate this reasoning by the fact. Congress have, by one corporation, subtracted from the fund made liable by the constitution to state taxation, thirty millions of specified right, by the instrumentality of power implied or not prohibited. The same species of instrumentality, not being prohibited, may also be implied in behalf of the states. And to place the federal and state governments in the constitutional relation existing between them previously to its exercise, the states ought to subtract thirty millions also from the specified fund exposed to federal taxation; a precedent by which one fund is diminished to the extent of thirty millions, and by the capacity of an incorporating power to diminish it without limitation, decides the fate of either of these sovereign spheres, which should be deprived both of resistance, and every countervailing expedient. Revenue is the sustenance of power. The old congress dwindled into imbecility, because the states could subtract from its funds without limitation; and the old states will ultimately suffer the same fate, if the new congress may by corporations subtract from their power to raise a revenue, without limitation. The position between these two spherical sovereignties would be exactly reversed, and however it may be justified upon the principles of retaliation and revenge, the reciprocity of defeat would, by the humiliation of the state governments, inflict greater evils upon the people, than they suffered from the humiliation of the old congress from a similar cause. Our experience had taught us the necessity of an independent revenue for the support of power; and the constitution under the conviction of experience, invested each sphere, sovereign say the court, with this paramount necessity, in terms the most distinct; but, if another paramount necessity for creating corporations, shall be able to subtract what it pleases from the paramount necessity for revenue, these spherical sovereignties will occupy the stations of England and Ireland, whilst the former took away revenue from the latter, by quartering a substantial, though not a nominal, corporation of pensioners upon the Irish funds. Had it been proposed in the convention, still further to reduce the fund for revenue left with the states, by investing congress with a power of subtracting any portion or the whole of internal state funds for raising revenue; or had such a construction been put upon the constitution whilst under the consideration of the people, it is impossible to hesitate in our opinions as to the results; and this unavoidable retrospective impression is no slight proof of its real intention.

Sometimes the court reject a restriction imposed upon particular words by the general tenour of the constitution, and at others endeavour to destroy the most liberal rights, though according with the general tenour. An exception excludes that which it does not contain. A delegation of power does the same. The prohibition to tax exports and imports leaves untouched every other species of taxation. The delegated power of taxation to congress, contains no new prohibition upon the states. The intention in both cases is literally expressed. The reservation of all powers not delegated to the United States, nor prohibited to the states, is a third literal restriction of the prohibition to tax imports and exports, to the things actually prohibited. Add to the positive letter the consideration, that sovereign states were delegating limited powers; and the idea, that both the specifick prohibition upon the states, and the restricted delegation to congress, may be defeated by an implication, hostile to both, and contrary to the rules of construction, seems entirely inadmissible. Had the framers of the constitution conceived, that the state taxing power, originally unlimited, could be limited by implication, a far more specious foundation for this doctrine was furnished by the power given to congress to regulate commerce; as the taxation of exports and imports by the states might have been " incompatible with and repugnant to" this constitutional power; and by not confiding in this implied species of prohibition, they positively reprobate it. The implication in this case would have been specially confined to imports and exports, had the constitution failed to prohibit the states from taxing them; but as it does contain this limited prohibition, I cannot conceive by what train of ratiocination, the limited prohibition expressed, can be made to beget an unlimited power in congress further to restrict the original state right of taxation.

It has been proved, that the English spherical sovereignty rejects any claim of sovereignty by one sphere over another, and limits the means of each, by the sphere of each. Admitting a sovereignty composed of spheres to be still one and indivisible, then a spherical sovereignty of spheres here would also be one and indivisible. Unity is an innate quality of sovereign power, as it is of legislative, though it may be compounded of individuals. Thus the moral or political beings called a sovereignty or a legislature are units, of whatever individuals composed. Such is the case with the sovereignty of the people. As this is composed of natural individuals, a sovereignty of spheres is composed of individual spheres. Neither of these can possess a better right to assume by any means a superiority over co-spheres composing a sovereignty, than one citizen under the pretext that he also is a component part of the sovereignty of the people can assume a superiority over other citizens. In both cases, however, a love of power has suggested a multitude of means, by which both the individuals composing the sovereignty of the people, and the individuals composing a sovereignty of the spheres, have violated their allegiance. Sovereignty here resides in the people, or in our individual political spheres. If in the people, these spheres are limited departments only, not having more power individually, than if they participated as is contended of sovereign power. If we even enlarge this power, by endowing our political spheres with sovereignty, then one sphere, being only an individual of the sovereignty, has no controuling authority over the others; such an authority, however disguised, would destroy a sovereignty of spheres and establish a sovereignty of one sphere; and this sphere would be a despot over the others, just as one citizen, who obtains a controuling authority over the rest, is also a despot. The case is precisely the same if one sphere of action can by any means obtain a controuling authority over the other spheres of action; the rights of the controuled spheres, derived from the sovereignty of the people, would be made dependent upon another sphere of action, created by the same authority. Thus a citizen having social rights loses them, if another citizen has by any means obtained an authority of controuling them. It follows from both aspects of the case, one of which must be admitted, that political spheres, constituting a spherical sovereignty, must controul and restrain each other; that political departments, circumscribed by the sovereign power of the people, must still more clearly controul each other; that is, spheres of action must controul each other; and that the means of each of these individual moral beings, must also be controuled and restrained by the means of the others; because an authority capable of controuling the rest, obtained by one, destroys the end and design of either political system.

The argument in reply to this reasoning is, that unless a supreme authority is allowed to the federal legislature and federal courts, to controul the legislatures and courts of the states, subordination will not exist, and sundry inconveniences would result from its absence. This argument would be sufficiently answered by asking for the words in the constitution, by which one sphere of action is made subordinate to another; or by which one is invested with the exclusive authority to restrain the rest within their proper spheres. But it overthrows itself by its own force, and by proving too much, proves nothing. It implies, that every division, balance, restriction or check of power by power, which has been or can be invented, must be wrong; and that subordination is preferable to them all : that Mr. Hamilton is wrong in observing that " power " controuled or abridged is almost always the rival and enemy " of that power by which it is controuled and abridged," and ought to have pleaded in favour of removing all restrictions by supremacy, for the sake of establishing subordination ; and that he was still more wrong in supposing, that power could only be controuled by power. It is not uncommon to destroy the highest attainable temporal blessings, by selecting and displaying the imperfections of which all human institutions participate. Thus the inconveniences of co-ordinate and balanced departments, and the conveniences of subordination are both

magnified. Individual spheres or departments are easily persuaded, like kings, that a subordination to themselves would
be better for a nation, than the occasional collisions produced
by a division and limitation of power. The federal and state
governments might both be induced to believe, that its own
supervising supremacy over the other would produce more good
to the people, than the plan adopted by the people themselves.
And thus an object of the first necessity or convenience, that
of a free, moderate and limited form of government, might be
sacrificed for such pitiful objects, called objects of necessity
or convenience, as transmitting the publick money by banks,
staying judgments and executions, making a road or a canal,
creating fraudulent corporations, and absolving their great
wealth from taxation, whilst very poor people are contributing
to the support of government. Usurpation begins with weav-
ing a shroud for free principles by the woof and warp of little
conveniences and pretended necessities, and ends by inflicting
the slavish quietism of a perfect subordination.

The court has cautiously forborne to define the origin, or the
extent of spherical sovereignty. By denying the argument of
the counsel, " That the people had bestowed sovereignty on the
" state governments, and therefore had none left to bestow on
" the federal government," it clearly asserts, that the people
do not lose their sovereignty by creating a government. By
contending that the federal government, created in virtue of
their retained and inherent sovereignty, has acquired any
species of sovereignty, it as clearly asserts, that they do lose it.
By asserting, that our political spheres are limited by their constitutional spheres of action, it admits, that they are not invested with sovereignty. By investing them with the right of
creating corporations, as resulting from the power appertaining
to sovereignty, it declares that they are. This sample of its
appurtenances, and the general position that it may employ any
means which it chooses, or may think necessary or convenient,
leaves the capacity of the new political structure called spherical sovereignty, quite indefinite. 1 have heard of a lady
desirous of having a new house, and unable to prevail on her
husband to build it, who persuaded him at length to suffer her
to repair the old one. With the help of an ingenious carpenter,
under her own influence and direction, she went to work; and

proceeding by cautious degrees, not to awaken her husband's attention, so altered and enclosed the old one, that when he at last discovered the artifice, he found himself obliged to pull it down and throw it piece by piece out of the windows. Thus the indefinite attributes of a sovereignty of spheres, will gradually usurp and supplant the attributes of the sovereignty of the people. The old principle of limited ends will be thrown out of the window by the new principle of unlimited means; and the right of the old sovereignty to create bodies politick, will be swallowed up by a new spherical sovereignty.

Of this sophistical spherical sovereignty, the instances abound; and we find it in every case to be the identical machine, by which all free and limited governments have been overthrown. The conventions of France (elected to form a constitution) upon the ground of representing the people, assumed a spherical sovereignty with its attributes as settled by themselves ; and exercised unlimited power, under a nominal acknowledgment of the sovereignty of the people. Bonaparte, both in his sphere of consul and emperor, took their votes, and thus owned the sovereignty of the people. But what was the value of the allegiance professed in either case, united with a choice of means, necessities, and conveniences, by these spherical sovereignties? The same as that of the divine right of sovereignty in kings, nobles and political spheres, from the beginning of history to this day.

The reader is reminded, that although I have adopted the phrase " spherical sovereignty" and supposed its existence, with a hope of proving that even this concession does not warrant the judgment of the court; yet I do not thereby design to admit of its application, under any definition, to our system of government; because its meaning is so utterly equivocal, as to be innately incongruous with the idea of limited powers, of which this system is composed. I contend that the idea of one or many spherical sovereignties is an adulteration of the sovereignty of the people ; that a limitation of spheres of action, is a limitation of means of action ; that no sphere can do any thing, because it may be convenient or necessary, unless it be constitutional ; that no sphere can invade another by means however beneficial, because it would be unconstitutional ;

that no sphere has a power of doing what is good or bad, generally, but constitutionally only ; and that if these principles can
be overturned by an ingenious management of words, all our
checks, balances, limitations and divisions of power, are good
for nothing.

SECTION 9.

THE BANK DECISION.—SUPREMACY.

"The people have said, "This *constitution* and the laws of the
" United States *made in pursuance* thereof, shall be the *supreme*
" law of the land." " *It is a question of supremacy.*" " It is
" of the very essence of supremacy to remove all obstacles to
" its action within its own sphere, and so *to modify every power*
" *vested in subordinate governments, as to exempt its own*
" *operations from their influence.*"

"It is a question of supremacy." This expression, being
unequivocal, had it remained unmodified, would have submitted to the publick consideration the plain question; whether
the constitution of the union had, or had not, invested the federal government with a supreme power over the state governments. National questions ought to be candidly and fairly
stated, to obtain a genuine national opinion. Out of complai-
sance to national opinion it was conceded by the court, that
both the federal and state governments were sovereign within
their respective spheres, to obtain as an attribute of sovereignty,
a mutual right of creating corporations, and conciliate the
usurpation practised by both. But, after allowing to both this
attribute of sovereignty, a variety of equivocations are resorted
to, for inhibiting to the states its other attributes, and assigning their exclusive enjoyment to the federal government. The
means, the necessities, and the conveniences of the federal government as attributes of sovereignty are dilated, and those of
the state governments consigned to oblivion. The federal government is acknowledged to be limited; but then it is said,
that there is no phrase in the constitution which excludes incidental or implied powers, without admitting, that no enlarge
ment of power can be inferred from this assertion in favour of
the federal sovereignty, in which the state sovereignties would
not participate. It is conceded, that the power of internal

taxation is not abridged with respect to the states, by the grant of a similar power to the government of the union, and that it is to be exercised concurrently by the two governments ; but the concession is retracted, by inferring from the constitutional abridgment in the subjects of imports and exports, a right in the federal government still farther to abridge the concurrent right of the states to an unspecified extent. It is said that the power of the states is subordinate to, and may be controuled by the constitution of the United States; but then it is inferred, that it is also subordinate to and may be controuled by the federal government. But, as this alternation between concession and retraction was liable to formidable objections, it is finally abandoned, or shielded against confutation, by the assertion " that it is a question of supremacy, and that it is of the very " essence of supremacy to remove all obstacles to its action " within its own sphere, *and so to modify every power vested* " *in subordinate governments, as to exempt its own operations* " *from their influence.*" The sweeping power asserted in the conclusion of this extract, is obviously distinct from a power of *removing obstacles within its own sphere*, previously asserted ; and is another instance, in which unlimited power is attempted to be inferred from a power acknowledged to be limited. Thus the wisdom of concession and the ingenuity of retraction are so constantly blended, as finally to invest a government acknowledged to be limited, with an unlimited power over the very restrictions imposed upon itself; and also over the state governments, acknowledged also to be its co-sovereigns. To fortify this mode of reasoning, it became even necessary to find a higher power than sovereignty, in order to controul the admitted sovereignty of spheres; and though hitherto thought not to exist, it is supposed to be found in the words "paramount and supreme" so sublimated, as to reduce the sovereignty both of the state spheres and of the people to mere glow worms.

The declaration of independence declares the colonies to be free and independent states ; the constitutions of many states assert the sovereignty of the people; and sovereignty has hitherto been considered as the highest political degree. In that sense it has been claimed, held and exercised by the people of every state in the union from the revolution to this day. The attempt made by the court (before considered) to transplant sovereignty from the people of each state, by whom it has been and may be exercised, to the people of the United States, by whom it never has been nor can be exercised, under our present system of government, might fail of success; and therefore a new mode of destroying the sovereignty of the people is resorted to. Its jealousy is first appeased by the acknowledgment of spherical sovereignties, and then its degradation is finished by subjecting these sovereignties to supremacy. If the ground is a good one, all the states of the union took bad ground both in establishing and sustaining their independence. Supremacy was the literal claim of the British parliament over the colonies; and these colonies having only established sovereignties (an inferior political degree) have in fact tacitly acknowledged the British claim, which, being thus recognised, may be still prosecuted. It is also probable that the treaty failed to acknowledge our title to paramount and supreme power. If the treaty and the declaration of independence had not unfortunately committed this oversight, it would have narrowed the question considerably, by excluding from it a necessity for this entire section. Had these instruments declared the states to be sovereign, independent, *paramount and supreme*, then the language of the court's admission must have been correspondently changed; and instead of admitting that both the federal and state governments were each sovereign within its sphere, they must have admitted that each was sovereign, paramount and supreme within its own sphere. But, if this language, to give each word its excessive meaning, would have been tautological; then these instruments have committed no error, but merely avoided repetition, by rejecting useless synonymes. To admit, that the words " sovereign, paramount and supreme" are synonymes, to express the highest degree of political power, bestows on the two latter their most excessive meaning; whilst there is no excess at all in allowing that meaning to the first; therefore this admission bestows on the doctrine of the court the utmost force of which it is susceptible. And yet after thus doing for it all that can be done, and more than it can claim, it is obviously defeated by the error of giving to one synonyme a different meaning from another; just as it is impossible to prove, that though three apples are of the same weight, yet that one may be made heavier than the others, by calling it a supreme apple. But I shall endeavour to prove, that even this ground is stronger than the opinion of the court is entitled to, by shewing that " sovereignty" describes a higher power, than " paramount or supreme," and therefore that it was never intended to be subjected to them.

The word "paramount" is not mentioned in the constitution, nor any where adopted, that I recollect, by our political phraseology; wherefore in considering the leader, it will be unnecessary to pay much respect to a feeble ally. Hence I proceed to shew, that the word " supreme" is invariably used by the constitution, not in a paramount but in a subordinate sense to sovereignty.

" The *constitution*, and the laws of the United States which " shall be made *in pursuance thereof*, and *all treaties made* or " which shall be made, *under the authority* of the United States, " shall be the supreme law of the land, and *the judges*, in " every state, shall be bound thereby, any thing in the consti- " tution or laws of any state to the contrary notwithstanding." This is the clause of the constitution, supposed by the court to confer on congress a power over the state governments and state sovereignties. These state sovereignties made, may revoke, or can alter the constitution itself, and therefore the supremacy bestowed upon the constitution, being some power subservient to the state sovereignties, demonstrates that the word " supreme" was used in a sense subordinate to these sovereignties; and being used in that sense, it is impossible that the people intended it as a revocation of those powers, or of any of their appurtenances, or of the spherical sovereignties, previously bestowed, never recalled, and specially reserved to the state governments, by the sovereignties, to whom the whole constitution and all its words, are subordinate. According to the construction adopted by the court, the stile of the constitution ought to have been this. " We, state sove- " reignties, do hereby establish a federal government invested " with limited powers, and retain our state governments, with " all their powers not delegated to the federal government, " each of which governments shall be sovereign within their " respective spheres, but over these sovereignties, we also cre-

" ate three supremacies; one a supremacy of the constitution;
" another, of the laws `of the United States; and a third of
" the treaty-making power." It is hard or impossible to serve
two masters only. The court has turned the federal and state
governments into sovereignties, and placed over all, three supremacies. The difficulties of such a system would be insurmountable: whereas, by acknowledging one master only, in the
sovereignty of the people, and confessing ¡the obligation of the
political departments created by that sovereignty, to move
within the orbits assigned to them, as great a degree of order
may ensue, united with liberty, as is attainable by human
wisdom.

Are these supremacies of co-ordinate and equal power; or
are laws and treaties subordinate to the constitution ? The
constitution, the laws and the treaties are all declared to be
the supreme law of the land, and therefore, as it could not
have been designed to bestow on laws, an authority equal to
the authority of the constitution, no construction can be correct,
which does not sustain both the superiority of the constitution
over laws, and also a perfect equality as to the obligations
imposed by the supremacy declared; and such a construction
is I think quite visible. The supremacy is not bestowed upon
the federal government. It is a moral and not a personal
supremacy which is established. It was not intended to confer
on one department, sphere, sovereignty, or organization of
persons, any superiority over another department, sphere,
sovereignty, or organization of persons; and was merely a
declaration of the respect to which the recited moral beings
were equally entitled. The constitution cannot be personified,
so as to be reduced to a supreme body politick distinct from
the people; and if laws are to be personified by congress, and
treaties by the president and senate, their supremacy would
either be of a different nature from the supremacy of the
constitution, or these two departments, neither of which, nor
both constitute the federal government, would be made supreme
over the federal and state governments, and equal to the
supremacy of the people, if they are to be considered as the
representatives of the supremacy of the constitution. But as
no additional personal or national power was conferred by
declaring the constitution to be the supreme law of the land,

it proves that no additional personal or spherical power was conferred by declaring the laws and treaties to be also the supreme law of the land. The declaration, that the constitution was the supreme law, confirmed all its limitations, divisions, restrictions and limitations of power, and it never was intended that either should be altered in the least degree by laws or treaties, or be placed under the power of those who should make laws or treaties. On the contrary, the laws were to be made *in pursuance* of the constitution, and the treaties, under *the authority* of the United States. The United States have no authority, except that which is given by the constitution. Both the laws and treaties to be supreme must, therefore, be made in conformity with the powers bestowed, limited and reserved by the constitution, and by these we must determine whether a law or a treaty has been constitutionally made, before the question of its supremacy can occur. The judges are expressly referred to, as the curators or executors of this moral supremacy, and no other department is by the least hint recognized, as being able to impair or enforce it. And finally, all officers, legislative, executive and judicial, take an oath to support the constitution, which is a moral sanction in favour of a moral system ; and none take an oath to acknowledge any species of personal or spherical supremacy. This clause then amounts to no more, than that the constitution shall be the supreme law of the land. As proceeding from the sovereignty of the people, the highest political authority, the term was proper ; because it was paramount and supreme over whatever should proceed from any inferior authority ; and as the constitution embraced our whole system of government, both state and federal, by delegating and reserving powers, the supremacy bestowed on it was intended equally and co-extensively to protect and secure the powers delegated to the federal government, and those reserved to the states. In this construction of the word " supreme," the court itself has literally concurred, in asserting " that it would be its duty to "declare an unconstitutional law void." The right of doing this arises from the supremacy of the constitution over law; from the restriction it imposes upon political departments or spheres to confine themselves within their limited orbits ; and from its intention that each department or sphere should controul another, if it trangresses its boundary. Upon this ground the court has asserted this constitutional power in its own sphere. It can be defended upon no other; because the constitution does not say, that their judgments shall be the supreme law of the land. If the ground be solid in relation to the judicial sphere, it is equally solid in relation to the limited federal and state spheres. If the legislative federal sphere have no supreme power over the judicial federal sphere; because its power is limited by the constitution, and not extended beyond these limitations by the clause of the constitution under consideration; it follows, that neither the federal nor state spheres derive any supremacy over the other from the same clause, whilst acting within their limited boundaries.

In fact, the opinion of the court admits the soundness of this construction, though it qualifies the admission by an unexplained ambiguity, which ingeniously keeps the question out of sight. "It is a question of supremacy." But it does not explain what this supremacy is, nor how far it extends. "It is of the very "essence of supremacy to remove all obstacles to its action "*within its own sphere.*" By the words "within its own "sphere" the court seems to admit, that a sphere ought to act within the boundaries prescribed to it, without suffering any hindrance from another sphere. This is all for which I contend; and if this be allowed (and it must be allowed to justify the judicial sphere in annulling an unconstitutional law of congress,) then neither the federal nor state spheres whilst acting within their spheres, are subjected to the impediments of the other, and each has a right to controul such impediments. But then the court produce the ambiguity by adding, that a supreme sphere may "*so modify every power vested in* "*subordinate governments,* as to exempt its own operations "from their influence." It is useless to concede principles if they can be evaded. The court had previously admitted that the federal and state governments were "*both sovereign* with "respect to the objects committed to them, and *neither sove-* "*reign* with respect to the objects committed to the other;" but now it takes it for granted, that the federal sphere is *supreme,* the state spheres *subordinate,* and that in consequence of this supremacy and subordinacy, the federal government has a right "so to *modify every power* vested in the

"state governments, as to exempt its own operations from
" their influence."

Power in the exercise of verbal construction, and in deducing inferences from particular phrases, like a fine lady admiring a casket of jewels, very easily discovers whatever it
wishes for, to be right, convenient, useful and necessary. Particular texts are often tortured to appease conscience, or to
gratify prejudice; and good or bad intentions are equally
fertile in expedients for surmounting obstacles. A single word
is often so indefinite, that its meaning is controuled by another.
A single sentence may generally be twisted into an enmity
with principles plainly asserted, in any book; but the defects
of language do not equally extend to an entire treatise. Thus
the imperfections of isolated words and sentences, and the
frailties of mankind unite to teach us, that the licentiousness
of construction can only be controuled by an impartial estimate
of a whole, and a candid comparison of its parts. If the reader
shall examine the federal constitution by this rule, and should
discover that it delegates a power to the federal government
"so to *modify every power* vested in the state governments as
" to exempt its own operations from their influence," he must
conclude, that the decision of the court, founded upon the
existence of this power in the federal government, is correct;
but if the constitution invests the federal government with no
such power, then it follows, that this decision, founded upon a
supposition that it did, must be unconstitutional. This is in
fact the very essence of the question; as interferences by the
federal or state governments with powers delegated to the
other, are in truth modifications of those powers; and it is
extremely important to ascertain, whether a power so enormous and unspecified is common to both, or exclusively conferred upon the former. The latter is asserted by the court for
the purpose of modifying the state right of taxation; by those
members of congress who supported a bill for prohibiting slavery in a particular state, and is the ground upon which alone all
interfering with the police of states can be defended.

It will be allowed, that the people of each state had, and
exercised the right of modifying the powers vested in the state
governments. If the federal government now have it, the most
unexpected consequences will ensue. The people can no

longer exercise the right, because they have given it away. If
it be a concurrent right, should they exercise it, the federal
government may re-modify their modifications. The state governments will be responsible either to the federal government
singly, or both to this government and the people for their
conduct. It was quite idle to reserve to the state governments
the powers previously bestowed, if they were at the same time
subjected to the subsequent modifications of the federal government. And the meditated check upon the federal government
by the powers reserved to the state governments would be
equally insignificant. These consequences of the construction
given to the word "supreme" by the court, so completely
subversive of the essential principles of our system of government, are a sufficient exposition of its incorrectness.

But the argument becomes stronger, when we resort to the
provisions of the constitution. I shall venture to test the
position relied on by the court, by the mode before practised of
confronting it with a contradictory position; so that one or the
other must be disallowed. It is a question of supremacy; the
constitution has invested the states with a complete, and the
state governments with a limited supremacy, over the federal
government, and expressly subjected its *operations to the
influence* of the latter, in sundry important instances. The
states by common consent may dissolve or modify the union,
over which, by the natural right of self-government, which they
have never relinquished, they retain a complete supremacy.
By the constitution, the state governments are invested with
the rights of appointing senators and electors of a president,
for the very purpose of influencing the operations of the federal
government for their own security. They may forbear to
exercise this right, and thus dissolve the federal government.
They may elect the members of the house of representatives by
a general ticket, and thereby very considerably influence its
operations. They may compel congress to call a convention.
They may ratify changes of the federal government, without
its consent. They may affirm or reject amendments proposed
by congress. They have a concurrent right of internal taxation with the federal goverment, and these concurrent rights
may deeply influence each other; and they are exclusively
invested with the appointment of all the officers of that force,

upon which the safety and liberty of the nation depend. These powers seem to me, to invest the state governments with a limited supremacy over the federal government; at least it must be admitted, that they are such as may and do deeply influence its operations. The constitution gives no authority to the federal government to exercise such powers over the state governments. Can it then be true, as the position of the court declares, that the federal government have a right so *to modify every power vested in the state governments, as to exempt its own operations from their influence?* Upon the ground of this doctrine, the supreme court of the federal government has attempted so to modify the concurrent right of taxation reserved to the states, as to exempt the incorporating power assumed by congress, from its influence. This is one of the enumerated powers invested in the states, by which it was certainly foreseen and intended, that they might influence the operations of the federal government; and if in this case such an influence justifies a modification of the state power of taxation by the federal government, and even by one of its departments, the same reason will justify a modification of all the rest of the enumerated influencing state powers. The supreme court might by the same principle, appoint senators, electors, and militia officers, should the states neglect to do it; in order, by modifying these powers of the state governments, as being subordinate to the supposed supremacy of the federal government, *to exempt the latter from their influence.*

If, therefore, it should have been proved, that the federal government is not invested with a power of modifying the powers bestowed by the people on the state governments, the pretended supremacy, supposed to bestow a right so unlimited, does not exist; the modification on the state power of taxation was of course unconstitutional; and the question would seem to be settled. But it starts up again, in a new form; and though it should be allowed that the entire federal government do not possess a right to modify the state constitutions, yet it is still contended, that one of its subordinate departments does possess it; and its supreme court have accordingly modified and restricted the power of internal taxation bestowed by the state constitutions on their governments. This power under the state constitutions was unlimited. It is not limited by the federal constitution. But the federal court have adjudged, that it is either necessary or convenient that it should be limited; and for that reason they have modified it by a precedent sufficient to justify other modifications of state powers to any extent, upon the ground of possessing an unlimited supremacy over the legislative and judicial power of the states.

The supremacy we have examined is confined to the constitution, the laws, and treaties. It is not extended to judicial decisions. Suppose congress should pass a law declaring such state laws as they pleased, to be unconstitutional and void. An excessive interpretation of the word "supreme," might give some countenance to so evident an usurpation; and as one branch of the federal legislature is elected by the people, it would afford some security, however imperfect, against such a prostration of the state governments at the feet of the federal legislative power. But neither this excessive supremacy, nor this defective security, plead for lodging the same unlimited power in the federal courts. Were they to possess it, they might modify the state governments, in a mode, contrary to the will of congress, as is exemplified in the case under consideration. In creating the bank of the United States, congress did not endeavour to prohibit the states from taxing the property employed in that speculation. Had the state right to do so been considered in that body, its constitutionality might have been decided in the affirmative. The court, therefore, in assuming a power to restrain this state right, may have violated the will both of the federal and state legislature, and modified the state constitutions, contrary to the judgment of both. The state law asserted the right, the federal law is silent, and the court imposes a constitutional rule on both (as if it were itself a constituent or elemental power,) objected to by one, and never assented to by the other. This outstrips even the arbitrary principle laid down by the court itself "that the supreme "government may modify every power vested in subordinate "governments, to exempt its own operations from their influ- "ence." It will not be asserted that the federal court is the supreme government, or that it has operations to carry on, which ought to be exempted from the influence of the subordinate state governments. If these governments are not subordinate to that court, it cannot modify their powers, even under its own principle; and if the federal government possesses this modifying power, it ought to be exercised by congress, before it can be enforced by the court. The court at most can only execute, and have no power to pronounce the modification. Congress might have intended, that the power of taxing the United States bank, like that of taxing state banks, should remain as a concurrent power, like the other concurrent powers of taxation. If that body conceived itself possessed of a power to modify the state power of taxation, it could only do so by its own act, and that act ought to have been explicit, that the people might, by election, have expressed their opinion concerning it. But when the modification is expressed by the court, the chief remedy for deciding spherical collisions,and for restraining each division of power within its own orbit, is wholly evaded, and completely transferred from the people to the judges.

But, though it should be allowed, that the court derives no supremacy from that clause of the constitution, which bestows it upon the constitution itself, the laws and treaties, yet it has been claimed under another. " The judicial *power of the Uni-* " *ted States* shall be vested in *one supreme court*, and in *infe-* " *rior courts.* The judges, both of the *supreme* and *inferior* " courts shall hold their offices during good behaviour." And in the next clause, this "*judicial power of the United States*" is defined and limited. By this clause, a judicial power is vested. Was it a limited or an unlimited power? It is expressed to be " *the judicial power of the United States.*" In the second section of the same article, the judicial power of the United States is expressly defined and limited; and this defined and limited judicial power, is that which is vested in *the supreme and such inferior courts as congress may from time to time establish.* The word " supreme" is evidently used in reference to " inferior." The supremacy bestowed is over the inferior courts *to be established by congress,* and not *over the state courts,* either supreme or inferior. This is manifested by the division of jurisdiction between the supreme and inferior courts. In cases " affecting ambassadors, publick ministers and " consuls, and where a state shall be a party, the supreme court " shall have original jurisdiction. In all other cases *before* " *mentioned* the supreme court shall have appellate jurisdic-

" tion." " Before mentioned." Thus expressly limiting the jurisdiction of the supreme court of the United States, to the subjects defined in the preceding article. If, therefore, any thing in the federal constitution is plain enough to be understood, I think we may certainly conclude, that the word " supreme" was not intended to extend the power of the federal court in any degree whatsoever. That court by declaring every local or internal law of congress constitutional, would extend its own jurisdiction; a limitation of which, attended with a power to extend it without controul, by a supreme power over the state courts, would be no limitation at all; since the power of supremacy would destroy the co-ordinate right of construing the constitution, in which resides the power of enforcing the limitation. A jurisdiction, limited by its own will, is an unlimited jurisdiction. As a further evidence of this conclusion, it may be observed, that if this word had bestowed " a supreme jurisdiction," there would have been no occasion for a subsequent delegation of jurisdiction to the sepreme court; and that, as by the subsequent jurisdiction bestowed (in the few cases of original jurisdiction given to the supreme court excepted,) the power of the inferior courts is made the basis of the appellate jurisdiction, given to the supreme court, it follows, that if the word " supreme" does not extend the jurisdiction of these inferior courts, it does not extend the jurisdiction of the supreme court. As the word " supreme" is not applied to the inferior courts, it cannot invest them with any power over the state courts. And as the appellate jurisdiction of the supreme court is limited to the cases before mentioned, of which the inferior courts can only take cognizance, it cannot invest the supreme court with any power over the state courts, unless it has also invested the inferior courts with the same power.

The federal constitution does not say, " that the legislative power shall consist of one supreme and inferior legislatures;" because it considered the state and federal legislatures as independent of each other, within their respective spheres. Had it considered the state legislatures as subordinate to the federal legislature, the supremacy of the latter would have been declared, and the subordination of the former expressed, as objects upon which this supremacy was to operate. If one federal court only had been allowed by the constitution, the word " su-

preme" would have been unnecessary. In creating and specifying the objects, namely, the inferior federal courts, upon
which the supremacy was to operate, all other objects are
excluded. The judicial federal power therefore stands in the
same relation to the state judicial power, as the federal legislative power does to the state legislative power; and if either
be independent of the other whilst acting within its own sphere,
both must be also independent of the other. If congress cannot repeal or injoin state laws, the supreme federal court cannot
injoin or abrogate state judgments or decrees. If the federal
legislative power be limited, the federal judicial power must also
be limited.

For the elucidation of this very important part of the subject, I shall resort to authorities, as respectable as authorities
can be.

Fed. p. 72. M. " The jurisdiction of the general government,
" *is limited to certain enumerated objects*, which concern all the
" members of the republick, but which are not to be attained
" by the separate provisions of any."

Fed. p. 208. M. " The local or municipal authorities form
" *distinct and independent* portions of the *supremacy no more*
" *subject within their respective spheres, to the general authority,*
" *than the general authority is subject to them within its own*
" *sphere.*" In the same page, however, Mr. Madison makes what
the lawyers call an *obiter* observation, that is, he drops an opinion
by chance, apparently without due consideration. " It is true,"
says he, " that in *controversies* relating to *the boundary* between
" the two jurisdictions, the tribunal which is ultimately to de-
" cide, is to be established under the general government."
Perhaps I mistake his meaning. If he mean, " controversies
" between two state jurisdictions," I admit that their decision
is vested in the federal judicial power. But if, as I confess it
appears to me, he meant " that the federal judicial power was
" vested with a right of deciding controversies between itself
" and the judicial power of the states," I must with much confidence, yet with great respect, differ with him in opinion.
The point ought to be determined by the constitution itself.
Mr. Madison asserts that, " the jurisdiction of the general
" government is *limited to certain enumerated objects.*" Is this
case comprised within that enumeration ? Is it said, generally,

" that the state judicial sphere shall be subject to the controul of
the federal judicial sphere ?" Or is it said, specially, that controversies as to jurisdiction between these two spheres shall be
decided by one of the parties? Are controversies between the
state and federal legislative spheres to be also decided by one
of the parties? Neither conclusion can consist with the preceding opinion of Mr. Madison, that " the local or municipal *au-*
" *thorities* form *distinct* and *independent* portions of the *supre-*
" *macy no more subject* within their respective spheres, to the
" *general authority*, than the general authority *is subject to*
" *them* within its own sphere." However, therefore, we shift
our words or phrases, in describing the powers delegated to the
federal government and reserved to the states; whether we
call them sovereign, supreme, legislative, executive or judicial;
they still retain their spherical, limited, co-ordinate and independent nature, in relation to each other, according to the
construction of contemporary writers of the best authority.
Fed. p. 456. H.   " There is not a syllable in the plan which
" directly empowers the national courts to construe the laws
" according to the spirit of the constitution, *or which gives*
" *them any greater latitude in this respect, than may be claimed*
" *by the courts of every state:*" Unequivocally rejecting the
idea of judicial spherical subordination.

But this constitutional question is deliberately and distinctly
stated, apparently upon the most profound consideration, in a
style, and with a precision, which it would be presumptuous in
me to defend, in certain resolutions of the Kentucky legislature, passed in the year 1798, said to have been drawn by Mr.
Jefferson, and bearing internally, evidence of flowing from an
enlightened mind. The first is in these words :—" Resolved,
" that the several states composing the United States of Ame-
" rica, are not united on the principle of unlimited submission
" to their general government ; but that by compact under the
" style and title of a constitution for the United States and of
" amendments thereto, they constituted a general government
" for *special purposes*, delegated to that government certain
" *definite powers, reserving each state to itself the residuary*
" *mass of right to their own self-government ;* and that when-
" soever the general government assumes *undelegated* powers,
" its acts are unauthoritative, *void and of no force* : That to this

" compact each state acceded as a state, and is an integral
" party, its co-states forming, as to itself, the other party ; that
" the government created by this compact *was not made the*
" *exclusive or final judge of the extent of the powers delegated*
" *to itself ;* since that would have made its discretion, and not
" the constitution, the measure of its powers; but, that as in
" all other cases of compact among parties having no common
" judge, *each party has an equal right to judge for itself,* as
" well of infractions as of the measure of redress." The co-
ordinacy of institution, the independence of each other, and
the mutuality of the right of construing the federal constitution,
are thus recognised and asserted, as existing in the federal and
state governments; and the principle, which pervades the whole,
must also pervade the parts. If the entire federal government
possesses no supremacy over, and can require no subordination from the entire state governments, whilst acting within
their respective spheres, no part or department of that government can exert a supremacy over, or exact a subordination
from, the corresponding parts or departments of the state
governments. The federal legislature having no supremacy
over the state legislatures, the federal judicial power can have
no supremacy over the state judicial power. The same prohibition of such claims, co-extensively forbids to both an enlargement of power by trespassing on the state sphere or state
departments. It arises from the limited powers bestowed on
the legislature and judiciary of the federal government, and
the reservation of the residuary mass of right to the states.

With this construction, the oath of office prescribed by the
federal constitution is a remarkable coincidence. Both legislators, judges and other officers, of the state as well as the
federal governments, are required to take an oath to support
the federal constitution; but neither federal legislators, judges
nor other officers, are required to take an oath to support the
state constitutions. The reason of this distinction is, that
state legislators, judges and officers, have some duties assigned
to them by the federal constitution, and would necessarily
have others, arising from the laws of the United States; but,
that federal legislators, judges or officers, having no duties to
discharge under the state constitutions or laws, but being confined within the limited spheres defined by the federal consti-

tution, no allegiance to state constitutions was necessary on their part. I cannot imagine a power more inconsistent with republican principles in general, and with ours in particular, than that claimed over the state laws, and consequently over the state constitutions, by the supreme federal court. It is under no obligation or responsibility of any kind to respect either. If it should violate its legitimate federal or spherical duties, it violates its oath ; and is liable to trial and removal from office. But, in virtue of its supposed supremacy over the state courts, it might be tempted to annul state laws, to advance the power of congress, by whom it is paid and tried ; and it might alter the institutions of the people according to its own pleasure, without even breaking an oath. The case is analogous in all its aspects to the claim of the British parliament, neither bound by an oath, nor elected, nor paid, nor removable by the people of the colonies, over the legislatures of these colonies ; which were elected, paid and removable by the people, and also bound by an oath. A judicial power, though under the obligation of an oath, paid by the king of England, was justly considered in Massachusetts, as an outrage upon the principles of justice and liberty. It was a feather to one, created by and accountable to a native distinct government, emulous (as is the nature of man) of power, possessing a supreme power, over the laws of a collateral government, without being under any influence or responsibility to observe those laws.

But cannot judges declare unconstitutional laws void ? Certainly. Constitutions are only previous supreme laws, which antecedently repeal all subsequent laws, contrary to their tenor ; and the question, whether they do or do not repeal or abrogate such subsequent laws, is exactly equivalent to the question, whether a subsequent repeals a previous law. Therefore, judges, juries and individuals have a correspondent power of deciding this question in all legitimate occurrences. But the constitutionality of state laws cannot legitimately be decided by the federal courts, because they are not a constituent part of the state governments, nor have the people of the state confided to them any such authority. They have confided it to the state courts, under the securities of an oath, and of various modes of responsibility. The people also have confided to the federal courts a power of declaring an unconstitutional federal law void, under similar securities; but where such a power is neither bestowed by the people, nor any security against its abuse provided, its assumption by inference is repelled by the absence of every regulation for moderating its exercise. In fact, the spheres of action of the federal and state courts are as separate and distinct, as those of the courts of two neighbouring states. Because the judges of each state are empowered under certain regulations to declare a law of their own state void, it does not follow, that the judges of another state can abrogate it. The federal judges owe no allegiance to the state governments, nor are more a component part of them, nor are more responsible to them, than the judges of a different state. Ramsay's United States, Vo. 1. p. 202. " Great Britain contended, that her " parliament, as the *supreme power*, was constitutionally in- " vested with an authority to lay taxes on every part of the " empire." " If the British parliament, said the colonies, in " which we are *unrepresented*, and *over which we have no con-* " *troul*, can take from *us any part* of our property, they may " take *as much as they please*, and we *have no security* for any " thing that remains." p. 303. " That by the *novel doctrine* " of parliamentary power, they were degraded from being the " subjects of a king, to the low condition of being *subjects of* " *subjects*." p. 306. " Where *parliamentary supremacy ended,* " and at what point *colonial independence began*, was not ascer- " tained." p. 307. " The *omnipotence* of parliament was so " *familiar* a phrase, that few in America, and still fewer in " Great Britain, were impressed, *in the first instance*, with the " illegality of taxing the colonies." Let us parody this quotation. The federal court contends, that as the *supreme power*, it is constitutionally invested with an authority to abrogate state laws, and contract state revenue. If, say the states, this court, *over which we have no controul*, can take from us *any law*, or any revenue, it may take away *as many or as much as it pleases*, and we *have no security* for retaining any. By the *novel doctrine* of federal judicial supremacy, we are degraded from the right of internal self-government, to the low condition of being *subjects of subjects*. Where the federal *jurisdiction ends*, and where *state jurisdiction* begins, is ascertained by the federal constitution, but the *omnipotence* of federal supremacy, legislative and judicial, may become so *familiar* a phrase, that few may be impressed, *in the first instance,* with the consequences to which it tends, or the evils in which it may terminate.

The first instance of a spherical supremacy which I recollect, was the claim of the treaty-making power, to bind the taxing or legislative power, by stipulating in a treaty for the payment of money. This was a dispute between two federal political spheres ; but the principles, upon which it has been or must be settled, are those by which the rights of the federal and state political spheres can alone be ascertained. In both cases, to find where powers begin and end, we must either conclude, that one sphere cannot be let into another under a claim of supremacy, or by any verbal construction, so as to abridge rights bestowed by the constitution ; or concede, that the constitution has unsuccessfully attempted to establish divisions of power between political departments. The federal legislative and treaty-making powers are obviously more interwoven with each other, than the federal and state powers delegated and reserved ; yet the federal legislature would not be at a loss to find limits for the treaty-making power, nor to discern the powers confided by the constitution to itself. As the federal legislative sphere may justly deny to the treaty-making power, a right to abridge the powers delegated to itself by the constitution, under a claim of supremacy, or by any species of construction ; so, the state spheres may justly deny to the federal legislative or judicial spheres, a right to abridge by similar modes the powers reserved to them. Suppose the treaty-making power should stipulate with England to declare war against France ; would that deprive congress of the right of preserving peace, with which it is invested by the constitution ? Suppose in like manner that congress should stipulate with a corporation by one of those laws called charters (in awkward imitation of monarchical sovereignty,) that its property should not be liable to state taxation ; can that deprive the states of a right as distinctly given to them by the constitution, as the right of declaring war is given to congress ? Previously to an incorporation, its funds, of whatever species of property composed, were by the constitution subjected to state taxation. Could congress or the supreme court have exempted this property, directly, from the state constitutional right to tax it? If they could not, can they do it by the circumlocutory contrivance of using two words " corporation and charter ;" neither of which is recognized by the constitution ? Cases might be stated to shew, that there are many objects within the reach of a supreme or sovereign treaty-making power, to which ours does not extend ; such as, stipulating to keep on foot standing armies ; to raise armies and navies as foreign auxiliaries against nations with whom we are at peace ; or to destroy the union by ceding states to form a kingdom for some foreign prince ; and these powers may as correctly be implied because they are not prohibited, as the powers of supremacy claimed by congress or the court. If we must resort to the obvious ends, the general texture, and the special divisions and limitations of the constitution, to avoid these violations of its positive principles, by a treaty-making supremacy ; the same remedy exists to defeat the evils, equally indefinite, which would arise from any other spherical supremacy. We have a multitude of political spheres, state and federal ; and if the orbit of one does not terminate where that of another begins, I am unable to discern any boundaries between them, so *convenient or necessary* for preventing a political chaos. If either of these spheres may create corporate political spheres, capable of corrupting, or of diminishing the powers of constitutional spheres, the musick, after which we have been dancing for almost forty years, will I fear become so harsh, as to make us weep. The licentiousness to which construction may be carried is remarkably exemplified, by its attempts to invert the climax of supremacy, established by " the constitution of the United States." " The consti-" tution, the laws made *in pursuance thereof*, and the treaties " made under *the authority* of the United States, shall be the " supreme law of the land." Under this clause, treaties have aspired to a supremacy over laws, and laws to a supremacy over the constitution, though both the legislative and treaty-making spheres have no powers, except those given by the constitution, and are limited by the authorities it bestows. It would seem therefore perfectly plain, that neither is invested with a supremacy, able to justify an abridgment of a power given by the constitution to the state spheres, and that these may resist such attempts, upon the same ground that the legislative federal sphere resists an attempt of the treaty-making sphere to abridge its constitutional rights.

The argument of the court may be thus condensed. The federal and state governments have limited powers under the federal constitution. The powers of both are attended by such a portion of spherical sovereignty, as is necessary or convenient for their execution. Sovereignty can legitimately use the means it may choose, for the execution of the powers it legitimately possesses. So far nothing is gained; because the sovereignty bestowed, and the means it may use, are limited by the spheres of action bestowed upon each government. But the difficulty is gotten over, and the court's own argument overthrown, by thrusting the word " paramount" into the constitution. The mutuality and equivalence of the spherical sovereignties allowed to the state and federal sovereignties is revoked; and one is made an absolute sovereign over the other, by a construction of the word " supreme" and an interpolation of the word " paramount ;" which must be unconstitutional, if the limited spherical sovereignties, previously assigned to each, are sustainable by a correct construction. To say the most for " paramount and supreme," they are only tautologies of " sovereign ;" and being so, shed no new light upon the case. Had the court declared, that the federal and state governments were each paramount and supreme, within their respective spheres of action, it would have only been a repetition of its assertion, " that they are each sovereign, within their spheres of action."

The reader perceives that the enquiry is reduced a plain question. Is our system of government founded in the principle of co-ordinate political departments, intended as checks upon each other, only invested with defined and limited powers, and subjected to the sovereignty, supremacy, paramount power, superintendence and controul of the people; or in the principle of a supremacy in the federal legislature or judges, with its concomitant controul over the state legislative and judicial departments? If the division of powers among a great number of political departments, endowed with rights independent of each other, constitutes its chief beauty, its distinctive superiority, and its soundest security for human happiness; then the absence of supremacy or sovereignty in one department over the rest does not require the expedient of shuffling words and phrases for the purpose of getting rid of an imaginary defect, by introducing the very evil intended to be avoided. If words are to be tortured or borrowed, let it be done to sustain, not to subvert the essential principles of our political system; if we continue to love that, which other nations admire. Should congress assume a paramount or supreme power over the state governments, it would acquire the authority of the people themselves, naturally possessed, never transferred, specially reserved, and necessary for the preservation of their liberty. Even the English monarchy derives all its eulogies, and owes all its benefits to the want of supremacy and subordination between its political spheres, and to the collisions which their absence produces. By extending the same principle, our system of government has obtained greater eulogies, and diffused greater blessings. Of these eulogies and blessings, the checks and collisions between several legislative branches ; between legislative, executive and judicial departments ; and above all, between the federal and state governments, are the sources. To this principle we owe the valuable judicial right of restraining legislatures within their constitutional powers. To the same principle we have resorted for the same purpose, by dividing powers between the federal and state governments. Are the state spheres less respectable than the supreme court, or less able to restrain congress within its limits, that they must be doomed to subordination because of the great powers of the federal legislature; whilst the court feel their capacity and avow their resolution to controul these powers, if unconstitutionally exerted ? If congress in consequence of the great power of the federal government possess a supremacy over the state governments, what must be the power of the court, which claims a supremacy over congress ? As supremacy has been found to govern sovereignty, it is necessary to find some word, by which the court can govern supremacy. By turning our attention from a complexity of words and phrases, to the true principles of the federal constitution, we shall find one by which the federal court, feeble as it is, is able to controul the federal legislature, powerful as it may be ; a principle, in which the court confides so firmly, as to express its prowess for vindicating its spherical rights. Feeble also as the state governments may be, they are protected by the same power upon which the court relies, and have no reason to be less firm and loyal in discharging the duties with which they also are entrusted. The strength of the government lies in the people. They are the protectors and supervisors of the collateral political spheres, which they have created. If one of these spheres could acquire sufficient power to controul the others, it would, like an officer of a monarch, who can controul all the other officers of the government, obtain a supremacy over the monarch himself; as many prime ministers of kings have actually done. Every inference deducible from the inconvenience of conflicting powers, and every reason in favour of a regular series of political subordination between the several departments of a government, applies as forcibly against the check of one legislative chamber upon another, and of judicial upon legislative power ; as against mutual checks of the federal and state governments upon each other; and to supply, what the reasoning of the court craves, the whole system of division and limitation of power must be destroyed. If it should make a breach at one point upon this principle, especially at the strongest, there can either be no talisman able to save the weaker from destruction, or there is one upon which the strongest may rely.

I cannot discern any difference between a supremacy in one man, or in one political department; between a singular or a plural absolute power. The divine supremacy both of kings and of popes have been limited by the more divine supremacy of human nature. Neither the uniformity of religion, nor a complete subordination of one civil department to another, has, by any modern writer of credit, been considered as equally beneficial to mankind, with the principle of limiting power, whether it be entrusted to one person, or to a political department. The bulls of the pope claimed supremacy; but the conclave of cardinals claimed and exercised a supremacy over these supreme bulls; and the Roman catholick countries found it necessary to limit both these supremacies. The laws of congress claim a general supremacy, but the supreme court claims and exercises a supremacy over them; and the division of powers by the constitution, like the catholick nations, possesses a right to limit, and has limited both these supremacies also. The supremacy of the pope, and of the kings of England, waged a long war against the sovereignty of nations and the rights of

human nature, claiming a power to remove all obstacles which
should impede its will, and to exempt its operations from controul; but the war of these allies terminated in their defeat.
The supremacy of congress and of the court, in alliance also,
has declared war against the sovereignty of the states; but how
it will terminate, is hidden in the womb of time. We must
enlist either under the banner of spherical supremacy or of a
limitation of political power.

Previously to the union, the states were in the enjoyment of
sovereignty or supremacy. Not having relinquished it by the
union, in fact having then exercised it, there was no occasion,
in declaring the supremacy of the constitution and laws made
in pursuance thereof, to notice that portion of state supremacy,
originally attached to, not severed from, and of course remaining
with the powers not delegated to the federal government;
whilst it was necessary to recognize that other portion of supremacy, attached to the special powers transferred from the
states to the federal government. But, by recognizing the
supremacy transferred, it was not intended to destroy the
portion of supremacy not transferred. The supremacy retained,
and a choice of means convenient or necessary for the execution of the powers reserved, was as indispensable an appendage
of state rights, as of the limited powers delegated to congress.
And in fact the unqualified supremacy, bestowed upon the constitution, is equally a guaranty of state and of federal powers,
as is demonstrated by the positive limitation of the supremacy
bestowed on federal laws, to such as were conformable to the
restricted legislative power, created by the constitution. Suppose a state should declare war, tax imports, or regulate commerce; or, that congress should tax exports, alter the course of
descents, or liberate the negroes; would these be questions of
supremacy, unconnected with the powers actually delegated
and reserved? If not, supremacy is limited by these powers,
and cannot extend them. In like manner, neither the federal
nor state courts, can under colour of supremacy, exceed its
own sphere. If one should assume admiralty jurisdiction, and
the other the distribution of intestates' estates, the party usurping could not constitutionally defend its usurpation under
colour of supremacy. Unconstitutional judgments, like unconstitutional laws, are null and void, and both courts are mu-

tually bound by their oaths to the constitution, and have a mutual right to resist and defeat, by every means in their power, unconstitutional laws, falling within their respective jurisdictions. Had an oath of loyalty, not to the constitution, but to the supremacy of one court, been imposed, it might have been otherwise. An exclusive right in either to ascertain the extent of its own jurisdiction would leave its jurisdiction without limits, and the rights of neither judicial sphere can be defended against the other, except by using all the means it possesses; just, as a senate and house of representatives can only defend their respective constitutional rights. The supremacy of the constitution is not confined to any particular department or functionary, but extends to our entire system of political law. Under its protection, the federal senate has a right to defend itself against the house of representatives; and the federal judicial power against the federal legislative power; and if so, it seems impossible to doubt, that the same sanction invests the state and federal judicial powers with a mutual right of self defence, against the aggressions of each other.

I renounce the idea sometimes advanced, that the state governments ever were or continue to be, sovereign or unlimited. If the people are sovereign, their governments cannot also be sovereign. In the state constitutions, some limitations are to be found; in the federal constitution, they are infinitely more abundant and explicit. Whatever arguments can be urged against the sovereignty of state governments, stronger can be urged against the sovereignty of the federal government. Both governments are subjected to restrictions, and the power by which both were constituted has entrusted neither with an exclusive power of enforcing these restrictions upon the other, because it would have conceded its own supremacy by so doing, and parted with its inherent authority.

No derived power can be greater than the primitive power. No state, nor a majority of states, had any species of primitive sovereignty or supremacy over other states. Elections by states, therefore, cannot confer upon a majority of congress a supremacy never possessed by a majority of states, especially as from the form of the senate, the representatives of a minority of people may pass a law, and this representation of the minority might, if it possessed a legislative supremacy, exercise a sovereign power over the majority. If federal legislatures do not possess an absolute supremacy, federal judiciaries cannot possess it, since judgments cannot enforce that which is not law. In conformity with this reasoning, neither federal legislative majorities, nor a majority of the states, can amend the constitution, because it was a compact by which each state delegated for itself only limited powers to the federal government; attended by a supremacy not of any political sphere, but of the constitution, limited and confined to the powers delegated, and not extending to the portion of primitive state supremacy, never delegated. Thus it happened, that no state was bound by the constitution, until it had acceded individually to that compact. And hence it results, that the right of construing the constitution within their respective spheres, is mutual between the state and general governments, because the latter have no supremacy over the state powers retained, and the former no supremacy over the federal powers delegated, except that which provides the stipulated mode for amending the constitution.

It is objected, that if the supreme federal court do not possess an unlimited or unchecked supremacy in construing the constitution, clashing constructions will ensue. This is true; and yet it is not a good reason for overturning our system for dividing, limiting and checking power, if that system be a good one; and if it be even a bad one, the people only, and neither one of their departments separately, nor all united, can alter or amend it. The objection applies as strongly to the other departments of our government, as to the judicial. If the federal legislature and executive do not possess an absolute supremacy over the state legislatures and executives, clashing constitutional constructions will ensue. The jurisdiction of the federal judicial power is as expressly limited, as the legislative and executive federal powers. There is no judicial supremacy recognized in the supreme federal court, except that over inferior federal courts. And, if the supremacy of the constitution bestows upon any federal department a supremacy over the correspondent state department, it must bestow upon every federal department, a similar supremacy over the other correspondent state departments.

It is therefore obvious, that the subject proposed by the objection for consideration is, whether it is better to abandon our primary division of powers between the state and federal governments, to prevent clashing constructions; or to retain this chief security against a gradual introduction of oppression, trusting to the mutual prudence of these governments, and the supreme authority of the people, for meeting the inconvenience, as it appears. The greatest scope of human wisdom is, to compare evils and choose the least. I cannot discern the wisdom of one who cuts off his head, lest his face should be scratched occasionally as he journeys through life. Montesquieu has somewhere said, that when the savage of America wants fruit, he cuts down the tree to obtain it. Shall we act with still less foresight, by cutting down the division of power between the general and state governments, calculated to produce the fruit of moderation in both, that one may cram us with the fruits of supremacy?

How or when have co-ordinate political spheres existed, with a supremacy in one over the others? The idea involves a contradiction. Indeed, the regal sphere in England has often attempted to reconcile it in various ways, and with temporary success. Henry the 8th exercised a supremacy over the two other spheres (at length by rebellions and civil wars rendered co-ordinate,) strongly resembling that now claimed over the state spheres; and the blessings reaped from his success, and the success of his daughter Mary, and of the Stuarts, in removing the evil of clashing powers, by the help of supremacy, were such as we shall reap by pursuing the same policy. It is very true, that the federal and state courts may occasionally carry on little wars with the weapons called injunction and habeas corpus, which both have an equal right to use; but then these weapons cannot shed blood, confiscate property, nor burn hereticks, as supremacy has frequently done; and besides, the states can at any time force the combatants to lay down their arms.

The mutuality of the right of construction in the several departments of the state and federal governments, was the reason, which suggested the section of the constitution of the United States requiring that, " the senators and representatives " in congress, and the members of the several *state legislatures,* " and all *executive and judicial officers, both of the United*

" *States, and of the several states,* shall be bound, by oath or
" affirmation, to support the constitution." The mutuality of
the oath, by imposing a common duty, implies a common right;
because the duty cannot be discharged, except by exercising
the right of construction. To impose the duty by the highest
sanction, and yet to have impliedly designed that its performance should be rendered null and void, by a constructive
supremacy in one political sphere over the others, would
amount to the same thing, as if the oath had been, that the enumerated spheres should be subordinate to one, invested with
a supremacy over the rest. Would this latter have been equivalent to the actual oath ? If not, can a construction by which
it is substantially enforced, be correct ? By the actual oath, the
constitution, in conformity with its great principle of a division and co-ordinateness of powers between the state and
general governments, divides also its confidence for its own
preservation. The same confidence is divided by the special
powers invested in the states and in the general government
for its execution. If the oath binds the federal judicial power
to disregard a mandate from a state judicial power, prohibiting
the exercise of its constitutional powers ; it also binds the judicial power of a state, to disregard a similar mandate from the
judicial power of the union ; and compels both to protect the
officers and individuals upon whom their respective jurisdictions may operate : otherwise, one jurisdiction may supersede
the other. This would be certainly a greater evil, than even a
necessity for a reference to the people to settle a collision.

If a greater sphere of action conferred supremacy according
to the constitution of the union, and if the federal government
possesses the greater sphere of action, (the positions upon which
the court relies as justifying its decision,) where was the necessity for declaring the constitution and the laws made in pursuance thereof to be the *supreme law* of the land ? The supremacy had passed, as the court asserts, attached to the greater
sphere of action. If it was attached to this greater sphere of
action, it is not bestowed by this clause ; and yet this clause is
referred to by the court, as auxiliary to their implied supremacy.
In the several mixtures of truth and error to be found in the
opinion of the court, this has been managed with the most ingenuity. The supremacy expressed has been united with the

supremacy implied, without any examination of the nature of the first, or of its great difference from the latter. A government of laws and not of men, is a definition of liberty ; a government of men and not of laws, of despotism. The expressed supremacy asserts the first principle ; the implied supremacy of the men composing the legislative or judicial federal departments, asserts the second. By blending them, their extreme contrariety is endeavoured to be obscured, and the clause conferring *supremacy on the constitution and the laws made in pursuance thereof*, is very ingeniously changed from a restriction, into an amplification of power. Yet it is under the supremacy conferred upon the constitution by this very clause, that the federal judicial sphere exercises a controul over the federal legislative sphere in the case of unconstitutional laws, because the difference between a supremacy of the constitution and a supremacy in congress, is manifest; whilst the same court insists upon a supremacy in congress over the powers reserved to the states, and denies to congress a supremacy over the powers delegated to itself. This seems to me to be obviously incorrect, because I consider the constitution to have derived from this clause an absolute supremacy for the preservation of the powers reserved to the states, as well as of those delegated to the general government; and not as bestowing on any one sphere, state or federal, an exclusive right to ascertain the extent of those powers; such a right being in fact a despotism of men.

Important as this subject is, to avoid prolixity, I shall overlook sundry features of the constitution, and only add a few observations to those already urged. A union of states clearly admits the sovereignty and equality of the parties uniting. A union does not, as a consequence of union, tacitly and impliedly, reduce these sovereign and equal parties to subordinate corporations; because in that case, they could not alter or dissolve the union, without the consent of the power, to which they would be subordinate. The federal government is allowed by the court to be limited. Can it be limited by a power subordinate to itself, or is it only limited by the didactick lessons of the constitution? The Federalist speaks of the jealousy which would arise between the federal and state governments, because they would be mutual checks upon each other, as co-ordinate powers always struggle for sovereignty; and of the great security for a free government, arising from this feature of the con stitution. But a paramount or supreme power in congress obliterates this feature. And of what avail is a preceptive limitation, bereft of the co-ercive resource for its execution? If congress be a paramount or supreme judge of its own legislative power, its power is unlimited. We have no conception of an unlimited power, beyond one, limited only by its own will. If the jurisdiction of the supreme federal court is limited only by its own will, it is in like manner unlimited. Power can never be checked by itself, or by its own subordinate instru-ment. The constitution certainly intended to invest the legis-lative and judicial spheres of the federal and state govern-ments, with distinct and independent objects of legislation and cognizance; but, these mutual rights however clear can never be preserved, if one party possesses a supremacy over the other, and the other, no power of resistance. Mr. Locke has some-where said, " that no man has a right to that, which another " has a right to take from him."

The art of melting up brass with gold, and calling the whole mass gold, is not a new one. When good and bad principles are thus fused together, it requires some intellectual chymistry to separate them. The court say, " the result is a conviction " that the states have no power by taxation or otherwise to retard, " impede, burden or in any manner controul, the operations of " the *constitutional laws* enacted by congress to carry into exe- " cution the powers vested in congress. *This we think the* " *unavoidable consequence of the supremacy which the consti-* " *tution has declared.*" The supremacy which the constitution has declared! This phraseology conveys a different idea from " the supremacy of the constitution." The foregoing part of the extract only amounts to an assertion, that congress have a right to pass constitutional laws, and that the states have no right to resist them. So far the metal is pure. But, instead of declaring that these conclusions result from the powers dele-gated to congress and prohibited to the states, they are said to be " an unavoidable consequence of the supremacy which the constitution has declared;" as if it had declared any species of supremacy to which it was itself subordinate. Here lies the essence of the question, and here the court are silent. They have not informed us, whether the declared supremacy created a sphere able to legislate or to judge unconstitutionally; nor pointed out the remedy, in case any such sphere should attempt to do so. There is no such question as the court have stated, namely, whether constitutional laws are supreme or obligatory. The true question is, whether any one political department is invested with a supreme power of deciding, what laws are constitutional, and of course obligatory. Now, if the supremacy of the constitution be really the declared supremacy, the court ought to have ascertained the objects upon which it was intended to operate, in order to decide this true question. These undoubtedly and principally are both the state and federal political departments or spheres, all of which being themselves subordinate to the declared supremacy of the constitution, no one could derive from that declaration a supremacy over the rest; and what would be still more absurd, a supremacy over the constitution itself, which would be involved in an exclusive right of deciding upon the constitutionality of laws or judgments. The declared supremacy of the constitution embraces the rights reserved to the states, as well as those delegated to the federal government; and therefore, if the administrators of the delegated rights derive from it any species of supremacy, the administrators of the reserved rights must derive from it the same species of supremacy, because both are guaranteed by the same sanction; namely, the supremacy of the constitution.

That the phrase " the supremacy which the constitution has declared" was intended by the court to convey a very different idea from " the supremacy of the constitution," is demonstrated by the following quotation from its opinion. " That the power " to *tax* involves the power to *destroy*; that the power to " destroy may *defeat and render useless the power to create ;* " that there is a plain *repugnance* in conferring on one govern- " ment a power to controul the *constitutional* measures of ano- " ther, *which other, with respect to these very measures, is* " *declared to be supreme over that which exerts the controul,* " are propositions not to be denied." And yet I think that all of them are deniable or of no weight. It is denied, that the federal government is declared to be supreme over the state governments. It is even denied, that the federal government is declared to be supreme in the exercise of its *constitutional* powers, any farther than the state governments, are declared to be supreme in the exercise of their *constitutional* powers. It is contended, that the constitution, and not either of these governments is declared to be supreme, and that its supremacy is an equivalent guaranty of the division of powers it has made. And it is concluded under the arguments previously urged, that the *repugnance* to the constitution is exactly the same, whether the federal government shall controul the constitutional measures of the state governments, or the state governments shall controul the constitutional measures of the federal government. It was to prevent evils thus repugnant to the nature of the constitution, that the powers of each were made co-ordinate, and a mutual right of construction delegated and reserved. If the remedy be defeated, the repugnance follows. The propositions " that the power to tax involves the power to " destroy, and that the power to destroy may defeat and render " useless the power to create," appear to me to be both incorrect and irrelevant. Shall not civil government tax, because a power to tax may destroy? Have not both the state and federal governments a power to tax; can they therefore destroy? Does not our political system contain remedies against an abuse of the power to tax? Can either government destroy by unconstitutional laws or usurpations? If we have legitimate modes of preventing it, why should an apparition terrify us into an abandonment of these modes? May not a power in the federal government to destroy state laws, defeat and render useless, the state power to create laws? May it not defeat and render useless, the power of the states to create a new constitution? How does a power to destroy, defeat and render useless a power to create? Is not the destruction of the old, and the creation of our new confederation, a refutation of the assertion? Did not this power reside, and does it not yet reside in the states? Is it not recognized by the constitution? Has not the constitution by this recognition, and by depending on the states for senators, and other materials for sustaining the federal government, admitted the state power to destroy and create? If the states have this power, where is the danger of their exercising it indirectly by opposing a constitutional law of congress? On the contrary, is not their acknowledged power over the constitution, a security for a temperate and conscientious opposition to unconstitutional laws? These general propositions, therefore, do not prove their conclusion of a supremacy in the general government over the state governments; but the first, however irrelative in its present shape, may, by a small alteration be rendered extremely applicable. A power to prohibit a government from taxing involves the power of destroying that government. If congress may take from the states, by virtue of the spurious supremacy assigned to it, one object of taxation, they may take away all; and I know of no better weapons to be employed by co-ordinate powers, always struggling for supremacy, than a right in one and not in the other, to withdraw from its competitor, by corporations, subjects of taxation.

But this argument is foreseen and opposed in the opinion of the court. That opinion declares, that "all subjects over which the "sovereign power of the state extends are objects of taxation; "but those, over which it does not extend, are upon the soundest "principles, exempt from taxation. The sovereignty of a state "extends to every thing which exists by its own authority, "or is introduced by its permission; but does not extend to "the means employed by congress to carry into execution "powers conferred on that body by the people of the United "States. We find on just theory a total failure of the original "right to tax the means employed by the government of the "union, for the execution of its powers. The principle for "which the state of Maryland contends, is capable of arresting "all the measures of the general government, and of *prostra-* "*ting it at the foot* of the states." If I understand the assertions of this extract, (as to which I am extremely doubtful,) they either apply against the paramount or supreme power claimed for the federal government, or are incorrect in point of fact. " All subjects, over which the sovereign powers of the "state extends, are objects of taxation." Whether sovereignty be natural or conventional, I have endeavoured to prove, that it resides in the people of each state. The conventional sovereignty created in each state, embraced and *extended to* every species of property, real, personal and mixed. Therefore, property of every kind was an object of taxation before the confederation. Have the states relinquished by that compact a right to tax any species of property, except imports and exports? If not, *as the sovereignty of the states extends to all internal property*, and as *all objects to which it does extend are objects of taxation*, a conclusion adverse to the conclusion of the court is unavoidable. To avoid it, the court subjoin, that which they seem to consider as a new and explanatory position. "The sovereignty of a state extends to every thing which exists "by its own authority, or is introduced by its permission ; but "does not extend to the means employed by congress to carry "into execution powers conferred on that body by the people "of the United States." The first member of this assertion is merely a repetition of the idea of sovereignty, as whatever it *extends to*, may be said *to exist* by its authority. Hence, the observations just urged apply to this modification of the same idea; to which it may be added, that property, so far as it is a conventional or social right, may be said *to exist by the authority of the sovereign power*, with peculiar propriety. So far, the positions of the court seem to be conclusive against its decision. But here a new, authoritative, and unconsequential assertion is advanced. "The sovereignty of a state does not "extend to *the means* employed by congress to carry into exe- "cution the powers conferred on that body by the people of the "United States." What! not if these means contract or destroy the state sovereign right of internal government ? It is difficult to discern, what is meant by the inexplicit word "means," nor could any have been selected, more suitable for establishing a precedent without limits, and a judicial supremacy without controul. If it includes men or property, so far as congress may employ either as *means* for executing its powers, then the assertion is incorrect ; because, the sovereignty of the states does extend both to men and property thus used as *means*. If a federal judge commits a crime or incurs a debt, he is amenable to the jurisdictions of state sovereignties. All resident federal officers are liable to pay a state poll tax, and the taxes imposed for supporting the poor, and keeping up roads and bridges. The property, real and personal, of all these descriptions of persons, to which we may add the president and members of congress, is liable to state taxation, and their persons exposed to state jurisdictions. Are none of these persons *means* employed by congress ? If they are, where is the distinction to be found in our system of government, under which all the means expressed, to be employed for its own execution, imports excepted, are left as they were found, exposed to state sovereignty, by which under cover of implied means, congress may remove either persons or property, beyond the reach of state sovereignty ; and liberate them from its cognizance, whilst both themselves and their property remained subordinate to it ? Are bankers more worthy *means* to be employed for executing the constitution than judges ?

But, suppose we admit " that the state sovereignty does not extend to means either expressed or implied, employed by congress," and allow that banking may be correctly numbered among the latter ; I would ask, whether it is the persons or the property of the bankers, which are thus absolved from state allegiance, and excluded from state jurisdiction? If the former, they may be killed with impunity ; if the latter, it may be plundered without redress. The federal government have no jurisdiction as to local wrongs, and the states can have no jurisdiction as to objects over which they have no sovereignty. If, however, they do possess a sovereignty, able to protect persons and property, though employed by congress as means to effect ends, that sovereignty extends to taxation, as protection and contribution are reciprocal political principles, and it would be unjust to the rest of society, to establish a sub-society, entitled to the one and absolved from the other.

Far from admitting, however, a position which would produce such consequences, I contend that the state sovereignty extends to all the *means* which congress can employ. It is necessary to protect the lives, the limbs, and the reputations even of the standing army; and to secure every atom of property, from which the federal government can extract resources. Except for the protection of state sovereignty, even imposts would fail. Whatever is not a subject of a sovereignty, is not entitled to its protection. Congress cannot pass a municipal law to protect persons or property, because the federal government is in no respect a sovereignty. Private property exists by, and is subject to state sovereignty. With this opinion the Federalist, formerly quoted, when explaining the concurrent power of the state and federal governments, as means for effecting the ends respectively confided to them, explicitly concurs. To me it seems, that the two governments are designedly blended and interwoven with each other, that each may contribute towards the preservation of the other ; and that a claim of independence, sovereignty or supremacy, in favour of one, is unfriendly to the federal constitution in general, and to the federal government in particular. If this be true, is there not something invidious and reprehensible in this expression used by the court? " The principle for which the " state of Maryland contends, is capable of arresting all the " measures of the general government, and of *prostrating it at* " *the foot* of the states." Without enlarging upon the fact, that the federal government is dependent upon the states for its existence, this principle may be compared with that contended for by the court. The state of Maryland contends for its original and reserved right to tax property. The court asserts, that congress by creating corporations may diminish or destroy the state resource for raising revenue, co-extensively with its own pleasure. By the first principle, the pecuniary resources for sustaining the federal government are untouched ; by the second, those of the states become dependent on the federal government. By the first, the power of both governments, either original or delegated, as to revenue, remains concurrent; by the second, congress assumes a power of placing whatever property it pleases beyond the reach of contribution for the support of either. By the first, a sovereignty which created private property, retains its rights ; by the second, a right is claimed on behalf of a spurious sovereignty to create private property, or rather to rob the legitimate sovereignty of that which it had previously created. If congress be indeed a limited sphere, as the court admit, it can neither create private property, nor absolve it from taxation, because these are attributes of sovereign, and not of limited spheres. Let the reader consider whether the principle of the court is not capable, in theory, of *arresting all the measures* of the state governments and *prostrating them at the foot of congress*. I say in theory, because I trust that in practice, all efforts for rendering these departments, equally necessary for our liberty and prosperity, jealous of, or hostile to each other, will be unsuccessful ; and that both will cultivate, not the means of acquiring a paramount or supreme power over each other, but those for advancing the publick happiness.

But the court, instead of confiding in the arguments which I have attempted to examine, endeavour to supersede them all, by observing that " the legislature of the union can be trusted " by the people with the power of controuling measures which " concern all, with the confidence that it will not be abused." Can be trusted by the people! The reiterated attempts to distinguish between the people and the states, to sooth and flatter the former by compliments to their elective sagacity, and by insidious blandishments to seduce them from the substantial ground of checks and balances, into the intricate and slippery paths of passion and confidence, are sufficient to awaken all the vigilance of those who believe, that power must be divided, limited and controuled, to keep it within bounds. In its every stretch, it uniformly solicits the popular confidence by protestations of integrity and promises of moderation. But, in considering the rights under the constitution of the federal and state governments, an estimate of the confidence due to either is certainly inapplicable to the subject, and productive of a malevolence, to be deprecated as the greatest national misfortune. Shall we exchange our constitutional compact, for a succession of artifices to win popular favour, or to take advantage of popular folly? Is not an appeal from an investigation of constitutional principles, to an estimate of fluctuating popular confidence, an acknowledgement of diffidence in the arguments previously advanced? If, however, a scramble for popularity is to be substituted for a limitation of powers, let us beware how we stake the federal government upon the event of the confusion. Mr. Madison, p. 252 of the Federalist, has observed, that " the powers delegated to the federal government " are few and defined. Those, which remain to the state " governments, are numerous and indefinite, and extend to all " the objects which, in the ordinary course of affairs, concern " the lives, liberties, and properties of the people." And in page 251, " the state governments may be regarded as consti- " tuent and essential parts of the federal government; whilst " the latter is in no wise essential to the operation or organiza- " tion of the former." The reader will see in these quotations an affirmation of the principles for which I have contended in this section; and he will also discern, that the popular confidence has been extended in a greater degree to the state than to the federal government, both in the mass of powers bestowed, and also in the dependence upon the former to which the latter is subjected. I forbear to enumerate the advantages which the states possess in this struggle for confidence, because I earnestly hope that the ever-to-be-avoided contest will never occur. They are perhaps too copiously remembered in the book last quoted. Let me, however, remind the reader, that the same book describes the superior sagacity and intelligence of the state legislatures, for detecting and repelling artful and insidious violations of the federal constitution, as a feature of our political system, most happily contrived to prevent the bad effects universally experienced from tornadoes of antipathy, affection, prejudice and zeal, to which even representative absolute power has been universally subject; and by which a mighty effort in France to establish a free government was frustrated. How can this feature of our political system, so highly eulogised in the Federalist, be preserved, if the *means* for giving it efficiency should be taken away from these same state legislatures, by investing the federal judges with a supreme power over these means? Ought this inestimable feature of our government, by which deliberation is substituted for passion, intelligence for prejudice, and restraint for unshackled ambition, to be exchanged for a confidence, in a single legislative department? Yes, says the last extract from the opinion of the court, it will be advantageously bartered *for a power in the legislature of the union to controul measures which concern all, because the people can possess a confidence that it will not be abused.* But, the constitution intended, according to the Federalist, that the legislatures of the states should be a check upon the legislature of the union, and when this check is endeavoured to be defeated by the words " confidence and supremacy," it only illustrates the absurdity of construing it by an excessive interpretation of particular terms, instead of adhering to its obvious intention.

The convenience or necessity of uniformity is the great argument, upon which this vital change of the federal constitution is contended for. Archbishop Laud, under the supremacy of Charles the second, attempted to effect a religious uniformity by the instrumentality of judges, and drew for that purpose a great portion of the business of the common law courts, into the ecclesiastical, having at their head one supreme court. His object was to establish arbitrary power; and that his means were as wise as they were wicked, is proved by the necessity of a long and bloody civil war to defeat it. The rights of the puritans under Charles's supremacy, experienced the fate to be expected by the rights of the states subjected to the jurisdiction of federal judges, under a supremacy in congress. One sect, subjected to the laws and judges of another sect, or one government, subjected to the laws and judges of another government, may consider its rights as equally secured or lost. The English saw the consequences of the judicial usurpations by the ecclesiastical courts, and many great men, though adverse to the puritans, united with them to defeat a progress so obvious towards arbitrary government. Every stretch of the jurisdiction of the federal courts, in virtue of the supremacy of congress, must operate upon state constitutional rights, as accessions of ecclesiastical jurisdiction, in virtue of the supremacy of Charles, operated upon common law rights in England. The uniformity attempted is as impracticable and chimerical in one case as in the other. If religious sects, severed by speculation, cannot be reconciled by any thing short of tyranny, how can great states, severed by local interests, be coerced within one bandage by a weaker power? The remedy in one case is, to let the opinions and the internal self-government of churches alone. The remedy provided by the federal constitution for the other, was also to let alone the local interests and internal self-government of the states. If one state, or a majority of states, under the contended-for supremacy of congress, to be enforced by the federal court, should interfere with the internal affairs of another; it cannot be justified by any mode of reasoning; except one, which would prove that one church, or a majority of churches, may rightfully and beneficially interfere with the internal affairs of another. Mankind have discovered, that equal or co-ordinate religious rights are preferable for human happiness, to uniformity; and every sect treats the idea of submission to another sect, with scorn and derision. Laud lost his head for assailing an opinion so natural, by ecclesiastical supremacy. Will the notion in the states of their natural right to internal self-government be more conquerable, by federal supremacy? Religious uniformity was recommended as a good thing by cunning knavery or fanatical zeal; but neither philosophical theory nor fanatical zeal will advocate the uniformity to be produced by the supremacy of congress or the federal court. Solid selfishness, and not moral reasoning; to destroy, and not to nurture our constitutional checks and divisions of power, will be the motive for assailing state rights. No important collision would ever happen between the federal and state governments, if it was referred to the arbitrament of the common good or general interest only. To keep the peace between them, it is only necessary to discern whether they are embroiled by honest patriotism, or by the pretended patriotism of monopoly, speculation, selfishness or ambition. Even churches have been much oftener involved in controversies by fraudulent and pernicious designs, than by honest and intemperate zeal. There was no remedy against such fraudulent arts, except that of preventing the artificers from getting any thing from their occupation, by allowing to these churches the natural right of internal self-government. So, by a sacred adherence to the right of the states to internal self-government, the manufacturers of broils between them and the federal government, would be disabled from getting any thing by the occupation, and then the business will cease. In times of ignorance, mankind have been bitten by a political or religious tarantula, and either cured or made worse by sounds; but now, their knowledge is such, that they can keep both their temper and their honesty with great philosophy in all discussions, which do not involve some exclusive advantage for themselves.

Besides the counterpoise intended by the federal constitution to be established between the federal and state legislatures, two clauses of the constitution seem positively to have renounced the idea of any species of sovereignty or supremacy, by which congress could create or regulate property. It must purchase with the *consent* of the state legislatures real property, *however necessary or convenient in its opinion for the common defence or general welfare.* As this consent is necessary to subtract real property from state resources, and subject it to federal legislation, it follows, since the state internal power is the same over both real and personal property, that the latter cannot be subtracted from the state internal power, and transferred to the exclusive legislation of congress, without any state consent. Congress may dispose of, and make regulations concerning the *property of the United States*, implying, very distinctly, that it cannot dispose of, or make regulations concerning the property of individuals, embraced by the states. These, and other specified powers given to congress over persons and property, seem to demonstrate, that it does not possess any unspecified power over them derived from the words "sovereign and "supreme."

Finally, it ought to be observed, that the constitution does not invest the federal court with any jurisdiction, in cases of collision between either the legislative or judicial powers of the state and federal governments; and as such a jurisdiction would be infinitely more important than any other with which it is endowed, the omission is not sufficiently accounted for by saying, either that the case was overlooked, as never likely to happen, or, that though its occurrence was foreseen as extremely probable, this important jurisdiction was bestowed by inference only, whilst cases of jurisdiction comparatively insignificant were minutely expressed. But the omission is well accounted for, if we consider the constitution as having contemplated the state and federal governments as its co-ordinate guardians, designed to check and balance each other; since, having established that primary and important principle by the division of powers between them, it would have been as obvious an inconsistency to have bestowed a power on the federal courts to settle collisions as to their mutual rights, as to have reserved the same supervising power to the state courts.

I hope the reader has perceived the propriety of my endeavours to ascertain the principles of our form of government, as preparatory to a consideration of the supremacy claimed for congress, supposed by the court to justify its decision ; and as necessary to enable us to determine, whether the ground it has taken is real or imaginary.

SECTION. 10.

BANK DECISION.—COMMON DEFENCE AND GENE-RAL WELFARE.—NECESSARY AND PROPER.—CONVENIENT.—NATIONAL.

I turn with sorrow from the construction of an entire system, to the science of verbality; from a consistency of meaning, to the artifice of verbalizing a single word, to destroy that consistency; and proceed to examine a mode of managing controversies, into which prejudice, ambition and self-interest continually strive to drag reason. The frippery of precedents, like the tinsel patched upon lord Peter's coat; here a bank, there a road, yonder a canal, bounties for these, their payment for those, now an epaulet of sovereignty, and then another of supremacy, may bespangle our form of government with armorial ensigns of despotism, and yet leave much of its original substance perceivable ; but the art of verbalizing single words into a different system, may render the constitution as unintelligible, as a single word would be made by a syllabick dislocation, or a jumble of its letters ; and turn it into a reservoir of every meaning for which its expounder may have occasion. I admit that wise and good men may entertain a great respect for the British form of government; and may conscientiously believe, that it would improve the constitution of the United States to draw it by construction towards that model: but yet I contend it would be proceeding too impetuously, to borrow its modes of construction practised in its most oppressive periods, and resisted by its best patriots.

In the time of James the second, all the judges of England (except one) decided "that the laws of England were the "*king's laws*. That it is an inseparable branch of the *pre-*"*rogative* of the kings of England, *as of all other sovereign* "princes, to *dispense* with all penal laws in *particular cases,* "and on *particular occasions*. That of *these reasons* and *neces-*

"*sity* the king is the *sole judge*. That this is not a trust now "invested in and granted to the present king, but the ancient "remains of the *sovereign power* of the kings of England, "which was never taken from them, *nor can be.*" Is not this decision a parallel both in language and substance with the decision of the court, and a complete precedent for its defence, except that the mode of construction it adopts is no longer justified in England? The harmony between the words "sove-"reignty, particular cases, prerogative, reasons and necessity," used by the English judges, and the words "spherical sove-"reignty, supremacy, convenience and necessity," used by the decision, strikes the ear, and settles in the understanding. Prerogative arises out of the king's sovereignty; supremacy out of the spherical sovereignty given to congress. This sovereign power of the kings could not be taken away; that of congress may remove all obstacles to its action. Of particular cases, occasions, reasons and necessity, the king by virtue of his prerogative arising out of his sovereignty, is declared to be the sole judge; of convenience and necessity, congress in virtue of its supremacy, arising out of spherical sovereignty, is declared to be the sole judge. The king may dispense with the penal laws of England; but the decision does not declare that congress may dispense with the constitution. It only invests congress with a spherical sovereignty begetting a supremacy for removing all obstacles to its action, and establishes the premises producing the conclusion, that congress may dispense with the rights reserved to the states. The English judges reasoned illogically, by inferring only from their premises that the king could dispense with penal laws; but the decision of the court, rejecting an error so apparent, does not limit the supreme power of congress, but leaves it co-extensive with the premises asserted. Thus, as the king's sovereignty made the laws of England his laws, so the supremacy of congress makes the constitution of the United States, its constitution.

Though this mode of construction be exploded in England, yet as it is revived here, I shall endeavour to bestow on it the consideration merited by its consequences.

"To provide for the *common* defence and promote the *general* welfare," powers are bestowed upon the federal government, with a right to make all laws which shall be *necessary* and *proper* for carrying the delegated powers into execution. Some sound principle, sufficient to ascertain the true construction of these expressions, ought to be settled. The constitution consists of correlative rights and duties, divided between the state and federal governments ; and neither allotment was intended to become the prey, directly or indirectly, of the other. This division was a limitation of the powers of both, and the laws to be made by either could not violate it, because a legal power in either of that character would have rendered the division itself utterly inefficient. The federal government cannot diminish the right of taxation reserved to the states, nor the state governments, the right of taxation delegated to the federal government, because these rights clash ; since their clashing being foreseen as certain, was not intended to be prevented by the division. The division of powers was not intended to be subordinate to a clashing of rights, but a clashing of rights was intended to be subordinate to the division of powers. These positions are entirely reversed, if either party received with its share of powers a supremacy able by inferences to be made by itself, to remove all obstacles to its action ; because all the clashings of powers, certain, foreseen, and not provided against by the constitution, would become accessions of power to the construing party and defeat the division itself. It would be exactly the case, as if the senate or house of representatives, between whom powers are divided and clashings arise, as in all such divisions, should either of them usurp a supremacy over the other, to remove the obstacles to its action, produced by these clashings. The ideas of limited powers and unlimited inferences being irreconcilable, any construction of particular words or phrases, which would unlimit the limitations expressed, is unconstitutional, if the constitution intended to make any substantial division of power. The field of expediency and convenience belonged exclusively to the framers of the constitution, and was shut by the constitution, against the trustees subsequently appointed to execute it, because otherwise it would have been no constitution at all.

The principle "that clashings of rights are subordinate to "divisions of power" is applicable to the structure of the state and federal governments, and restrains their legislative, executive and judicial departments within their proper orbits. If either could make the rights of a co-ordinate department subordinate to itself, by inference or expediency, those constitutional divisions of power would be destroyed. I therefore contend, that no construction of particular words or phrases can change or abolish the division of power between the state and federal governments, without changing or abolishing an essential principle of the constitution itself.

It seems to me, that constitutional law, enacted by the people, is as binding upon political departments, as civil law is upon individuals; and that none of these departments have any better right to discharge themselves from its observance by the plea of convenience, than an individual would have to disobey a civil law under the same plea.

The states united "to provide for the *common* defence and the *general* welfare." The words "common and general" can only refer to the parties uniting, and these were the states. Therefore, if these words bestowed any power, instead of only reciting the ends intended to be accomplished by the union and its terms, it could only extend to interests "common and general" to all the parties, in their state associated individuality. But they have been construed as conveying some local and internal powers over persons and things, and if they convey any, it must be admitted that they bestow all powers of this character. To determine the propriety of this construction, we can only advert to the nature and compass of the powers delegated to the federal government, and reserved to the states. No power is given to the general government to pass a law for the regulation of private property, or the security of personal rights; therefore, "common defence and general welfare" did not include these important objects of welfare and defence; and they are provided for in the reservation to the states, because they are not included by these terms. These terms of course have in view the defence and welfare of the states, as states, and not the internal government of the individual states. The provisions of the constitution, in relation to foreign nations and domestic insurrections, are analogous to this construction. Had these words conveyed power, there would have been no occasion for the provision in the case of insurrection; and this special power of internal interposition, excludes a general power of the same tenour. A similar exclusion is contained in the special power bestowed upon congress to legislate for the ten miles square "in all cases whatsoever." As this anomalous district would lose state care and protection, it is thus specially provided for, because the words under consideration gave no power to the federal government. Had they done so, no specification of federal powers would have been necessary; and if they do so, the subsequent specifications mean nothing. Under the first supposition, the convention needed only to have organized the government after the first clause of the constitution, to take care of the common defence and general welfare, which would have comprised unlimited power. And if the second supposition be true, then a catalogue of powers was superfluous, because these words covered both those specified, and all others not specified, which might advance the general welfare. It follows, either that these words convey no power, or that the subsequent definitions of the powers delegated restrict their meaning. In fact, they are obviously introductory, and not decretal. The ends in view are recited, and then follow the means for effecting those ends. If these means should prove to be insufficient, the constitution, far from confiding to its officers a power to supply deficiencies, provides for the occurrence. In all questions, therefore, concerning banks, roads, canals, taxes, agriculture, manufactures and internal or local prosperity, the construction of *the constitution* ought to be confined to its decretal sections. In these we find two concurrent provisions. Both congress and the state governments may tax the same property and suppress the same insurrections. And the specification of these two instances of a concurrent power excludes the idea of a concurrency of power, in the other enumerated cases.

But, if the sweeping powers said to be conveyed by the ntroductory clause of the constitution cannot be proved, their absence is said to be nearly supplied, by the power given to congress to make all laws, " which shall be *necessary* and *proper* " for carrying into execution the *foregoing powers.*" I shall endeavour to prove that these words, far from enlarging, restrict the legislative power of congress; and that, coupled with other parts of the constitution, they also limit the jurisdiction of the federal courts. 1. They expressly limit the legislative power of congress to laws necessary and proper for executing the *delegated* powers, and bestow no authority to assume powers *not delegated.* 2. The jurisdiction of the federal courts under laws, is limited to " the laws of the United States," meaning such laws as these states by their representatives in congress have a right to enact. They have only a right to enact laws " for carrying into execution the *delegated* powers." 3. Congress have no power to enact laws " necessary and proper for " carrying into execution" the powers reserved to the states, as their legislative powers are limited to the *foregoing* or delegated powers; and in cases concerning which congress have no power of legislation, the federal courts have no jurisdiction. 4. The states possess an exclusive legislative power with respect to the powers reserved to them, with the appurtenant right of passing all laws, which shall be *necessary* and *proper* for carrying into execution such reserved powers. 5. The jurisdiction of the state courts is limited to the execution of the laws which the state governments have a *right* to pass, as the jurisdiction of the federal courts is limited to the laws which congress have a *right* to pass; and neither of these courts can derive any powers from laws, which the respective legislatures under which they act have *no right* to pass.

The remarks, in defence of these propositions, must be more concise than their importance merits. The division of delegated and reserved powers between the federal and state legislatures would have been quite nugatory, without a division of the right of legislation respecting them; and except for both divisions, the principles of representation adopted by the federal government would never have been approved of. These are calculated for external objects, or objects common to all the states, as to which a consentaneous interest and feeling would prevail among the representatives; and in the power of taxation necessarily bestowed on congress, precautions are taken to prevent the ill consequences which might be produced by the absence of those ingredients, necessary to secure legislative impartiality. These precautions shew, that the framers of the constitution were conscious, that the principles of representation in congress were so defective as to require some safeguard beyond the usual confidence in representation, against the abuse, even of a power of taxation for the benefit of the union.

The constitution contains no provision whatsoever for the exercise of the rights reserved to the states, nor any stipulation respecting it. Can it be imagined, that, having expressly placed them without the compass of the compact between the states, it meant impliedly to bring them back under the power of congress, without subjoining any provision for its defective form of representation, as in the case of taxation? Numerous and important powers and rights are reserved to the states, to secure which the members of congress are bound by no sanction, nor any sympathy. The slave question, and the unlimited right of taxation reserved to the states, are among the number. Mutual prejudices, separate interests, different circumstances, and want of local information, all operate against the idea that the constitution intended to invest congress impliedly with a power of local and internal legislation. But arguments abound to prove, that the representation in congress is devoid of every principle of representation, in respect to these objects, or the powers reserved to the states. Local laws, passed by the representation in congress, could only operate upon the representatives of a single state. The sufferers under such laws could not by election influence the legislature. The qualifications, required by state constitutions in legislative representatives, would be wholly abolished. The necessity of residence would be superseded. In short, the representatives from Georgia in congress might legislate as to the local and internal concerns of Massachusett's bay. Every relation between constituents and representatives would be violated by a power of local or internal legislation in congress. Both in theory and practice, it would approach near to that detestable virtual representation, under which the British parliament claimed a power of local and internal legislation over the colonies. Implied, inferred, and virtual representation, are substantially equivalent. No express power was given to congress to legislate in reference to local or internal objects, or to objects reserved to the states; because that body was not organized by any representative principle in reference to these objects. All the reasons which excluded an express, exclude an implied power of local and internal legislation. Implication cannot transform congress into a representation of local state rights, when they are not so recognized by the constitution, and are devoid of every quality and character of such a representation. In legislation they are therefore limited to the delegated powers, in the execution of which they have no right to usurp any power of local or internal legislation, as in the cases of roads and banks, because there is not in that body any species of local representation.

The acquisition of powers either not delegated, or inconsistent with the powers reserved to the states, or incongruous with the nature of the representation in congress, must all be very different from the execution of the powers bestowed. Congress may " make all laws which may be *necessary* and *proper* for carrying into execution the *foregoing* powers." Suppose the clause had thus proceeded. " And may also invest themselves " with other powers by implication, inconsistent with the princi- " ples of representation." Would this addition have altered its meaning? If so, what does it mean as it stands? If I have proved that the powers of congress cannot, under colour of legislating for the execution of the powers delegated, be extended to powers not delegated and reserved, it follows that the jurisdiction of the federal courts cannot be extended by a species of legislation which is unconstitutional and void. The special objects of jurisdiction given to the federal judicial power, have no connexion with their jurisdiction founded upon the laws of congress. An act or law of congress, which is unconstitutional, is agreed to be no law at all. Suppose congress should pass a law to liberate the slaves of a particular state, or to give the land of A to B? Would the federal courts derive jurisdiction from it, or would the state courts retain their exclusive jurisdiction between the people or citizens of their own state? But is there not an appellate jurisdiction lodged in the federal supreme court, able to reach cases in which the federal judicial powers have no original jurisdiction? The reasoning upon this point seems to be superseded by a complete perspicuity in the constitution. We have seen, that the legislative power of congress is limited to the delegated powers, and that the federal judicial power under the laws of congress only extend to such as come within the limitation. Such is its original jurisdiction. The constitution declares, " that the appellate jurisdiction of the supreme court," shall extend to the cases *before mentioned.* The jurisdiction arising under a law of congress is that, with which the argument is concerned. To bestow the original jurisdiction, the law must conform to the delegated powers. Therefore, the appellate jurisdiction cannot take cognizance of a case, in which the original jurisdiction has none. The federal courts derive no jurisdiction from state laws. Their jurisdiction, arising from law, is limited to laws passed by congress in conformity with the delegated powers. On the contrary, the jurisdiction of the state courts is limited to state laws in conformity with the reserved powers. Neither of these courts has an appellate jurisdiction from the other. As the federal and state legislatures have a right to legislate within their respective orbits, independently of each other, the respective judicial powers have a right to execute these independent laws, independently also of each other. It is said, that some supreme power is *necessary* to prevent collisions. A saying of the Marquis of Halifax (a man renowned for understanding) recorded by Wrangham, fits our case. " The word " *necessary*, is miserably applied; it disordereth families and " overturns governments by being abused." Necessities are, strictly, things unavoidable. In practice, they may be divided into absolute or imaginary. In relation to the principles of government, they are all of the latter class, as governments are capable of endless modifications. In this case they are only expedients. The plain question, divested of verbal evolutions, is, whether congress are invested with the supreme power of altering or mending the constitution, should they imagine it to be expedient? The same management is used to excite the doubts, which have been laid hold of to produce a radical change in our constitution. As *necessity* is used instead of *expediency*, *collision* is used instead of *check*, whereas in political effect they are essentially the same. A supreme power able to abolish collisions, is also able to abolish checks, and there can be no checks without collisions. The checks resulting from the co-ordinacy of the lords and commons of England, could not produce any good, if a *political department* existed able to controul those collisions, and much less, if one of these bodies possessed a supremacy over the other. In that country, checks attended with collisions, are preferred to subordination, under a very imperfect supremacy, hardly acknowledged or capable of acting, called publick opinion. Here, also, we have preferred checks and collisions, to a dictatorship of one department, under the supremacy of the people, fully acknowledged, and acting without difficulty. If the inconvenience of collisions between co-ordinate political departments begets a *necessity* for the supremacy of one, and this necessity will justify its assumption, the scheme of checks and balances is entirely chimerical, and a political fabrick built upon that theory must fall. Necessity, inference and expediency never fail to beget an endless successive progeny. Roads are necessary in war; therefore congress may legislate locally concerning roads. Victuals, manufactures, and a certain state of national manners, are more necessary in war; therefore congress may legislate locally, concerning agriculture, manufactures and manners. The favour of the Deity is more necessary than either; therefore congress may provide salaries for priests of all denominations, in order to obtain it, without infringing the constitutional prohibition against an establishment; or they may incorporate sects, and exempt them from taxation. Roads are more necessary for collecting taxes than even banks. Taverns are very necessary or convenient for the officers of the army, congress themselves, the conveyance of the mail, and the accomodation of judges. But horses are undoubtedly more necessary for the conveyance of the mail and for war, than roads, which may be as convenient to assailants as defenders; and therefore the principle of an implied power of legislation, will certainly invest congress with a legislative power over horses. In short, this mode of construction completely establishes the position, that congress may pass any internal law whatsoever in relation to things, because there is nothing with which, war, commerce and taxation may not be closely or remotely connected; and the constitution does not contain any prohibited degrees of consanguinity. The personal departments established by the state constitutions seem indeed to be without the scope of this mode of construction, which can only strip them of their whole wardrobe of rights, and reduce them to a sort of naked political skeletons.

I see no end to the power of necessity, armed with supremacy. It seems already to have carried us nearly a thousand years backwards in the science of political justice. In 846, Ethelwolf established tythes, and exempted the property of the clergy from taxation. Bankers are said to be useful and convenient to the government. The established clergy are still thought so by the English government. Governments and nations very often differ in opinion as to conveniences.

The argument of collision would reach a multitude of cases. As an instance. It has been judicially and practically established, that both congress and the state governments have a right to tax carriages. Suppose the states should impose a tax on them amounting to a prohibition. Would this state law be void, because it might defeat the law of congress? Collisions between concurrent and co-ordinate powers, are natural and certain, and must have been foreseen by the framers of the constitution. Moderation and the people, are the only arbiters they thought safe or necessary. But a conflict between a positive and an implied power, is the question we are considering. Can the latter abrogate the former under any pretext whatsoever?

Let us consider the subject in this new light with some attention. The natural rights of nations, in respect to each other, are more evident, better understood, and more universally recognized, than the rights of individual men ; because a nation can more conveniently exist independently of other nations, than one man can of other men. Accordingly they are acknowledged by all political writers to confer on nations the character of individuality, and the utmost degree of independence, of which human nature is susceptible. The United States, whilst provinces, were imperfect nations. Under charters, they obtained and exercised a separate and distinct national character, in relation to internal affairs, yielding to Great Britain the management of their external national rights. By the revolution, each state became a perfect individual nation, possessed of all the natural rights of nations. As perfect nations, they have entered into two confederations, both influenced by the principles to which as colonies they were willing to have conformed in a union with Britain. By these confederations, they relinquished several national rights, and retained all not relinquished. As to their natural rights retained, they remain perfect nations; or in other words, their national individuality and independence of each other, respecting these rights, are unchanged. A conveyance of one portion of an estate, by metes and bounds, does not impair the title to the portion not conveyed, especially if attended with a positive reservation. Had they entered into a similar union with Britain, their inter-

nal and local rights must have been specified, as not having
been settled; and they would have been justified in asserting
and maintaining the specifications against any implications, for
which an assumed British supremacy, or the appellate jurisdiction of the king in council might have contended. But, no
specification of the state rights reserved was necessary in
establishing our union, because these rights were not conceded, as being national and antecedent to the compact. Being
natural and national rights, and also never delegated, but reserved, they are held by the states in their original character,
as perfect national rights. This amounts to a plain specification
of the powers of the states, and a positive prohibition bearing
upon those of congress. The conflict, therefore, is not between
implication and implication, but between specification and implication. Ought the positive stipulations of contracts to be
supplanted by doubtful conjectures? " Congress shall have
power to make all laws which shall be necessary and proper
for carrying into execution the delegated powers," says the constitution; and also, subjoins the implication, " power to make
all laws necessary and proper to contract the powers reserved
to the states." The chief forces on the two sides of the question are thus opposed. The states are armed with their original
national rights; congress with conventional rights. The states
have a natural right to make all necessary and proper laws
within their national powers reserved; congress a right of legislation limited to delegated powers. Implied powers may be as
copiously extracted from the rights of the states, as from those
of congress; but if their absolute and conventional powers are
independent of each other, their powers by implication must
also be liable to the same limitation. If congress cannot directly
contract the state power of taxation, being a national right,
they cannot have an implied power to do it indirectly. But if
congress can by implication assume a power of passing any
local or internal law beyond the specifications of the constitution,
it must be admitted that they have a right to undertake the
care of state prosperity in relation to agriculture, manufactures,
private property, corporations, roads and canals; as it is impossible to find a justification for one case, which will not extend to
the others. Suppose the clashing laid hold of, for introducing
a catalogue of implied powers, under the supremacy of the

very power intended to be checked, was not between specification and implication, but between specification and specification. This supposition places the subject upon much stronger ground in favour of the doctrine of implied powers, in congress only (forgetting the equal right of the states to them,) than has been yet taken. Congress have no specified power to create a corporation, but they have one to impose a tax on stills and whiskey. It will not be denied that the states have a concurrent power to tax the same objects. Suppose they should impose on them a tax amounting to a prohibition. It would defeat a law passed by congress for taxing them. This would be a conflict between specification and specification, or between two powers, undoubtedly residing in the respective governments. Could the federal court defeat the state law, upon the ground " that the states have no right by *taxation* or otherwise, *to* " *retard, impede, burden, or in any manner controul* the opera- " tions of the *constitutional* laws enacted by congress," as the court has declared? In this case the law of congress would be *constitutional*, and the argument deducible from it surrenders the objection arising from the unconstitutionality of the bank law. If the question be answered in the negative, it follows, that if no power resides in congress or the federal court to abrogate a *constitutional* state law, thus impeding and controuling a *constitutional* law of congress, the argument is insufficient in every other similar case. And if I am not mistaken in the reason of its insufficiency, neither the *constitutionality* of the law passed by congress, nor its *impediment nor controul* by the state law, ought to have any weight upon the subject. This reasoning establishes an essential conclusion, towards which all my arguments have been directed. It is this. Powers are delegated or reserved both to the state and federal governments to make laws. Under the concurrent power of taxation, they may each pass a law, both of which may be constitutional, and yet these laws may clash with, or impede each other. The same thing may happen in many other cases. For this clashing the constitution makes no provision. The right of passing constitutional laws which clash with the constitutional laws of congress, is not prohibited to the states; nor is the right of passing constitutional laws, which may clash with the constitutional laws of the states, prohibited to congress; because the evil of clashing, balanced, or checked powers, appeared to its framers, to be inconsiderable, compared with that of an absolute supremacy. I have called the first an evil, in a spirit of concession, but I think it the only security for the whole catalogue of social blessings; and not to be counterpoised by a concentrated supremacy, which would be obviously a step towards consolidation and despotism. As the constitution has not provided for the clashing of constitutional laws, it may safely be demanded, by what authority either the state or federal legislative or judicial power, can abrogate one constitutional law because it clashes with another? After the people have invested two legislatures with the power of passing laws within specified orbits, who but themselves can circumscribe those orbits? If the constitutional rights and powers, established by the people between legislative, executive and judicial departments, and between state and federal departments, do in the language of the court *retard, impede, burden or controul* each other, where does the authority lie for removing the inconvenience, admitting it to be one; in the people, or in an implied supremacy of one of these departments, intended by the people to be controuled? If in the latter, the constitution is exposed to be altered by laws or adjudications without restraint. If in the former, then it can never be a question before any judicial department, whether a law is void because it retards, impedes, burdens or controuls another law; and the only chaste question is, whether or not the obstructing law is itself constitutional. Supposing then the bank law to be constitutional, and also that the national right of the states to impose internal taxes is not surrendered, and of course constitutional also, neither congress nor their courts can modify this state power without invading the sovereignty of the people.

In some of the West India islands, as I have heard, the power of an executor extends to all the testator's estate, real and personal; and to such an extent has legal chicanery been carried, that he can easily cheat the devisees out of the whole. A rich father on his death bed informed an only son, that he had given a moderate legacy to one of his friends and appointed him his executor, but that he had devised to him (the son) the whole residue of his estate. The son, thanking his father for his good intentions, but recollecting the sophistry so successfully practised on behalf of executors, besought him to alter the will, to give him the small specifick legacy with the appointment of executor, and to make his friend residuary legatee. The federal government is the specifick, and the states the residuary legatee. If the former can transfer to itself such portions of the residuary estate as it pleases, either by its own will, or by judges appointed, paid and removable by itself, the fate of the latter must be that of a West India residuary legatee. I know of nothing, equivalent to this West India precedent, more in point for construing our constitution, so as to transfer the residuary estate to the special legatee. And yet even this precedent does not go far enough. The legal power of the executor extended to the whole estate, whereas the constitutional power of congress is prohibited from touching the powers reserved. Much less ingenuity was therefore necessary to hold a legal possession contrary to justice, than to acquire possession contrary to law. The executorial power of this country is more like the power of congress. It does not extend to real estate. When an executor or administrator here shall deprive the heirs or devisees of their lands, we shall have a better precedent for establishing the right of congress or the federal courts, to deprive the states, or rather the people, of their natural, national and reserved rights. These are truly their real estate, far surpassing in value the administration of external concerns.

The court, probably without intending it, seem to me to have advanced a position which fully justifies the ground I have taken. They say, " let the *end* be legitimate, let it be with-" in the *scope of the constitution*, and all *means* which are appro-" priate, which are plainly adapted to that end, which are not " prohibited, but consist with the *letter and spirit* of the consti-" tution, are constitutional." It is plainly intimated in this extract, that whatever is constitutional, is valid ; and of course conceded, that in a conflict between two constitutional acts, neither can have any sovereignty over the other. The court indeed in advancing this doctrine, seems only to have turned its eye towards the constitutionality of the acts of congress, overlooking entirely the constitutionality of the acts of the state governments. But if constitutionality bestows validity, and if the state governments, and other political departments can perform constitutional acts, then the validity of these acts rests upon the same foundation, with the validity of the acts of

congress. By "ends" the court seems to understand expressed
powers, and by "means" the execution of those expressed
powers. What then are the powers expressed? Undoubtedly,
those delegated and those reserved. Unless the reservation be
an expression of powers, it can mean nothing. What are these
powers? They can be none others, but the national rights not
surrendered. Taxation is one of these: or rather the support
of the state governments by revenue may be called the end, and
taxation the means. *This end is legitimate, within the scope
of the constitution; the means are appropriate and plainly
adapted to the end, not prohibited and consist with the spirit
and letter of the constitution.*
The constitution has involved ends and means, in such a
manner, as to prove that it never intended that the latter should
beget any ends inconsistent with its great principle, express
letter, and obvious spirit; all uniting to establish a line between external and internal powers. The power of declaring war is an end for which the federal government was
instituted, and nothing could be more *necessary* for carrying this end into execution, than to raise armies, support them,
and to make rules for their government. Yet these means are
not left to be implied as necessary for the execution of the end.
The reason I take to be this. Wherever the means, such as
taxation for the support of armies, and a code of military laws,
would trench upon or circumscribe the national rights inherent
in the states, they are expressed and constituted into a delegated power. If such was the reason for specifying means of
this character, so necessary in war, it follows that no means
of the same character, namely, such as subtract from the national state rights, were intended to be inferred from *necessity.*
But the court, apparently wanting confidence in the words
necessary and proper, as being under an expressed restriction,
and subjected to a comparison with all the other parts of the
instrument, in which they are used; in order to determine their
meaning, have taken a ground so comprehensive, and so ade-
quate to the defence of any acquisition of unconstitutional
powers by congress, that if it be solid, every thing hitherto said
is immaterial. They add to the last extract, as conclusively
responsive to its doctrine, "that banking is a *convenient, a use-
"ful, and essential* instrument in the prosecution of fiscal ope-

"rations, is not now a subject of controversy." Of course a syllogism bounces unexepectedly upon us, out of the two extracts. Fiscal operations are within the powers of congress, and all *means* appropriate to that end are constitutional ; banking is a means convenient, useful and essential to fiscal operations; the conclusion is inevitable. But this interpolation of the words, "convenient, useful and essential," into the constitution, is in my view not even a plausible argument. It is merely a tautology of the phrase " necessary and proper," but excluding the restriction attached to the latter. If the tautology may be fairly used, it can only be as an illustration, since the word "proper" is equivalent to "convenient and useful" so far as they are applicable, and " necessary" to " essential." " Proper" indeed has a reference to the impropriety of swerving from the constitution, and the substitution of words otherwise equivalent may be so far ingenious. The substitution, however, is not a correct illustration of the constitution without the restriction. To reason from it, the court ought to have stated it thus. Congress may pass all laws, which shall be " convenient, useful and essential" for carrying into execution the *foregoing powers.* Thus stated, all the arguments, used in reference to " necessary and proper," plainly apply to the substituted words. And if no power, expressed or implied, be given to congress by the words used, to abrogate constitutional state laws, or to travel out of its delegated orbit into the reserved orbit, I think I may assert, that it cannot derive this power from the substituted words.

But whatever use can be made of these substituted words, it surely cannot appertain exclusively to the delegated powers, and must extend also to those reserved. These would be quite nugatory, under a prohibition to resort to that which was convenient, useful and essential for their execution or preservation. And the constitution having divided and balanced the powers between the federal and state governments, has united itself with common sense in dividing and balancing means, words, phrases and implications, by not investing either department with an exclusive use of these implements necessary to its existence ; foreseeing that powers in either case divested of means, would be inefficient ; but it did not intend that either should destroy the other with its means, though prohibited from doing it with its powers.

It is easy to see, that the court have erected a climax by the words "convenient, useful and essential," to unite an extension of power with an apparent adherence to the words of the constitution. We are gently led along from convenient to essential, as if all the three words were legitimate, because of the resemblance in the last to the word "necessary." Considering all three as restricted by the words "foregoing powers," this is not very material ; but yet, as the incorporating power of congress is deduced from these substituted words, the expediency of banking thus asserted by the court cannot be wholly passed over. I shall, therefore, subjoin a short catalogue of its inconveniences.

The court, with candour and justice, has limited the power of congress to create banks, to the circumstance of their being "convenient, useful and essential to fiscal operations," and forborne to urge their general utility as a reason for the exercise of that power, because it was conscious that the country was not ripe for that doctrine ; or that the constitution did not authorise the extension of federal power, upon the ground of internal social expediency ; and therefore, it was necessary to hook every implied, to some delegated power. Banking is of course suspended to fiscal operations. As to these, the eulogy is consequently wholly pecuniary; and can have no other meaning, than that banking will save publick money, by the facility with which it can be transmitted. And I admit that pecuniary frugality is convenient, useful and even essential to republican governments. This solitary argument for investing congress with the right to incorporate banks, if it can overthrow all those I have advanced, depends yet upon the fact, to which I shall therefore call the reader's attention.

The depreciation of money caused by banking, has been repeatedly and successfully urged both under the state and federal governments, as a reason, for an increase of wages and expenditure ; and has considerably aggravated taxation, both state and federal. Whatever increase of wages or expenditure has been produced by banking, has been nearly a total loss to the nation, unless it can be proved, that an increase of taxation is a publick benefit; a doctrine, which all governments have inculcated, and no nation has yet believed. The reader must compute the extent of this increased taxation, both state and federal, for himself. I can only furnish him with two facts. The federal expenditure in the time of Washington amounted to about three millions annually, and in that of Jefferson to about six. At the first epoch, the United States were paying the interest of their debt; at the second, both the interest and a portion of the principal. Now, the expenditure of the federal government exceeds twenty-five millions. The same candour which will admit, that only a portion of this rapid increase of taxation is attributable to banking, must also allow that much of it is so. I compute the additional taxation, state and federal, thus derived, at not less than five millions annually; paid for the facility of transmitting the publick money from one place to another. Neither our army, nor our navy costs so much. Whatever is the amount, it undoubtedly is directly the reverse of fiscal convenience or utility ; that is, in regard to the nation ; for I know that it is not rare for governments to consider an increase of taxation as " a convenient, useful " and essential *instrument* in the prosecution of fiscal opera- " tions," and that banking has therefore been very much of a favourite with those of the old world. I acquit, however, all our governments of this design, because I believe they never thought of it, however extensively their laws may have brought it about. It only happened from the circumstance, that similar causes, either in the west or east, will generally produce similar effects. In the east, exclusive privileges have invariably turned out to be publick grievances ; and aggravated taxation, legal extravagance and pauperism, have regularly brought up the rear of banking. But our legislatures have fondly hoped, that exclusive privileges, granted by good republicans, would be publick blessings.

It was once asserted, that banking would reimburse the loss it caused to the nation in aggravating wages, expense and taxation, by enhancing the price of our commodities ; and the argument kept its ground, so long as these brought a high price in Europe ; but woful experience has detected the delusion. It is at length demonstrated, that the price of our exports is fixed in foreign markets, and that banking does not, by enhancing it, reimburse the nation for the increase of taxation it causes. The argument of the court can derive no benefit from any utility in banking, except in *fiscal operations*, as it does not pretend a right to extend the powers of congress from any general considerations of national good ; but only as means appurtenant to an actual delegated power, which in this case it supposes to be the power of taxation, though called " fiscal operations." But, whilst the court, in sustaining this argument, is limited to the convenience of banking for the execution of a delegated power, in refuting it, all the national inconveniences it causes are fair counterpoises against its solitary convenience of transmitting publick money. This is, apparently, a pecuniary convenience ; but if we pay for it more than it saves, by the increase of taxation arising from the depreciation of bank currency, it is clearly a pecuniary inconvenience ; and it is not yet contended, that the powers of congress may be extended by implication to rights inconvenient and oppressive to the nation. No one, who computes impartially, will hesitate to conclude, that the increase of taxation, caused by the depreciation of bank currency, infinitely exceeds the saving of transmitting taxes by bank instrumentality. Waving the facilities arising from bills or orders, which would be considerable, I will venture to assert, that if it was removed under a military escort, the expense would be comparatively trifling.

To the increase of taxation by banking, another great item of pecuniary loss is to be added. The local depreciation of its currency causes us to pay an additional price for our imports. Sellers will reimburse themselves for this depreciation, to our excessive injury when the balance of trade happens to be against us, by asking a price sufficient to enable them to make remittances in specie. And exclusively of the diminution of the precious metals thus caused, the difference between their value and the value of bank paper is a large item of national pecuniary loss, independently of the pecuniary individual loss arising from the same cause.

Fiscal operations are the means, by which civilized nations are oppressed and enslaved. If a government may do whatever it pleases to think " convenient, useful or essential in the pro- " secution of fiscal operations," however inconvenient, useless and injurious to a nation, and however detrimental to the

morals, interest, and happiness of individuals, it is difficult to
conceive any limitations by which it can be restrained. The
framers of the constitution, aware of the necessity for restraining this dangerous instrument, confided to the federal government a fiscal power, defined and limited. In the division of
powers between the federal and state governments, the care
of the morals, interest and happiness of individuals is confided
to the latter; nor is any power over persons given to the
former, except for the carrying into execution the delegated powers, which were not intended to absorb a right to
take out of the hands of the states their national and original
right to provide for the morals, interest and happiness of the
individuals composing each state. Suppose experience should
disclose mischiefs and inconveniences to the people from the
circulation of notes payable to the bearer. Is the federal or
state governments to apply the remedy? The limited power of
the federal government over persons does not reach the object.
The state governments have endeavoured to prevent it, by prohibiting individuals or unincorporated banks from issuing such
notes. They might have suffered this, but congress could not.
It is merely an internal local regulation, like the transfer of
bonds, bills or notes, within the power of the state governments, and without the power of congress. The right of prohibition is consecutive to the right of permission; and congress
have no power to prohibit, because they have none to permit.
Whilst the care of the morals, interest and happiness of the
people internally, is confided to the states, it can hardly be
imagined that congress was invested with a power of legislating, so as to afflict all three in a mode, which they had no
power to prevent. They could not, constitutionally, even consider the inconveniences of banking under any power given to
them by the federal constitution, as to the morals, interest and
happiness of the people, because the care of these is reserved
to the states; and ought to have confined themselves to the
meagre point of its affording a facility in transmitting money,
as all its other effects belonged to the state orbit. In this view,
the decision of the court allows that congress may cause great
and general internal inconveniences, of a character beyond its
power to prohibit or even to consider; and that the states, who
can only consider these inconveniences, and cannot apply a

remedy under their internal power of forbidding the circulation of notes payable to order, often exercised and never relinquished.

Congress were never expected to consider those local frauds by which life is embittered and society corrupted; even the manners of the individuals who conduct its banks, are without its province and beyond its correction; and although the idea of correcting the frauds of institutions, shrouded in secrecy, is only a theory, yet this unfortunate fact is an unanswerable argument for a power of suppression in a government. Being of an internal nature, congress cannot exercise this power; yet evils ought to be suppressed. Is there a single case of a stockholder, defrauded by the management of these secret institutions, having been able to obtain justice? Whilst widows and orphans are pining in silence, under the distress of the spoliations they have suffered, the newspapers roar with the dolours of the patriots who have employed their property in unsuccessful speculations. Legislatures are invoked by arts and wailings from bankrupts of borrowed property, to have compassion on their aversion to the payment of their debts, to sequester a poor remnant which their unfortunate creditors may recover, and confiscate this remnant, by devising some depreciated currency with which to balance accounts.

Under our form of government, fiscal operations ought not to be considered in reference to the convenience or benefit of a government, as they are considered under European monarchies, but in relation to the convenience or benefit of the people. Now, though the government may suffer no inconvenience or injury from the increase of salaries and expenses produced by the depreciation of bank currency, the people from our peculiar situation may sustain both. Their funds arise chiefly from the exportation of agricultural or marine productions, by which they are enabled to pay their taxes. The price of these productions being limited by their trans-atlantick value, the people cannot be reimbursed by the depreciation of a local currency, for an increase of taxation chiefly paid out of this restricted price.

Again. The fiscal operations of a government may be nurtured by a corruption of manners, and a violation of justice among individuals. Unhappily, the revolutionary patriots were driven into the latter evil by necessity. But we have voluntarily introduced both without any. The United States have ascertained the effects of paper money by two experiments, and its character under a free government has been settled by both. By the first it is ascertained, that the most solemn national promises of redemption, without equivalent funds, cannot sustain its value, or prevent its fraudulent operation upon individuals : By the second, that a promise of redemption by the payment of specie will sustain its value, or delay its fraudulent operation upon individuals, so long only as the nation believes in the falsehood, that the banks are able to pay it. In a free country, the detection, sooner or later, is inevitable, and a heavy shock of factitious misfortunes ensues. Banks, managed by the power of despotism or of aristocracy, live long either upon delusion, or upon supplies extracted from the people. The same motives unite these parties in these means, for conducting their *fiscal operations.* Exposed to the scrutinizing eye of liberty, a detection of fraud will come at last. Under the iron rod of despotick governments, these institutions are deterred from committing any frauds, but in concert with their accomplices, both by the fear of punishment, and the influence of patronage; but under our mild policy, neither expiation nor bribery is practicable in the case of banks. Their crimes may possibly be numbered, but no figures can record their punishments, because they are never punished. Had the bank of the United States commenced its very career, by committing the most enormous frauds, congress might have been deterred by the magnitude of its offences, or an inability to do justice to the injured, even from making them publick.

A catalogue of the immoral tendencies of banking ought to be awful to a republican government, which many great writers assert to be incapable of subsisting long, except by the preservation of virtuous principles. Can these be preserved, by investing corporate bodies with the privileges of committing remediless frauds, of laughing at detection, and of retaining the pillage ? By nurturing and then ruining, pride, extravagance, speculation, folly, rapaciousness and dishonesty, as the arch fiend entices into guilt, and punishes those whom he has deluded ? By corrupting legislative bodies, the temporary representatives of the people, into an opinion, that they may prolong their power and establish their speculations, however detrimental to their constituents, for unlimited periods ? By deluging a whole nation with floods of depreciation usury, having first banished the only check by which it could be restrained ? By enlisting in the cause of this overwhelming system of usury, from which even those who never borrow cannot escape, a great portion of the talents of the country ; and teaching them to be satisfied with its intellectual pleasures, without salaries ? By rewarding atrocious frauds, sometimes with wealth, and always with impunity ? By first expelling specie, and then subjecting the nation to the alternative of suffering a great loss in getting it back, or of submitting for ever to banking prescription ? By bribing corporations with an absolute power of acquiring wealth by frauds with impunity, for the sake of a trivial political convenience ? By committing the national safety and prosperity to the care of individual character, without responsibility or controul, for indefinite periods ; except such as may be fixed by the will of temporary representatives ? By thus regenerarating the hereditary principle of subjecting mankind to the chance of being governed by knaves in the affair of money (so important to social happiness,) under an interest to do wrong, and under no compulsion to do right ? By substituting an arrogant divination for actual experience (the true source of human knowledge,) in usurping a right to pass irrepealable laws ? By staking the national prosperity on the maxim, that it may safely be intrusted to unchecked avarice ? By arranging society into debtors and creditors, bribing usury to lend, tempting indiscretion to borrow, protecting the former against the payment of its own debts, and producing by law a state of things, calculated for destroying a good government, or subjecting it to the clamours and threats of dishonesty ? And by making it improvident to be prudent ; as by endeavouring to provide for old age or misfortune, we should probably lose the whole, and certainly a portion of our labours ?

The facts, to justify these inconveniences produced by banking, are left to the recollection of the reader; but the expression " depreciation usury, " requires a short explanation. It refers to the loss sustained by the nation, from the depreciation of bank currency, beyond the interest paid for it by the borrower. This item of pecuniary loss, frequently repeated in the circulation of the paper, may possibly amount to as much as the additional taxation caused by the same depreciation. The two items and the interest paid to banks chiefly constitute the price paid by the nation for the *convenience* of transferring the taxes from place to place. It is probable that it amounts to thirty or forty per centum per annum, on a larger sum than the amount of taxes ; and equally so, that these taxes could be transmitted in the most inconvenient mode, which could be devised, at less than one.

Wherein consists the difficulty on this subject ? may the truth be permitted to answer the question ? Men incline to acquire wealth, without encountering the labours of industry ; as they incline to get to heaven, without discharging the duties of morality. Speculators for both objects are therefore greedily attended to, and often infuse tenets into nations so stubborn, as to divide society for ages into jugglers and dupes. Governments have repeatedly aggrandized themselves and enriched the initiated, under intricate and plausible schemes for enriching the nation ; and labour is induced cheerfully to exchange its earnings, for a dogma or a charm. When these schemes or incantations are directed against a foreign nation, the imposition is easy ; and governments generally cajole nations out of their property to a great amount, by ingenious lectures to prove that they will be reimbursed ten fold in heaven, or by other nations. Once taught that we may be enriched by the speculations of our government at the expence of foreigners, a transition from a dogma having a glimmering of truth, to one having none, becomes easy ; and we rashly believe that a patriotick magician can instruct a nation to enrich itself, by speculations upon itself ; that exclusive privileges conferred on an incorporated section of the national wealth will produce a greater degree of national prosperity, than equal privileges retained by the whole.

Congress, in rejecting lord North's insidious proposal for raising a revenue by colonial laws, observed, " that all history shews " that a *power over the purse is the best intercessor for a redress* " *of grievances, and a re-establishment of rights.*" Banking has gotten into its possession that which the national purse contained ; intolerable grievances have ensued ; the right to pri-

vate justice has been grossly violated, and no general benefit
has been produced. The revolutionary congress, that highest
emblem of wisdom and virtue, with which Providence has endowed man ; the fathers of our liberty, uninfluenced by avarice
or ambition ; the revolutionary congress decided, "that a
power over the purse is the best intercessor for a redress of
grievances and a re-establishment of rights." *The power over
the purse* has escaped from the people and their governments.
This best security against grievances and wrongs has been
transferred by legislatures to corporations. If they had a right
to transfer the best, they may transfer all other securities to the
custody of chartered bodies. Dazzled by a spurious lustre, we
have violated this sound maxim ; we have worshipped a demon
instead of a Deity ; and now that we are awakened by sensation from the infatuation, we are told that the altars of fraud
are sacred. Grievances and violated rights abound ; the principles of justice are prostrated ; but the hurricane of evils
claims a power founded in the imposition of calling a law a
charter, to molest an entire generation during its whole life,
without redress ; and the isinglass of construction is its ally
against the diamond of justice. Money governs the world. Is a
corporate despotism over the money or currency of a nation no
political power ? That which is able to do good or harm to nations, is power. All our constitutions have provided representation, checks and responsibilities, to *prevent grievances and
preserve rights.* Can representation invest corporations with
a power of doing good or harm to the nation for long terms,
without being subject to the constitutional provisions for preventing grievances and preserving rights ? No legislature is itself invested with any power, unsubjected to these provisions.
If legislatures can create a power beyond their own, the coercion of which is without the reach even of election, they may
thus overthrow every principle of our constitutions. Our constitutions unite in deciding, that political power ought to be
responsible, to be entrusted for short periods, to be controuled,
and to be punished if abused. In the legislative creation of
political corporations, none of these precautions has been regarded. We have had an irresponsible, uncontrouled, unpun-
ishable, unelected power over the national purse, in operation
for a short time. Compare the effects of the two principles,

exactly contrary to each other, and decide which is best. Can the evils embowelled in one, by having been littered over the land, hide the blessings which have flowed from the other ? This absolute power over the national purse was never before conferred on banking corporations, nor has a pecuniary despotism been before entrusted by any government, to such establishments. The banks, created by monarchies and aristocracies, have all been subjected to those governments, and subservient to their designs. The government directs their political effects: Private bankers are liable, personally, to the payment of their debts. Our bankers are neither liable to the controul of our governments, nor subject, personally, to the payment of their debts. A non-descript in their nature, they have of course been a non-descript in their consequences.

But, if these evils of banking are recompensed to the nation by its convenience in transmitting federal money from one part of the country to another, there would yet remain weighty constitutional arguments against it. The absorption of power by money was so very well known by the framers of our constitutions, that they studiously erected a circumvallation of restrictions, such as election, representation, sympathy, rotation, responsibility, checks, balances, divisions and limitations, around the power of the purse, when exercised by the governments they created, and these governments have bestowed that power on bankers, unattended by any restriction at all, in return for the convenience of transmitting the publick money. It is, as if a monarch had surrendered to a corporation all the principles by which his throne was secured, for the same mighty object. Weighty enough, as the court think it, to invest a government with the most dangerous and oppressive of all powers, that of granting exclusive privileges, and creating bodies politick; neither France, nor many other large countries, have ever thought of it; and the novelty of making an object, so diminutive hitherto in the history of mankind, a source of acquiring enormous powers, must be an evidence of the profundity or shallowness of the American genius. There is evidently much ingenuity in making the convenience of transmitting publick money, on the ground of the great extent of the United States, the matrix of the right to incorporate, because the state governments cannot, with any plausibility, avail themselves of the argument, the whole force of which must redound to the federal government; but yet I shall proceed to controvert it.

The mother bank of the United States, I suppose (for I have not the law before me,) may, or may not, estabish or abolish branch banks at its own pleasure. If so, it may, or it may not, at its own will, transmit publick money from one place excepted. I do not know whether the bank is compelled by the law, under a penalty to receive and transmit publick money, wherever it may establish branches; or whether the law is merely preceptive as to the point; but I suppose, that it can only be required to transmit what it receives, and that it is not bound to receive where it has no branch. If this should be the case, this compensation to be paid by the bank, as justifying its incorporation, may be extended or diminished at its own pleasure. It is true, that the profit arising from deposites of publick money, inspired a very reasonable hope, that the bank would send out branches to those places where most of it was to be received, and from whence it could most easily be transmitted; but hope is eventual, and the constitutionality of a law ought to be positive and not fortuitous, at the time it is passed ; not now constitutional and then unconstitutional, as the bank should choose to hook it to, or unhook it from fiscal operations ; and not constitutional in one state, or at one place, where the bank might choose to have a branch to aid those operations, and unconstitutional in another, where it might choose to, have none. However this may be, it must be admitted, that the size of the convenience can have nothing to do with its power to invest congress with the right of creating corporations, and that the transmission of a cent would be a convenience, as effectual to constitutionalize an incorporating law, as the transmission of a million. The constitution does not confine the virtue of this power-amplifying principle to conveniencies, or means of any specified degrees of magnitude, and each, however small, like every magnet, contains the power of attraction. The least convenience, therefore, in the exercise of every delegated power, will justify congress in granting individual or corporate privileges ; and those who will transmit federal horses, arms or victuals, (so much more cumbersome than money,) have a better right to them than the money-changers themselves. In short, if the argument of convenience be sufficient to establish the constitutionality of the law in the case of the banks, every power whatsoever, delegated to congress, may reward its co-adjutors with exclusive privileges, and embrace within its means, monopolies of every description.

It would be a subject worthy of mature consideration, whether a bank currency, such as we are suffering under, does not bear a strong analogy in its effects, to the monopoly of the colonial trade long held by the English, and which we supposed we had happily abolished by a long war. But it is too copious for the limits I must observe, and I only suggest it to the reader, that he may compare in his own mind, both the extent of the two monopolies, and the cost of getting rid of them.

A phalanx of words have been enlisted to assail the plainest provisions of the federal constitution ; but only one more shall be adverted to. The word "national," is often made an auxiliary of "sovereign, supreme, necessary and convenient," towards destroying or relaxing the restrictions imposed upon congress by the union. It is contended, that congress may exercise *national* powers. Where is this nation, of which gentlemen speak ? Is it composed of twenty-three individuals only ? If so, if the states made the union, and if congress possess no powers, except those bestowed by the union, then the term is only an expedient, like that in using the words sovereign, supreme, convenient and necessary, to convey to the federal government recondite, in the place of defined powers. All these words being equally sufficient to convey indefinite, instead of the limited powers really delegated to congress, why should we be led round the radii of a circle to get at its centre, omnipotence ? The premises being settled, the argument would terminate in a syllogism, and put us out of our pain. As thus: Such a thing is an act of power, congress is omnipotent, therefore it is within the sphere of congress. Is it not the same sort of reasoning to say, such a thing is an act of sovereignty, or of supremacy, or necessary, or convenient, or national ; congress may do what is sovereign, supreme, necessary, convenient, or national, therefore it is within the sphere of congress ?

SECTION. 11.

THE BANK DECISION.—PRECEDENTS.

I shall conclude this subject, by an examination of an argument with which the court began. It remarks, that "banking " was introduced at a very early period of our history, has been " recognized by many successive legislatures, and has been " acted upon by the judicial department in cases of peculiar de- " licacy, as a law of undoubted obligation." This remark must either furnish the conclusion, that precedents may change the federal constitution, or it has no weight. As it was intended to have weight, it deserves an attentive consideration.

In consolidated societies, subject to one sovereign government, having but one legislature, and but one judicial power, where law is omnipotent, the omnipotence of precedents is a component part of the form of the government; but in a federal republick, having two co-ordinate and distinct legislatures, and two judicial powers, where law is not omnipotent, and where the governments, instead of being sovereigns, are only invested with limited powers, it would be an incongruity with the form of government, to allow to precedents the same force. The constitution does not invest either the state or federal governments with an exclusive power of changing its principles by precedents, because it would destroy their co-ordinacy, disorder the division of powers, and subject one to the other. Nor can such a power be common to all these governments, because the different precedents, which would thence arise, must soon make as many federal constitutions as we have governments. In countries where the unity and sovereignty of the government is the primary political principle, these objections to precedents would have no weight; but here, where neither this unity nor sovereignty is to be found, they would, if used as they are used under those governments, destroy our existing system; because, a right to make precedents in any one of our departments is an acknowledgment of a sovereignty in that department. The reader will remark, that I am speaking of political precedents, which ought not to be confounded in any degree with municipal or forensick, established for ascertaining private rights, because we did not intend by constitutions to subject the national liberty to so uncertain a tenure.

If, however, we should even be governed in relation to charters, by the precedents of other nations, and other forms of government, they would furnish us with a volume of authorities, subversive of their sufficiency to sustain our banking corporations. In England, the granting of charters was an executive, not a legislative act; and as the English king, (the grantor) never dies, so his act could never be revoked. But all our legislatures die regularly, and the precedents of repealing laws are numerous enough, if the right of repeal depends upon precedents to establish it beyond a doubt. In England, it never was even contended, that the parliament could not annul charters, and therefore charters cannot have drawn from that country a sanctity for precedents, with the help of which they may annul constitutions.

It would be tedious to collect the changes made by laws in the English magna charta. This charter itself has been so entirely obliterated by laws, as to have become useless, and to deserve a very opprobious appellation bestowed upon it by an English judge, but yet so appropriate as to have been long commemorated. The commercial charters granted by queen Elizabeth, and other English monarchs, were often annulled or revoked by law; and even by the kings themselves, in spite of their legal immortality. The south sea charter was annulled, and remedies applied by the guardians of the publick good, to the evils of chartered frauds. Precedents therefore pronounce, that legislative power is not prohibited by corporation fictions, not even by the ancient fiction that the king never dies, "*intro-*" *duced at a very early period of our history, recognized by many* " *successive legislatures, and acted upon by the judicial depart-*" *ment, in cases of peculiar delicacy, as a law of undoubted* " *obligation,*" from shielding nations against any calamities produced by charters. The mischiefs of having south sea directors in the English parliament were so apparent, as to have suggested a law prohibiting the officers of revenue from even voting at elections ; and this is a very pointed precedent, applying to the case of filling our legislatures with bank directors and stockholders, who receive nearly the whole of our taxes both state and federal, and make a profit on all these deposites. So that like English revenue officers, the higher the taxes the greater will be their income.

Many precedents in relation to charters have been *"introdu-* *"ced at periods of our history"* still earlier than banking ; have *" been recognized by many successive legislatures,"* and have been *" acted upon by judicial departments in cases of pecu-* *" liar delicacy as laws of undoubted obligation."* Virginia, when a colony, oppressed by a mercantile or money-making charter, having the acquisition of wealth, and not the good of the colony for its object, was saved by taking refuge from it under a king ; even a king of the Stuart family. The same king divided Virginia in violation of charters. Carolina and other colonies were in like manner divided. All the colonies broke through charters to get at publick good and national safety. The effects of bank charters were not better understood when these laws, so nick-named, were passed, than the excessive extent of a few colonial charters, when they were granted. This unforeseen extent demanded and received remedies. Even since the revolution, it was a subject of debate in congress. The smaller states asserted, that justice demanded a restriction of the charters extending to the western ocean, and an application of unsettled territories to the general benefit ; and the states possessing such charters yielded to the call of justice, and the general interest. Is this a precedent for sacrificing both to banking charters, and for re-instating musty feudal errors, so very soon after we have subverted a host of them ; by subjecting our property and industry to a ruinous tenure, renewable forever by those who receive the rents ?

Let us look at the logick which supposes that acquiescence makes precedents, and that precedents make reason. All precedents or laws are at first theory, and acquiescence alone can convert them into practice. Banking began as a theory ; and political augurs differed in their prognostications of its effects. The worst precedents are often but little felt in their infancy, because they move with caution, until they gather strength ; and the worse they are, the more time is often required to develope their character. Some foretold that banking would be beneficial; others, that it would be pernicious to our country. It would be an odd judgment, however honest, which should assert, that fulfilment ought to destroy, and falsehood to establish an augury, because just at the time when experience has converted the theory of banking into evidence, both felt and understood, acquiescence has also mellowed the same theory into a precedent, and a precedent deprives us of the benefit of experience; so that the time, expended in ascertaining the truth or falsehood of an augury, renders it impossible to remedy its imposition, just at the moment when it is discovered.

Judicial precedents are commonly the work of one man or a very few men. An opinion becomes an authority, and as it rolls along, it magnifies by others which adhere to it, not because it is right, but because it is authority. In my view, it bears no resemblance to the species of consent by which we make constitutions.

The submission of the people is one argument of little or no weight to prove the constitutionality of laws. The influence of government, and not the approbation of the people, generally causes a submission to laws; and therefore, it is but a bad argument for sanctifying precedents. But under the federal constitution, the argument has moreover a fraudulent aspect, because its provisions for amendment have taught the people to believe, that there are no other modes by which the constitution can be altered; and lulled them into security against precedents. Expecting solemnities and publick discussions before their own solemn compact could be changed, they would be caught by the snare of precedents, from an opinion that no such snare existed. It would have been better to have declared, that all laws which should live to a certain age should be engrafted into the constitution, because it would have kept the people attentive to legislation, and induced them to save such laws as were good, and to check the vigilance of governments in making precedents favourable to power. Suppose, it had been proposed to amend the constitution in either of the prescribed modes, by investing congress with powers to create banks, to bestow bounties, to grant exclusive privileges, to make roads and canals, to annex conditions to the admission of new states into the union, and to prohibit the state governments from taxing the persons or property it should invest with exclusive privileges ; would all these powers have been as quietly and silently obtained in the constitutional mode, as by precedents ? There is no fair way of deciding the doubt, except one, which I wish to see resorted to, namely, a formal proposal in congress for conferring all these powers upon itself, by a positive amendment of the constitution. The inconsistency between limiting a government attended with prescribed modes of amendment, and the doctrine that this same government might extend its powers by its own precedents, is sufficient to have deluded the people into an opinion, if it be a delusion, that the constitution was not liable to be altered by precedents ; and that whatever law could do, law could undo. Precedents would make a strange species of constitution, according to our notions ; they would be repealable by the legislatures which made them. In those countries where the governments are absolute, this is no objection to them ; but here precedents are nothing but laws, and the question, whether they are constitutional or not, must forever remain attached to them, unless it can be proved that it is a question of no importance after they have obtained the title of precedents. It will then become a matter of very great importance, to ascertain by whom this title is to be bestowed.

The Stuart family were mighty sticklers for precedents, and sedulous builders of these political forts to hold the ground gained by construction from time to time, by its inroads upon constitutions ; because, successive encroachments terminate in conquest. To prevent these encroachments, as a fatal appendage to all governments invested with sovereignty, we have deprived ours of the right to modify our constitution by precedents, by prescribing the modes of modification. The precaution was suggested by two very important considerations. One, that every government which has possessed a power of modifying its own form, has used it fraudulently and oppressively : The other, that we having established co-ordinate governments, state and federal, a right of modification by precedents must either be equal or exclusive. If it was equal, inextricable confusion would ensue ; if exclusive, the principle of co-ordinacy would be abolished.

The distinction between limitations and restrictions imposed by the people on their governments by constitutions, and those imposed by the governments on themselves, by their own precedents, is manifest. There is no similitude between the cases. Constitutions and precedents perform contrary offices. The first tie, and the second untie. It has always been difficult for nations to tie governments by precedents; and to give them knives, for precedents are such, to cut these constitutional knots, would make every government an Alexander. Each administration would have as good a right to make precedents, as its predecessor; and this guillotine of restrictions would seldom lie idle. Veneration for our constitutions is the best security for the endurance of our free form of government, and the best infusion for elevating the national character. But, how can a nation love an embryo litter of fluctuating precedents, concealed in the womb of time, each of which as it grows, hustles some principle out of the constitution, as the cuckoo does the sparrow out of its own nest? Had Pygmalion's beautiful statue, after it was animated, been seduced to produce bastards, would he have loved her the better for it? What should we say to a husband, who should surrender the custody of his wife to a set of professed rakes? That which ought to be said of a nation, which entrusts its constitution to the care of precedents. They are only the projects or opinions of successive legislators, presidents, judges, generals or statesmen, none of whom will acknowledge that their laws, actions, decisions, orders or schemes are unconstitutional, though they will be forever as various and contradictory as the characters from which they proceed. Mankind have generally, however, confided in this chance medley current of governmental promulgation, for the preservation of their happiness; but we have preferred principles, maturely considered, carfully selected, cautiously approved, and distinctly defined, as a better security. Our mode of establishing the principles in which we confide is infinitely preferable to the European practice, of leaving them to be found and to be lost, by a succession of precedents; from the consideration, that our conventions have no other business, and reason acts, uncorrupted by avarice or ambition; whereas, after a government is in operation, the whole tribe of selfish motives becomes active, and time for inventing and practising stratagems is endless. France, by deviating from our mode, and investing her constituent assemblies with the current powers of government, received a lecture upon the consequences of deriving constitutional principles from the governing power, which she has cause to remember, and which we ought not to forget.

It is admitted, that precedents, both good and bad, ought to have weight in fixing our conclusions. They are practical demonstrations of wisdom or folly ; and constitute the fund of experience, by which the faculty of reasoning is supplied with materials. But discrimination is as applicable to precedents, as to any other species of evidence ; and if mankind have improved in the theory of political morality, their age only suggests a suspicion of their goodness, and the propriety of their rigourous examination. As rigourously ought current measures to be subjected to the test of an improved political system, because its value depends upon its practical effects. It is true, that power, to prevent this necessary examination of precedents, has in all ages attempted to fortify them by a spurious sanctity, for the purposes of fostering usurpations, and securing its acquisitions ; and that the worse they are, the more earnestly is their sanctity asserted. The exclusive power and wealth they obtain from the general evils they inflict, are zealous preachers in self defence, which never fail to convince themselves. Hence no improvement in civil government has ever been made, or can be preserved, but by a subversion of precedents, until a form is discovered incapable of corruption. Being numerous as foes, and few as friends of liberty, she must constantly have recourse to constitutional principles to keep them in check, or fall a victim to their power. By surrendering its constitution to precedents, a nation would surrender its strongest fortress to its strongest enemy ; and would subscribe to the opinion, that the best mode of defending itself, is to throw down its arms. Constitutions are exposed to the jurisdiction of experience ; but precedents presumptuously renounce it, and impiously say to improvement "stop ;" so that when experience has discovered an evil, our sensibility of its affliction is rendered more poignant by the veto of a precedent against the remedy.

An exaltation of precedents to an equality with constitutions would exceed their pretension, however it might dissatisfy their arrogance ; and yet a dignity so extravagantly gratuitous would not absolve them from construction by a reference to principles, nor entitle them to complain of a treatment, which they apply to constitutions. But, if we reduce precedents to their just rank, we shall discern that they are exposed to two tests, to which constitutions are not subject. They are amenable both to constitutions and expediency. The enquiry upon the first ground is not, whether the precedent is better or worse than the constitution, but whether it is conformable to constitutional principles; and if it is, the precedent is still amenable to the second enquiry, whether it is working good or evil. If a succession of wrongs can constitute rights under the name of precedents, as in Europe, then indeed they are beyond the reach of these enquiries, and have obtained a degree of insubordination, to which constitutions themselves do not aspire; otherwise, they are always liable to an arraignment for disloyalty to constitutions, or injury to society; and if found guilty, constantly exposed to the mild punishment of suppression. If they should slip by constitutions, upon the smooth profession of benefiting society, they ought certainly to be arrested, should the profession turn out to be fallacious.

But suppose, as the court contend, that banking " having been " introduced at a very early period of our history, been recog- " nized by many successive legislatures, and been acted upon by " the judicial department in cases of peculiar delicacy, as a law " of undoubted obligation," is settled by a cloud of precedents to be constitutional; and that the question should be considered under an admission so copious, of the efficacy of precedents. Yet this same efficacy is as strong to sustain *positive*, as to sustain *implied* constitutional articles. The court does not say that the federal constitution bestows a positive power on congress to create banks, and only asserts that " there is no phrase " in the constitution which excludes *incidental or implied* " powers," among which it includes banking. A concurrent right of taxation is a positive power given and reserved to the federal and state governments by the constitution. *It has been exercised to great extent from the commencement of our constitutional history; it has been recognized by many successive legislatures; and it has been acted upon by the judicial departments in cases of peculiar delicacy, as undoubtedly constitutional.* If a cloud of precedents can establish an incidental or

implied power, another cloud of precedents ought to establish
a positive and expressed power. The finest effort of ingenuity
to be found in the opinion of the court, is, that of availing itself of
precedents in a point only incidental, and of passing them by
altogether in reference to the true question to be decided. The
state of Maryland had not disputed the constitutionality of the
bank, but had exercised its concurrent right of taxation ; and the
court refers to the multiplicity of precedents as a proof of its constitutionality, and forgets the same species of multiplicity as a
proof of the constitutionality of the concurrent right. There was
a sound reason for doing so. The intended decision was to make
a new precedent, to overthrow the whole multitude of precedents
establishing the concurrent right of taxation, and therefore it
was wise to transfer our attention from the precedents applying
to the question, intended to be destroyed, to make a shew in
the back ground, as some generals have gained a victory by
formally arraying the scullions of their army, and deceiving
their adversaries into an opinion, that they were really soldiers.
Besides, it held out an aspect of paying respect to precedents,
under cover of which they were actually to be overturned.
There was no precedent at all by which the court could abridge
or modify the concurrent powers of taxation established by the
constitution ; but a multitude of precedents in favour of the
constitutionality of this concurrency, had arisen from its mutual exercise. Congress had established it by many laws, especially in taxing the state banks by a stamp act. If the establishment of state banks was within the state spheres, congress
had no right to throw *obstacles in the way of their sphere of action,* except by virtue of the concurrrent power of taxation ; and
if this power justified congress in taxing state banks, the same
power justified the states in taxing the banks of congress, though
these latter were also constitutional. But, the court, instead
of considering the precedents in relation to the concurrent
right of taxation, have insisted at large upon those which relate
to the constitutionality of banking, and adhered to the precedent of searching for a goose, when the thing lost was a cow.
The excessive departure from the true question by this process, will be seen at once by supposing all that it could prove,
namely that the constitution had given to congress a positive
power to create banks. We should then have seen it in

a state of equality, as to origin, rank and obligation, with the positive concurrent power of taxation; and the question would have come fairly forth, whether one power revokes another equal to itself, because they clash? If this question was answered affirmatively, and the revoking power ascertained, it would be easy to prove that very little of the constitution would remain. I suppose it will hardly be asserted, that an implied power is better than if it had been expressed, because though it may be moulded so as to defeat other implied powers, it can hardly be made to destroy a power expressed. The concurrent right of taxation reaches all property real and personal, and had banking been positively allowed, still it would not have followed, that any modifications of property thus subjected to taxation, by the state or federal government, should discharge it from the liability to which it is clearly subjected. The property could not evade the constitution by changing its shape. The authors of The Federalist have considered this concurrent right of taxation in the federal and state governments as a plain, positive and vital principle of the constitution; and the court has merged it in the implied constitutionality of banking, as by precedents established.

If I have overlooked any argument used by the court, it has been done undesignedly; and if I have any hope of victory, in a contest between a dwarf and half a dozen giants, it is founded in the following consideration. It seems to me that the argument of the court may be defined " an exquisite sample of " artificial phraseology;" and that the simplicity of ignorance may possibly break through fine webs spun from the wombs of single words, because truth can be seen without being dressed in such flimsy robes. Mystical interpreters extract from texts whatever doctrine is necessary for their purpose, but sound logick is not like money; an hundred light arguments will not make a heavy one, as an hundred cents make a dollar; and I cannot discern an argument in the opinion, which weighed singly, seems heavy. When I read those extracted from the words " sovereign, supreme, sphere, paramount, necessary and convenient," I thought I saw the end of the sound revolutionary good sense by which our governments were constituted, as Rome saw puns and quibbles substituted for the masculine eloquence which preceded the age of Augustus. It seemed like extract-

ing poison from vipers, under an opinion that it would be medi-
cinal. If I were asked, how it has happened that men in power
can inveigh against, oppose, support, and practise the same
maxims? I should reply, by artificial phraseology. How are
political parties drilled into contradictions? By artificial phraseology. How has the reasoning of the court been assailed, whilst
its conclusion is allowed to be correct? By artificial phraseology. How is the right of incorporating banks conceded, when
the mode of defending the right is censured? By artificial
phraseology. And what is this artificial phraseology? It is the
vocation of stripping evils of unseemly attire in order to dress
them more handsomely, or of subjecting the federal constitution to the needles of verbal embroiderers, in obedience to the
saying " the tailor makes the man."

SECTION 12.

PROTECTING DUTIES AND BOUNTIES.

The points presenting themselves in considering this important subject, are, first, whether either the federal or state governments possess a right to distribute wealth and poverty, gain and loss between occupations and individuals. Secondly, whether the federal government possesses this right. And thirdly, supposing both or either to possess such a right, whether it is wise, or honest, or beneficial to the United States, to exercise it.

To understand the rights of mankind, the powers of government, and the meaning of constitutions, we ought to ascertain the design of civil society. Man, by nature, had two rights; to his conscience, and to his labour; and it was the design of civil society, to secure these rights. In the case of religious freedom, we have seen one right; in that of the freedom of property, our vision is not so clear; yet both, as natural rights, stand on the same foundation.

By suppressing the distinction between occupations, and covering all by the inclusive term, labour, we at once discern the natural equality of the right. The occupations of men are the men themselves; and every free government supposes, that it is only distinguishable from a tyrannical one by equal laws, and equal rights in its citizens. Our societies grew up from this principle, and we find nothing in our constitutions by which it is abolished. Our governments received man, animated by the creator, with a free will over his mind and his labour; and were instituted to protect the divine bounty. The freedom of conscience was made complete, because no contributions from that natural right were necessary for the support of civil government; but the freedom of labour was incomplete, from the necessity of such contributions. For ages, governments used the division of mankind into religious sects, as a means for making some men subservient to the avarice of others. We have detected this fraud; but its principle is vindicated by our governments having used the division of mankind into different occupations, as a means for making some men subservient to the avarice of others. The natural rights of labour, in subjecting themselves to contributions for the support of civil government, never meant to acknowledge themselves to be the slaves of a despotick power. These contributions were agreed to, for the purchase of protection, and not to establish a power for transferring the fruits of labour from one man to another. When paid, the freedom of property, as a natural right, occupies in relation to the remainder, the same ground which is occupied by the freedom of conscience. There is no reason to make any deduction from the latter right, for the sake of civil government; the reason for doing so, as to the former, extends only to publick contributions, and when these are paid, the rights of property are the same as the rights of conscience. Had it been proposed in forming our constitutions, to invest government with a power (over and above the power of exacting contributions for publick use) of taking away the property of some and giving it others, it would have been rejected with indignation; yet this power is as much exercised by bestowing gratuities or exclusive privileges, as if the individuals, impoverished and enriched, had been named. This evasion of the freedom of property is particularly fraudulent, when a new society is constituted of men previously divided into distinct sects or occupations. Then the names of these sects or occupations are exactly the same as the names bestowed on infancy, as a medium for transferring property from one to another, and more difficult to exchange, in order to elude the imposition. Suppose, that at the period when the Highlands of Scotland were inhabited by a very few cognominal families, these families had united in a civil government by the names of tribes, either in the terms of the state or federal constitutions. In the first case, an assumption of power by their government to tax one family or tribe to enrich another, would have been exactly equivalent to state exclusive privileges in favour of some occupations, and injurious to others. In the second, an assumption of the same power would also have had this effect, and would moreover have resembled partialities on the part of congress for and against particular states. The endowment of one class of men by the names of their occupations, at the expense of another, is evidently the same in substance, as to tax the McGregors to enrich the McDonalds. All these cases, however modified, are an actual subjection of labour and free will for self good, to the use of avarice; and if this be not tyranny, I know not what is so.

Had beasts established a government among themselves, to protect each individual in the exertion of his own skill and industry, in gathering the fruits of the forest, and this government should have passed laws to prevent the majority of beasts from eating clover and cherries, and confining them to broom straw and blackberries, that a few might indulge in the most delicious fruits; would it not have been an arbitrary restriction of the desires and comforts bestowed on beasts by divine bounty, and a tyrannical abridgment of their natural power and liberty to provide for themselves? The case is much stronger, when the fruits are produced, not spontaneously, but by labour. Can it be less humiliating to reason than to instinct, to suffer this deprivation; or is the latter most capable of feeling it? Yet sophistry, or at least self-interest, has deluded several states into an opinion, that it is a blessing. But Doctor Rezio of Barataria could never persuade honest Sancho, that he would be made healthier or happier, by having good victuals or drink conjured away by the wand of power. Nations, excluded by prohibitory duties upon industry and free will, from enjoying the good things produced by different climates and different degrees in the arts, are placed in the situation of the beguiled and half starved Sancho. This is not surprising, when they are obliged to submit to doctors; but what shall we say to nations who boast of doctoring themselves? Are our comforts so numerous that they ought to be diminished? Yes, says the doctor, it will make you richer. When we reflect, however, upon the existence of an ocean for the diffusion of these comforts, and that man has been taught to walk all over the world upon the water, it ought to induce us to doubt, whether this worldly wisdom, even if it were not a fraud, of bartering comforts for deprivations, was preferable to the wisdom which has provided the means of bartering comforts for comforts.

The capacities of reasoning and labouring beget among men a relation founded in desires and wants, which designates them as constituted by nature, for society. Whether society be tacit or conventional, its end and design is to protect each individual of which it is composed, in the enjoyment and exercise of his primitive and natural faculties of labour and free will. Restraints upon these, so far and no farther, than to protect the same natural rights of other individuals, constitute social liberty; and restraints imposed, not for the end of this social protection, constitute tyranny. If the society has crept tacitly into existence, these two natural rights are the strongest of all limitations upon the powers of its government, because they are imposed by God; if it be conventional, the same limitations also remain, unless the compact should expressly surrender them. It would even be a doubt, if an existing generation should improvidently do so, whether future generations would be bound by the surrender; and the soundest opinion is, that they would not. Suppose the compact should say, that the government should have the power of taking away the life of one man for the private benefit of another; would this be a free government? But if it be silent upon the point, could the government exercise the power because it was not prohibited? And what prohibits it, but the natural paramount human right to the enjoyment of life? It is this paramount right, which has made it unnecessary to stipulate in our constitutions against the killing of one man for the benefit of another. The right of each man to his own labour, by which only his life can be preserved, is as much a natural right, as a right to life itself; nor was there any more need to stipulate in actual social compacts for its safety, than for the safety of life. It is an evasion of the right to live, to take away the products of labour by which men live, and to give them to other men. If a government can take some, it may take all; and bad governments, by this species of tyranny, do often starve men to death. But there is no difference in the principle, whether men are partially starved, or quite starved, to enrich other men. If the reader will recollect, and apply to this point what has been before said in relation to a bill of rights, he will discern that there was no reason to vindicate natural rights in that mode, because they remain, if not surrendered; and as the rights to our lives and our labour are not surrendered by our state constitutions, their design being on the contrary, to protect and preserve both, it follows, that these

paramount rights are limitations upon the power of state governments to invade, either by exclusive privileges or otherwise, to
enrich private individuals.

I might rest the argument here, and leave it to the reader to
determine whether the interest, liberty or happiness of any state
in the union can be possibly advanced by overturning these
principles ; but as the freedom of property is the object intended to be vindicated by this treatise, I hope he will have patience
with me in bringing it into view in as many shapes as I may
happen to recollect.

All, or most intellectual improvements, are referable to the
free exercise of each man's will, in procuring his own happiness.
It unfolds his understanding, increases his knowledge, and ani-
mates his virtue. By multiplying the relations between the individuals of the human family, the blessings of society are also
multiplied ; and an abridgment of these relations is a retro-
gade movement towards that savage state, in which they are
few. These relations are called commerce ; and all obstacles
thrown in its way are diminutions of an intercourse, from which
men have derived their accomplishments, and a capacity for
happiness.

Though a power of interfering in the intercourse between individuals by bestowing exclusive privileges on particular sects
or interests, civil or religious, is contrary to the rights of nature
and the end of society, and has produced oppression, when exercised in all other modes ; it is contended, that one mode remains, by which a bad principle may be changed into a good one,
and fraud white-washed into justice. By baptizing this bad
principle with the goodly name of " an encouragement of manufactures," avarice is supposed to be turned into patriotism, as
Jefferies was made an upright judge, by clothing him in ermine ;
or, as it was once endeavoured to be purified by the still better
name " religion." It behooves us, therefore, to consider this
new nominal modification of the same old tyrannical principle,
with great attention.

If men were classed by the colour of their hair, yet the generick term "man" would include them all. Classed by their
occupations, all are also included by the generick term " labour." They all have the same rights, whatever may be the
outlines of their physical or moral qualities, and to stretch or

contract their moral qualities by force, in order to pamper the passions of a particular sect, or their physical qualities to gratify those of a Procrustes, is one and the same act. It is the same thing for a government to grant exclusive privileges to a particular occupation at the expense of the others, as to the class of black-haired men, at the expense of those having hair of other colours, because the effect of both would be, to confiscate a portion of the faculties of some men to provide for their own subsistence and comfort, and to bestow the amount of the confiscation upon other men; and it exceeds in atrocity the contributions imposed by generals on conquered towns, because it cannot be defended by the right of conquest. We have been led into this error by the abundance and vagueness of words. The words "agriculture, manufacture, commerce, profession and science" have produced artificial distinctions, which have obscured the reach of the inclusive word " labour," and caused us to forget, that it is a natural faculty, like that of seeing, given to all men, that each might provide for his own individual happiness. I cannot see any difference between taking away from a man one of his eyes, if it could be done, and giving it to another; or taking away and giving to another fifty per centum of his labour. But this has been effected by making the plenty of words change the nature of things, although labour is in fact the only manufacturer. Workers upon the land, or upon the ocean, who give to things new forms or new places, are all manufacturers; and being comprised in one essential character, are entitled to the same freedom in free societies. It is this equality of rights, and nothing else, which constitutes a free, fair and mild government.

The power of a strong man to extort from a weak one, more labour than he gave in exchange, identifies the character of a government, which personifies the strong man, in depriving some occupations of free will in making exchanges of labour. It assumes that very practice of the strong man, which caused mankind to form themselves into societies, for the purpose of resistance. An exertion of this power first defrauded the sufferers of all the labour they had lost during the revolutionary war, by the circulation of certificates whilst they were depreciating; and secondly, of as much more by taxes imposed on the sufferers themselves, to raise an enormous bounty for the last holders. A certificate sect, strong in influence, used the power of government to transfer to itself a great mass of the labour of more useful occupations, like the strong unassociated man. The banking sect, also, has been able to convert the legitimate power of government to protect the freedom and fairness of exchanges, into an illegitimate power of destroying both, by enabling that sect to rob all useful occupations of a great portion of their labour, by means of false or depreciating tokens of value, drawing an interest paid by these occupations, in addition to their losses from depreciation and bankruptcy. But, the manufacturing sect do not propose to divert the power of government from the protection to the invasion of property in the same atrocious degree, and only asks it to compel all other occupations to exchange labours with it, not by the mutual valuations of free will, but by a compulsory, inadequate valuation ; and like a liberal, unassociated strong man, it is willing, for the present, to receive *annually*, from all other occupations, two measures only for one. In exchanges of labour, that which a freedom of intercourse can obtain, constitutes the only true measure.

The effects of this annual exchange of labour to a great amount, by a false, and of course, a fraudulent measure, are too extensive to be explained in this short treatise, and too intricate to be completely developed ; but some of its consequences are necessary to clarify the argument.

As all the other occupations, by being compelled to give two measures of labour for one, will sustain a great diminution of their means for procuring subsistence, competency or affluence, every individual belonging to them will immediately exert his ingenuity to evade the imposition, and to reimburse himself for his losses, at the expense of other individuals. He will endeavour to enhance the price of his own manufactures, whether agricultural, mechanical, commercial, scientifick or professional, in order to bring back exchanges from the false measure of legal compulsion, to the true measure of free will. If these other occupations could succeed in this attempt against the occupation obtaining the bounty by means of the false measure, the bounty or privilege would become abortive, and exchanges would be honestly made, measure for measure, as they were previously to the compulsion. In this event, the experiment would only have the effect of disordering for a time the only fair principle of social intercourse, and of exciting new arts for mutual imposition. If these other occupations cannot succeed in reinstating the golden rule of free will in the exchanges of labour, they will endeavour, like starving men, to prey upon each other; and the oppression of the bounty will fall heavily upon them a second time, by producing fraud ,and extortion among themselves. Those occupations, which cannot find at home objects on which to operate, to indemnify themselves for the extortions of the occupation which is privileged to mete in a smaller measure, than they are willing to receive by, cannot be reimbursed. The agricultural and commercial occupations are in this situation. Neither of these can for many years find objects at home for exchanges, sufficient to reinstate the freedom of intercourse ; and neither can indemnify itself for the coerced contributions to the domestic privileged sect, at the expense of foreign nations, because all exchanges between them and these nations must still be made and measured by free will and mutual computation, whilst the extortions they will suffer from the false legal mode of exchanges at home will remain. The agricultural class may indeed retain and employ its capital, subject to the contribution, but a considerable portion of the mercantile capital will be thrown out of employment ; and its owners must suffer miseries and losses from leaving a business in which they are skilful, for one of which they are ignorant. They will be emigrants from a highly cultivated to an unexplored country. Though the scientifick classes may make a few reprisals from the endowed class, and many inroads for indemnification upon the mercantile and agricultural classes, yet it will be incomplete, because they must participate of the loss sustained by their best customers. The valuable classes of ship builders, owners and navigators, subsisting entirely upon the capital of the mercantile and agricultural classes, must inevitably lose a portion of employment equivalent to the losses of their patrons or customers, without the smallest chance of reimbursement. These classes sell neither bread, meat, physick nor law, and their wages will be diminished by a diminution of employment. Such will be the effect until a sufficient number of these maritime manufacturers are starved, or thrown out of employment, to create a demand for the labour of the remnant.

The great argument, in favour of compelling all other occupations to pay double prices to that which is very incorrectly
called, exclusively, the manufacturing occupation, is, that the
imposition will be temporary ; for that when it has coerced
an emigration from other occupations into this, to stock the
market sufficiently with manufactures, the fraudulent measure
or compulsory price will disappear, and the fair measure, or free
will in computation, will be re-instated ; and an anticipation
of a recovery of the principle for which I am contending, is said
to be better than its actual enjoyment. No proverb has said,
that a bird in the bush is worth as much, as one in the hand.
This argument, containing the essential and solitary promise, by
which a protecting-duty policy is defended, is infinitely more fallacious than any I have ever met with, by which privileged sects
have heretofore dazzled reason, and defrauded ignorance. These
fungi have usually asserted, that their monopolies and exclusive
privileges were good, and proper for endurance. But this admits, that the privilege and monopoly it is striving to obtain
bad ; by asserting that it ought to be granted, because it will
in time cease to operate partially and unjustly upon the other
occupations of society. Let us, says its great argument, relinquish the good principle of exchanging labour by the measure
of free will, and undertake a journey, long or short, upon the
bad principle of forcing all other occupations to give two measures for one, to a certain detachment of manufacturers, that we
may get back to the same good principle from which we set
out. What should we think of the general of a vast army,
encamped on firm ground, who should march for many years
over bogs and marshes, in order to get back to the same ground ?
If he should even accomplish a project so profound, would
his getting back resuscitate or cure the soldiers who had died
or been crippled by the way ? A journey through exclusive
privileges, in order to get back to the principles of social liberty,
is even more hopeless than the march of an army round the
world, in order to get back to a safe station ; for this latter journey might possibly have an end. But where is the end of the world
of exclusive privileges? What man can hope to live to the end
of a journey through its protecting-duty region only ? If he
should survive the hardships and privations of this long and
perilous journey, could he be so infatuated as to expect, that

no new exclusive privileges will be invented by the way ? Will
avarice be glutted and put to sleep by its success in this instance ; or will that success beget a new progeny, and cause the
hopes of our traveller from good principles, to get back to the
same good principles, by the road of bad principles, to be more
extravagant than those of a turnspit dog, which expects that
every step will be his last, and that then he will eat the meat
he is roasting ? But why do I argue this point, when he who
gave to man the capacities of free will and labouring, hath
said, " with what measure you mete, it shall be measured
to you again ?"

Let us, therefore, proceed to the second point, namely,
whether the federal government has a right to regulate the
wealth and poverty of individuals, or of corporations, by protecting duties and bounties. And if it has, mark the consequence! Protecting duties for the encouragement or coercion
of manufactures are within the *sphere of action* of congress ; *the
supremacy of congress over subordinate governments entitles it
to remove all obstacles to its measures within that sphere ;*
therefore, the state governments cannot tax internal manufactures, because it would obstruct the intention of congress to encourage them by bounties. Here is a new case, displaying the
extent of the principles asserted in the bank decision, and
evincing that their power to enable congress gradually to strip
the states of the right of taxation is not ascertained, if according to that decision, it admits of any limitation. I hope the
reader, in considering this important point, will endeavour to
recollect the observations previously made, in relation to sovereignty, supremacy, and our distinction between local and external powers, which caused us to go to war with England,
and dictated much of our former and existing confederation.
He is not to determine, whether congress could create a bank,
or grant protecting-duty bounties, or gratuitously bestow the
property of the people upon revolutionary soldiers, as if these
were special and particular cases ; but, whether it has an unlimited right to establish monopolies, grant exclusive privileges to
persons, exempt capital or wealth from state taxation, and give
away the property of the people in any amount to whomsoever
it pleases. Such are the general conclusions arising from these
special cases, which seem to me to deserve the national
attention.

The truth of the following proposition, depends upon the intention of the federal constitution. Congress is only invested with *limited* powers *over persons and things,* for the purpose of executing the *defined* powers delegated to it. The 8th section of the first article of the constitution contains a list of these defined powers, amounting to seventeen; and the eighteenth clause of the section empowers congress to make all laws necessary and proper for executing the seventeen defined powers delegated. Thus, a correlative power of acting upon persons and things is attached to each defined power delegated, as a necessary and proper means for the execution of that power; and not as a means of obtaining power not delegated, or of destroying or diminishing any power reserved to the states.

The first power given to congress is that of taxation, to provide for *the common defence and general welfare of the United States.* Under this power, congress can act upon persons and things, so far as is necessary and proper to collect these taxes. It has however been often asserted, that the power given to congress to lay taxes is amplified by the words " to provide for the common defence and general welfare *of the United States.*" This construction is obviously erroneous. These words refer to the destination of the taxes, and are only a reason for the power of taxation. If they convey any power over persons and things, internally or externally, they convey all power over all objects; and under a construction of the latitude contended for the power of taxation, and all the subsequent powers bestowed in the same section, would have been quite superfluous. For, if these words comprise a grant of power to congress, the power is unlimited, and includes both all the specified powers, and also every other power, which in their opinion may be necessary and proper to provide for the common defence and general welfare. They would suffice to swallow up the treaty-making power, as well as the other specifications of the constitution; but, if they do not suffice to swallow up all the specifications and restrictions of the constitution, they are not sufficient to swallow up any one. Of course, they cannot absorb any portion of the local or internal powers, specially reserved to the states, among which that of making roads is undoubtedly one.

But, suppose we detach the phrase " to provide for the common defence and general welfare *of the United States*" from the power of taxation, and consider it as an isolated and distinct grant of power; it will then be necessary to ascertain whose defence and welfare was to be provided for; the defence and welfare of the individuals composing the states, or of the political individuals called states. I think the letter and tenour of the constitution correspond upon this point with perfect perspicuity. "The United States" are specified as the objects or individuals, whose *common* defence and *general* welfare was to be provided for. In the first clause of the constitution the same phrase is used: "The people of the *United States* to pro-"vide for the common defence and promote the general wel-"fare establish this constitution *for the United States of Ame-"rica.*" It was not, therefore, a constitution for the government of persons or things generally existing in these United States, but for the government of the states themselves, and in order to promote their common defence and general welfare. The words *common and general* refer to the objects or political beings, whose defence and welfare was to be provided for, as being in a state of union. And as no state of union or any species of social compact existed among the persons composing the states, inclusively, these words cannot be made to refer to them. They therefore restrain the power of congress to the defence and welfare of the states themselves, instead of enlarging it to include the defence and welfare of private persons.

The whole tenour of the constitution corresponds with this literal construction. All the powers given to congress point to the defence and welfare of United States, and those necessary for the defence and welfare of private individuals are reserved to the states themselves. If this construction be correct, it clearly follows, that congress can only impose taxes, constitutionally, for the defence and welfare of the states, and that an imposition of taxes for the purpose of enriching one state, one interest, or one individual, at the expense of another state, another interest, or another individual, is as unconstitutional, as it is adverse to the freedom and fairness of exchanges. In fact, this declaratory end is a complete key to the intention of the constitution, and locks out congress, in conjunction with the reservation to the states, from all constructive powers over persons and things, of a local and personal nature, especially the power of taxing either to foster political fungi, or to grant bounties or exclusive privileges.

Let us, however, look farther into the constitution, to see if it affords other proofs of the correctness of the construction for which I contend. Its terms, in creating the departments of the federal government, are the same with those used to define its design. " The house of representatives shall consist " of members chosen by the people of the *several states.* Repre- " sentatives and direct taxes shall be apportioned among the " *several states.* Until the enumeration, *the state of New* " *Hampshire shall be entitled to choose three representatives.* " When vacancies happen in *the representation from any state.* " President of *the United States.* Senate of the *United States.* " House of representatives of the *United States. And the con-* " *gress of the United States."* Now, can any fair reasoner contend, that the states are not here repeatedly recognized, as the authors of the federal government, and the federal government as a government of the states, and not of the people? Those who made it are its constituents, and over these constituents its powers are delegated. The states are expressly characterized as individual political beings, and every department of the federal government, even the house of representatives, is positively asserted to be the representative, agent or trustee of the states, and none are even insinuated to be the representative, agent or trustee of the people, except as comprised by the term " states." Congress is therefore a representation of those interests only common to its constituents, the states. But the framers of the constitution, lest this representation should usurp powers over private persons and internal concerns, carefully defined such common interests of these constituents, as were intended to be entrusted to their representative; and the question is, whether the doctrine of means to effect ends, can bring under the power of a representation of states, persons and things, neither its constituents, nor subjected to its power.

Let us look at a sample of this question.

Powers bestowed by the constitution.	*Powers claimed as means.*
Taxation,	Incorporating banks,
War,	Making roads,
Appropriating money,	Giving it away,
Regulating trade,	Granting monopolies,
Admitting new states.	Prescribing state constitutions.

In one column, we find objects of general concern to the states; in the other, said to be their legitimate progeny, objects merely personal or local. Now I contend, that the progeny of the parent powers ought to be sui generis; and that a progeny of means, which violate the powers reserved to the states, under the influence of a different species of lust, from that which excited the heathen gods, is no less spurious, than the fruit of their amours.

Let us deduce a few arguments from the following position. No powers, delegated to congress, are represented in the state governments; and no powers reserved to the states, are represented in congress. If this be true, it evidently follows, that the design of the federal constitution was to establish two communities, assigning to each a distinct representation, and entrusting each with distinct powers and duties, so modelled as to preserve the common interest, fellow feeling and sympathy, which constitute the essence of a true representation. Congress was entrusted with powers concerning the common defence and general welfare of the community of states, which it represents; and the state governments, with the common defence and general welfare of the communities of individuals represented by them. If the latter should exercise powers within the sphere of the former, under the pretexts that it would advance the welfare of the community of states constituting the union, and were means which might be inferred from the reserved powers, they would be acting for a community which they do not represent; and if congress should exercise any powers within the state spheres, under the same pretexts, it would in like manner be acting for a community which it does not represent. Now, as it is not pretended that either congress or the state governments can violate the principles of representation, by directly assuming powers assigned to the other, the only question is, whether either can do it indirectly, by the instrumentality of means. It seems to me, that both these governments must as well be the representative of means, as of powers, and this consideration is as much a restriction upon the former, as upon the latter. Means ought to be emblematical of the powers they commemorate, and the converting of them into powers which penetrate into the territories, either of rights delegated or rights reserved, is a species of political transubstantiation, transgressing the essential principles of representation. They are emanations from the powers delegated to congress or reserved to the states; but these emanations must surely be limited and restricted by the same principles which limit and restrict the powers themselves. The primary and obvious intention of the federal constitution was, to invest congress with such powers only, as equally affected the members of the community called the union; and to leave to the state governments, all those powers affecting the members of the community called the states. In both cases, this was necessary to sustain the principles of representation, and in neither can this primary and obvious intention be evaded by any means, without destroying both the positive division of powers, and the moral principle of representation. A legislation of either of these communities within the territory assigned to the other, is equivalent to a legislation by one independent nation over another. I now ask the reader, if monopolies, exclusive privileges, or bounties to persons ; or local improvements, such as roads or canals, and an encouragement of agriculture or manufactures ; are represented in congress ; and if congress in legislating upon such subjects, can possibly be invigorated by the community of interests, which ought to pervade that body in the discharge of its federal functions ? Are not the recited functions plainly local and personal, and would they not be exercised in congress by feelings and motives, entirely different from the common interest, fellow feeling and sympathy, essential to representation?

In the Federalist, pages 173, 176 and 177, Mr. Hamilton, who was neither disposed to diminish the powers of congress, nor to extend those of the states, has delivered the following contemporary construction of the constitution. " *The encou-* " *ragement of agriculture and manufactures is an appendage* " *of the domestick police of the states.* Exorbitant duties on " imported articles tend to render other classes of the com- " munity, *tributary*, in an improper degree, to the manufactur- " ing classes. They would be attended with *inequality*, be- " tween the manufacturing and non-manufacturing states." What a whimsical thing is party politicks ! This gentleman assisted in framing the federal constitution. He knew that the agricultural and manufacturing interests were not represented in congress, and that a patronage of either by that body, would therefore be an usurpation ; and having stated that they appertained to the states, he suggests the tyrannical effect of high duties, in making one state *tributary* to another. Mr. Hamilton had a clear view of the subject. As the states and not individuals were the constituents of congress, he saw that it could not legislate concerning the property, the persons, or the rights of individuals, of a local or internal nature ; because in such cases the relation necessary to bestow a right of legislation, between constituent and representative, did not exist. He saw that the absence of this relationship would, as it always does, make some people tributary to others. He saw that the care of agriculture and manufactures equally appertained to the states. And he knew that a right to encourage one involved a right to discourage the other ; and that, however modest and unassuming the first word might appear, it contained as much internal tyrannical power, as any degree of ambition could wish for.

But, may not the power of encouraging and discouraging both agriculture and manufactures, be common to congress and the state governments ? This is a doubt which deserves great attention, and will reflect much light upon the subject. We have not forgotten the assertion in the decision of the bank question, " that congress being elected by and representing all" may be trusted with internal powers, and therefore it behooves us to look into the constitution itself, to discover how far this is the case. When we do so, we at once discern that the elective and representative qualities of congress are not considered in the least degree as vehicles of powers ; but that defined and limited powers are delegated, adapted to the nature of its representative character, and of its constituents. The powers delegated are such, as would act upon the common interest of its constituents, and not such as would foster local partialities. And there is no concurrency of powers between the federal and state governments, except in the case of taxation; from whence it is fair to infer that none other was intended to exist. It will not be denied, that a right to encourage agriculture and manufactures, and to make roads, was possessed by the states previously to the union ; and that, as it is reserved by the constitution, it still remains. The concurrent power established from necessity in the case of taxation seems to exclude the idea of tacit concurrent powers. At least, these cannot be inferred from the representative nature of congress, without endowing that body with a concurrent power as to all the other powers reserved to the states; nor without exploding the reasoning which goes to prove that congress is the representative of federal, and not of personal or local interests. The meaning of the word " reserved" must also be overlooked. A has no right to participate in that which is *reserved* to B, and if congress be excluded from the exercise of the powers reserved to the states, and those encouraging agriculture and manufactures are among the powers reserved, its right to exercise either power cannot be established.

But, these powers have been claimed as an appendage of that to "regulate commerce," and as the power of taxation has been made to beget a power of creating corporations and granting exclusive privileges to persons and property, so this power to regulate commerce is supposed to contain both the latter power, and also that of inflicting a tax upon all other interests to enrich one. This art of making external and federal powers beget local and internal powers, resembles I suppose the ingenious process by which pigeon-breeders are said to be able to furnish birds of any colour; but it is not yet pushed quite as far in this instance as in the bank case. In the latter, taxation has begotten banks, and those banks have begotten a restriction of the right of taxation reserved to the states; a very anomalous progeny indeed; the right of transmitting taxes has taken away the right of imposing them. Thus, as two persons re-peopled a deluged world by throwing stones over their heads, the tossing about of words is made to revive all the powers prohibited to a federal congress by a federal constitution, and to resuscitate legions of those principles of despotism, which were intended to be suffocated by divisions and limitations of power. It is not uncommon for a skilful verbalist, to engraft upon an old root new scions bearing very different fruit; but we might as justly contend that an apple engrafted on a pear, would produce pears, as that a power to tax all other occupations to enrich one, engrafted on the power to regulate commerce, would be an imposition of duties "to pay the debts " and provide for the common defence and general welfare" of the United States.

During the pressure for money towards the conclusion of the revolutionary war, an ingenious member of congress, by way of amusement, informed a very rich friend of his, that congress had resolved to engraft, upon the words "general welfare," in the old confederation, an absolute power over private property; and that coerced by necessity, it had resolved, that the estates of one hundred of the richest individuals in the United States should be sold, and applied to the "common defence and general welfare" for which it was the duty of congress to provide. Being a gentleman of great ingenuity, he alarmed his friend by many plausible arguments to prove the existence of the power and a necessity for its exercise; and drew from him a serious and laboured answer. This case is evidently much stronger, than that under consideration, and afforded a wider scope for the verbalizing science. The words "to provide for the common defence and general welfare" are of larger compass, than the words "to regulate commerce." The application of the money, to be raised by this violation of private property, to the use of the nation, was more conformable to the constitution, than a transfer of private property to private people. And it was more equitable that the rights of one hundred men should be sacrificed to defend the nation, than that the rights of all other occupations should be sacrificed to enrich the manufacturing class.

Let us place before our eyes the root, and the scion proposed to be engrafted on it. The root is, "congress shall have power to regulate commerce;" the scion, "congress shall have power "by protecting duties to tax all other occupations for the pur- "pose of enriching the manufacturing class." But the power to lay duties had been defined and limited by the first clause of the section, and their application limited to national use. The power to regulate commerce could not be intended to convey to congress an indefinite power of taxation, because a definite power of taxation had been previously expressed. Specification precludes inference; at least, if the inference contradicts the specification. As the subject of taxation had been expressly disposed of, it cannot be fairly supposed that it was tacitly resumed; and as the specification appropriates duties to the use of the United States, this tacit resumption cannot also contain a hidden power, to lay duties for the benefit of a particular occupation. The recondite powers contained in the words " to regulate commerce" may find objects for their operation, as they are multifarious, without adding to the catalogue, a power expressly given in another clause; but, if they are allowed to be a root, capable of endowing congress with all powers having relation to commerce, they will convey many powers inconsistent with the tenour of the constitution.

They would invest congress with an internal power over persons and things, not represented in that body; and both prohibited to it, and reserved to legislatures in which they are represented. The whole property and wealth of the country are more nearly connected with commerce, than roads are with war; and the mode of reasoning in that case will embrace agriculture, and invest congress with a power of regulating that also, as is attempted by making it tributary to manufactures. The constitution has laboured to prevent this illicit intercourse between construction and a lust of power. "No " *capitation* or other direct tax shall be laid, unless in proportion " to an enumeration. *No tax shall be laid on articles exported.* " No preference shall be given, *by any regulation of commerce* " *or revenue*, to ports of one state over those of another." The intention of these restrictions was, to deprive congress of the power of exercising local or personal partialities. Protecting duties operate in fact as a direct or capitation tax, for the benefit of one occupation, imposed upon all others by legal necessity; and such taxes ought to be apportioned by the census, unless it be said that this rule is only required when the tax is imposed for public service, and may therefore be disregarded when it is imposed for the benefit of a pecuniary aristocracy. " No taxes shall be laid on articles exported." The value of agricultural staples must long depend upon exchanges with foreign nations. They are consumers of our breadstuff, cotton, tobacco, fish, and many other articles. Consumers neither exist, nor can be speedily created at home. These foreigners are utterly unable to pay us in specie for the products we can spare, and if they could, this specie would depreciate like paper money, unless we could export it, not to buy more specie, but articles of consumption. A prohibition, therefore, complete or partial, of the importation of the articles of consumption in which agriculturists must receive payment, is in substance a double tax upon exports. It lessens their value, and enhances the price of the few articles of consumption they can procure at home. It will have an effect similar to a diminution of circulating currency by banks, because it diminishes the currency, (the soundest imaginable,) circulated by the freedom of exchanges. It is an illusion to suppose, that this banishment of currency from the agricultural market of our country will not cause it to decline, because specie may still be brought in payment. The currency brought to this market consists of specie and articles of consumption; by banishing both, the market would be starved; by banishing one, it will be half starved. It is surprising that gentlemen who despise and deride a miser abounding in wealth, and yet denying to himself the comforts and delights of life, should recommend an example which they reprobate, for the imitation of their country.

" No preference shall be given, *by any regulation of com-* " *merce or revenue,* to ports of one state, over those of another." In all these prohibitions, we find the great principle of interdicting to congress a power of regulating the wealth or prosperity of particular states or occupations, carefully enforced. Ports is here put for people. Inanimate things have no rights, and can enjoy no preferences. A tax paid by agricultural to manufacturing states, if the bounty be sufficiently high to enable the manufacturing class to meet foreign competition, will operate as a favour to particular ports in the state where the manufacturers reside. The bounty, bestowed by the British parliament upon Irish linen exported, was a preference to the ports from which the exportations were made, of the same kind. And all such bounties, direct or indirect, have been considered universally as highly valuable local preferences. The weight of the restrictive clauses of the constitution, as an exposition of the intention to exclude congress from an exercise of power, internally, over persons or things, by which partialities or pecuniary inequalities among states or individuals might be cultivated, would be sufficient to over-balance a long list of verbal subterfuges, by which this principle, so anxiously enforced, is endeavoured to be eluded; even if literal prohibitions, exactly fitting every deviation from it, could not be found. Man's foresight cannot anticipate all the artifices of ambition and avarice; but the restrictive clauses of the constitution, compared with the limited powers bestowed, demonstrate an abhorrence of the idea, that the federal government should have a power of bestowing preferences of any kind upon states, districts or occupations. The restrictive clauses are precedents by anticipation, and the reason which suggested them, extends to similar cases. This was the division of powers between the federal and state governments, and therefore a construction so ingenious, as to elude the letter of the restrictive clauses, will still be incorrect, if it violates the reason which suggested them. Have protecting duties been imposed by congress under the expressed power in the first clause of the eighth section " to lay duties," or under the clause " to regulate commerce ?" If under the power expressed, their purpose must be " to pay the debts and provide for the common defence and general welfare of the United States;" if under a power inferred from that to regulate commerce, can the constitutional appropriation or purpose be thereby evaded or repealed ? To lay them for the purpose of paying the debts, enriching or advancing the welfare of particular persons or occupations, seems to accord as little with the words of the constitution, as with its spirit in creating a division of powers ; assigning to congress those exclusively relating to the defence, welfare and debts of the members constituting the union, called states ; and to the state governments, exclusively also, those relating to the defence, welfare and debts of individuals and occupations.

But the following argument seems to be conclusive. A government, which exercises a power of distributing welfare among occupations and individuals, must be sovereign and absolute over persons and occupations, to enable it to do justice by bestowing countervailing favours, because it must of necessity otherwise commit great injustice. Even the British government acknowledges the right to such equivalents, and accordingly endeavours to compensate the agricultural occupation by particular favours and a considerable monopoly, for the favours and monopoly it has granted to the manufacturing class. It is unnecessary to enlarge upon the intricate system of equivalents extended to a variety of interests in England ; and it is enough to know that this system must exist as an appendage of exclusive privileges, necessary to give them even an appearance of justice and equity. By this game of government, though played with professed fairness, the great body of the people do not appear to have been gainers. What then would be the effect of a power in congress to grant exclusive privileges to two occupations only, those of bankers and manufacturers, without any power to grant to other occupations or the persons engaged in them, the countervailing equivalents? We must therefore conclude, either that congress have no power to grant exclusive privileges to the individuals engaged in these occupations, or that the constitution has invested it with an absolute internal power over persons and property; because it can never be imagined, that its wise framers intended to invest congress with a power of granting exclusive privileges to two occupations, one of no value, and the other of inferior value, and to prohibit it from advancing the welfare of the agricultural, commercial, maritime, and scientifick occupations, of so much more importance. We must either embrace an absurdity so flagrant, or discern that our decision upon this point is reduced to a plain alternative; and that we are forced to conclude, either that congress may constitutionally incorporate, or grant exclusive privileges to every species of human occupation, or to none. By the first decision, congress will acquire an unlimited internal power over persons and things; by the second, the powers reserved to the states will be retained. The third opinion, that congress may grant favours to particular states or districts, by granting exclusive privileges to occupations locally prevalent, is inconsistent with a possibility of dispensing equal justice or general welfare among the parties to the union, not less forcibly impressed by the tenour of the constitution, than by common sense and sound policy. All places and all states are not susceptible of the same exclusive privileges, and these cannot therefore be equalized, except the power of granting them shall embrace the means by which only it can be effected. Each reader will select that of these opinions, which may correspond with the true intention of the federal constitution.

But, if all our legislatures have an absolute power over persons and property, and the freedom of exchanges is an imaginary notion; and if the federal constitution does empower congress to incorporate or grant exclusive privileges to all occupations, or to two only, it still remains to be considered, whether its exercise is wise, honest, or beneficial to the United States.

It is said, that protecting duties by their derangement of fair exchanges will be a bounty to starving and destitute manufacturers. I shall not stop to enquire into the power of congress to provide for the poor of all occupations ; nor to display the iniquity of taxing the poor of all other occupations to raise bounties for the poor of one ; nor to enforce a parallel between such a law, and one for taxing the dissenters, as they are called, to raise bounties for the poor of the church of England ; nor to press the existing similitude of these dissenters being taxed in England to raise bounties for the episcopal clergy, who more nearly resemble those who will get the protecting-duty bounties ; but passing over these fruitful arguments, come at once to facts.

It will hardly be imagined, that the workmen in manufactories wrote the multitude of pamphlets and petitions, which have appeared in favour of the protecting-duty mode of bestowing bounties upon the occupation of manufacturing; and if the phenomenon does not arise from the concert and avarice by which exclusive privileges have been hitherto moved, it may have been produced by a pure and disinterested benevolence in their employers, of intending to enhance the wages which they are themselves to pay. Allowing a motive so gratuitous and disinterested for the expenditure of talents and waste of vehemence brought forth by the occasion, it will be useful to these gentlemen to enquire, whether their charitable purpose is attainable by the mode they have recommended ; because if it be not, as they have no mercenary design, it will be doing them a service to cool a consuming zeal, and save them from the shock of a sore disappointment. It will undoubtedly dismay them to be told, that all the bounties arising from the protecting-duty project, must inevitably settle in their own pockets ; and that the wages of their poor workmen (the objects of their solicitude) will ultimately be diminished by it. Yet such will certainly be the consequences.

As consumers must pay these bounties, and as a majority of consumers are poor, it follows, that if additional wages could have been bestowed upon the workmen in manufactories, by an impost on consumptions, it would have still diminished the comforts of more poor men than it would have relieved ; and this observation derives additional force from the fact, that whilst our manufactories are young, and their fabricks coarse, they will be chiefly consumed by the poorest classes in society. Our capitalists so well skilled in figures may therefore very easily discover, that their project is on the debit side in the account of benevolence. Their poor workmen, like all other poor people, are consumers themselves, and a tariff to bestow bounties by a general monopoly will reach and tax them, with the exception of the solitary article manufactured by each. Thus each workman will pay two measures of labour for one, on a multitude of articles, even if he should receive two measures for one, on a single article. What a number of these double prices, for instance, will be paid by the poor grinder of snuff, for that portion of the double price which may get into his pocket! Such is the theoretical benefit to the poor workmen; practically, even this poor benefit does not exist.

The theory supposes, that the workmen are to get the whole excess of price arising from protecting duties, but as they have a violent tendency to aggravate taxation and provoke a taste for expense in the government; and as the system can only be enforced by a great increase of publick officers, the share of these burdens, which would fall on the workmen, would probably balance or certainly diminish the bounties very considerably.

But the system must encounter a still more formidable fact. It must meet and destroy a principle much sounder than itself, before it can fulfil its promise to enhance the wages of the workmen. The wages of labour are not settled by law, but by circumstances over which law can possess but a very feeble and transient influence. As the level of wages among labouring occupations had been settled previously to protecting-duty laws, the circumstances by which it had been effected were too stubborn to be suddenly subverted; otherwise, when fifty or an hundred per centum had been added to the price of a manufacture by law, the same addition would have been uniformly made by employers to the wages of their workmen. We know that this is never the case. Even a struggle for the bounty seldom ensues between the employers and their workmen, and it was never seen that the workmen have gotten it all. Now, all could not possibly be more than sufficient, to reimburse the workmen, for the loss they sustain by the increased expense of government, and by the additional price they must pay for the articles they consume, but do not fabricate; and if the employers get any part of the bounty, the labour of the workmen will not go so far in providing them with subsistence, as it would have gone, had not the price of consumptions been enhanced by protecting duties; and although the wages of manufacturing labour should be somewhat raised, above the level of those paid to the workmen in other occupations, the retrenchments would exceed the accession, and leave the workmen less to subsist upon, than when their wages, expenses and taxes were all lower.

Suppose however, that the whole tax collected by a multitude of monopolies from the community should go to the workmen, without their employers being able to intercept any portion of it, and suddenly create a great inequality between the wages of manufacturing workmen, and the workmen in other occupations; yet the circumstance of abundance, which so absolutely diminishes the price of labour, would tread upon the heels of the acquisition, and very soon defeat it. An enhanced price suddenly removes scarcity, begets plenty, and terminates in cheapness. Therefore, when merchants design to obtain an article at a low rate, they wisely begin with giving a high price. The bait fills the market, and they avail themselves of the abundance to buy cheap. So in this case, if the wages of the workmen should be raised far above the level of the wages of labour in other occupations, the bait would suddenly draw an abundance of workmen to the manufacturing occupation, and this abundance would immediately reduce the wages to the rate dictated by the necessity for subsistence, or by a comparison with the wages of labour in other occupations, leaving to the employers the whole of the bounty. The most favourable operation of the protecting-duty system, as to the workmen, is, that the whole body of consumers in the community, including themselves, will be taxed to raise a great annual bounty; that this will augment the expenses of government of which they must bear a share; that this bounty may draw an abundance of workmen to the market; that this abundance will certainly reduce their wages lower, comparatively with the expense of subsistence, than when there was a scarcity of workmen;

and that the bounty will infallibly settle in the pockets of their employers. Thus the system eventuates as all other exclusive-privilege projects, in an absolute conspiracy against the interest of labour, by inflicting on it an additional burden, precisely of the same character and effect, as if the sum paid to employers had been added to the salaries of the officers of government, or given as a bounty to any two or three hundred men by name.

A few facts will be the strongest arguments in support of this reasoning. Society may be divided into the classes of rich and poor; both are consumers; but as the poor class is by far the most numerous, it is of course the greatest consumer; and therefore, it must pay the greatest portion of the tax imposed by the protecting-duty system, especially as that tax falls chiefly upon coarse fabricks. In iron foundries for instance, as in all other manufactories, the workmen belong to the poor class, and consume more of the taxed articles of home manufacture, than their employers; upon all of which they pay the tax. As to the tax upon iron itself, it is chiefly paid by the poor of the whole community, because they consume more of it than the rich. This instance is adduced to establish the fact, that the poor class, including the workmen in all the manufactories, instead of receiving, actually pay the largest portion of the protecting-duty tax.

The manufacturing workmen in England are among the poorest of the poor class, although the prohibition against the importation of their fabrications is complete. Why has not this prohibition enriched the workmen? Because it has established a monopoly which operates only in favour of their employers, increases the expenses of government, and feeds unproductive capital by sacrificing productive labour. It keeps down the price of labour both by a concert among employers, and also by a comparison with its price employed in other occupations; and subverts the pretence, that the same system will produce opposite effects in this country. It is evidently a system in favour of the rich, and against the poor class, because the first class possess the capital which the system nourishes, and the second perform the labour, which supplies the nourishment.

Employers are called capitalists with great propriety, because more capital is necessary to establish a manufactory, than to employ ourselves in individual occupations. Few or none, therefore, of the manufacturing capitalists can belong to the poor class of society. The mercantile occupation requires capital in the next degree, and of course furnishes the next fewest number of individuals belonging to the poor class. The scientifick and professional occupations include the next fewest number of persons assignable to the poor class. And the agricultural occupation contains a much greater number of individuals belonging to the poor class, than either of these, because no capital, except bodily labour, is necessary to go to work ; and a very small sum suffices to procure means sufficient to employ ourselves in that occupation, to the utmost extent of bodily capacity. Of the variety of other occupations, highly useful, but yet containing a still greater number of individuals belonging to the poor class, I shall specify two, for the sake of an observation suggested by each. The seafaring occupation is chiefly composed of people having very little capital except their bodily labour. If a bounty should be given to this occupation, by taxing all other occupations, these other occupations would presently exclaim, that the law of plenty or scarcity, which governs the price of labour, would certainly enable its employer, the rich mercantile occupation, to appropriate this bounty to itself, by diminishing wages from an estimate of the bounty, and of other wages ; and that, under pretence of favouring poor sailors, the poor of all other occupations would be taxed, for the benefit of the richest merchants. I see no difference between capitalist merchants and their sailors, and capitalist manufacturers and their workmen. The carpenter occupation, like the agricultural, contains a large proportion of the poor class. A law laying a heavy duty upon the importation of houses, as a recompense for the tax these poor people pay through their consumptions to the manufacturing capitalists, would be equivalent to laws laying duties upon the importation of bread-stuff, tobacco and cotton, to reimburse the poor agriculturists for the same tax.

The wealth of the owners of manufactories, having conferred upon them with great propriety, the title of capitalists, I cannot see the policy, wisdom or justice, of taxing the whole class even of the rich in all other occupations, to make them wealthier ; but when the tax producing this effect, is extended to the poor of all other occupations, it is something worse than a fraud, and becomes a grinding oppression. Morality may calmly disapprove of the rich plundering the rich, but humanity shrinks with no little impression of abhorrence, from the idea of the rich plundering the poor. If avarice should endeavour to conceal this appalling spectre from herself, by the flimsy pretence, that the manufacturing poor and not the manufacturing rich, will get the protecting-duty tax, it only proves that a very small matter of reasoning, attended by a great sum of money, will satisfy her. Where is the justice or policy of taxing the great body of the poor class, included in all other occupations, for the benefit of the small number of poor, included by the manufacturing occupation? Suppose two capitalists, having each a million of dollars, and a law should pass for taking from the one and giving to the other only half a million. How would he feel, though he would have more than enough left? Bodily labour is all a poor man's capital. In taking away a moiety of this, though for the purpose of giving it to another poor man, a more cruel injury is committed, because he has not enough left. It is not an excision from a superfluity, but from the necessary natural capacity to labour, and strongly resembles the Abyssinian morality of feeding upon an animal which is still living. To tax one poor man for the benefit of another, each having no other capital, but his natural ability to labour, in its degree of oppression, is the same to the sufferer, as if the tax had been appropriated to the rich ; but the distinction is of no consequence, because the fact upon which it is surmised does not exist. The whole community, poor and rich, is taxed by the protecting-duty system. Had the small body of poor comprised in the manufacturing occupation received this tax, they would have ceased to be poor. If such be the case, there is no further occasion for the tax ; but if their poverty continues, we can no longer reason upon a supposition, that the protecting-duty tax is received by the poor manufacturers; and we are forced to conclude, that it is a tax upon the poor and rich of the whole community, all being consumers, for the exclusive benefit of the rich of one occupation. This is aristocracy in its worst character.

To corrupt our political system by the principles of aristocracy is, of itself, sufficiently immoral and unwise. The struggle for wealth between individuals is chastened by laws and restrained by punishments; but a struggle for wealth by combinations is fostered by laws, and encouraged by rewards. The first is incapable of begetting civil wars or political revolutions; the second acts with a concert, an influence and a force, able to corrupt principles, subvert governments, and dispense general oppression. As combinations multiply, they become chafferers among themselves for a division of national spoil, and measure out their own privileges and emoluments by their own will. In legislative bodies, they exactly resemble religious sects, invested with a power to regulate the rights of conscience; and by the same corrupt devotion to their own exclusive interest, regulate the rights of property. All their compromises are dictated by this design. Civil combinations indeed invariably promise to invest nations with the riches of earth, as religious promise to endow them with the kingdom of Heaven; but all history informs us, that one promise terminates in adding to the mass of wickedness, and the other in adding to the mass of poverty.

Let us enquire whether the peculiar situation of the United States holds out to them this historical experience as an admonition, or a policy worthy of imitation. We know that combinations, by the force of concert acting against disunion, have been able in all ages to delude or purchase allies enough, to enable them to pillage and oppress majorities. If they can in this country enlist whole states under their banner, they will become infinitely stronger here, than in countries where no such allies are to be obtained; but, as other organized states, intended to be the victims of their avarice, will act in concert in opposition to the design, the resistance will also be stronger than in countries where no such organized interest exists. Hence would arise collisions between the general interest and the exclusive interest, infinitely more violent, than the collisions between these combatants in countries, where the general interest is unaided by organization and concert; and yet such collisions with weaker weapons have been sufficiently baleful to human happiness.

Combinations have hitherto succeeded by deluding particular states into an opinion, that they would be benefitted by serving under the banners of mercenary self-interest. The certificate peculators succeeded in establishing a system for liquidating the expenses of the revolutionary war, exuberantly partial to themselves, and atrociously unjust to a vast majority of the community; by urging the locality of their exclusive interest, as combined with the general interest of the states in which they resided. Banking combinations have by the same artifice cajoled towns, districts and states, to become partizans in favour of their selfish speculations, pernicious to the common interest. The acquisitions of all these projects have been paid by the labour, and the mischiefs they have caused, have been suffered by the people of the deluded states, together with the people of the other states; and the question simply is, whether it would be beneficial to the people of any one state, to create an order of bishops, or of useless officers, because these bishops or officers happened chiefly to reside in it. If I have proved that this pretence is a snare in the case of manufacturing workmen, it must be a deception still more notorious, when addressed to the people of a whole state. These workmen are placed much nearer to the benedictions supposed to emanate from a sect of privileged capitalists, than the great body of the people in any state; and if to them the dew of monopoly will be as little refreshing as the benedictions of the pope himself, I cannot conceive how the people of any state can imagine, that they will be reimbursed by this visionary manna, for the solid contributions they must annually pay to enrich a monopolizing sect.

But suppose, that the locality of the monopoly may be a pecuniary benefit, fully equal, in the case of a particular state, to the pecuniary contributions it will exact; it will then behoove the state, which may be so wonderfully fortunate as to balance its account of profit and loss with the monopoly, to consider, whether a pecuniary reimbursement will also comprise a compensation, for the political calamities the policy is calculated to produce.

The policy of fostering combinations by federal laws, has undoubtedly transferred, and continues to transfer, a considerable portion of the profits of labour, from one portion of the union to another; not to enrich the people generally of the receiving states, but to amass great capitals for a few individuals residing in them; towards which all the states contribute, and by which is artificially reared a monied interest at the expense of the whole community, which is gradually obtaining an influence over the federal government, of the same kind with that possessed by a similar sect over the British parliament. The operations of this sect, being already sorely felt, have already produced awful calculations in reference to a dissolution of the union. These arise from its new efforts to gratify an insatiable avarice, and its fears of the resentment it excites. It therefore craftily works upon the passions of the states it has been able to delude, by computations of their physical strength and their naval superiority; and by boasting of an ability to use the weakening circumstance of negro slavery, to coerce the defrauded and discontented states into submission. The indignation, excited by these threats, has suggested on the other hand estimates of resources and means of defence. The value of their exports; an ability to procure foreign cooperation for the protection of commerce; and an exclusion of the rapacious monied sect from a farther participation of their wealth; are suggestions natural to the occasion. Whence has arisen this ugly account, replete with other exasperating items; from the interest of the people of any one state in the union, or from the interest of a monied sect, embracing only an inconsiderable portion of these people? For what are the states talking about disunion, and for what are they going to war among themselves? To create or establish a monied sect, composed of privileged combinations, as an aristocratical oppressor of them all. I appeal to every disinterested man of common sense to say, whether the least cause for discontent or dislike between the states exists or has appeared, founded in any interest of which the people in any one state of the union generally participate? It is notorious, that all discontents between the states have been produced and fostered by pecuniary projects of a monied interest, the success of which, however beneficial to the individuals composing that interest, must be highly injurious to the majority of every state in the union. An intercourse upon fair and equal terms, between the sections of the union, founded in an exchange of agricultural labour, for naval, commercial and manufactural, is the basis of mutual prosperity, and utterly distinct from the speculations of a monied interest, whose prosperity is founded in principles, always hostile to the interest of labour. Shall honest labour and fair industry go to war with themselves to bestow a sovereignty over both, upon their greatest enemy? Charles the first lost his life and his kingdom by his infatuation for episcopacy, and suffering himself to become the tool of his bishops. If the United States should be plunged into a civil war, and lose the union by a devotion to capitalists, and by suffering themselves to become the tools of a monied interest, I will venture to predict, that future historians will degrade Charles from the summit of folly, which he has so long occupied without a rival.

I freely admit, that capitalists, whether agricultural, commercial or manufactural, constitute useful and productive classes in society; and by no means design, in the use of the term, to insinuate that it contains an odious allusion. It may even be applied to the man, whose bodily labour is his sole capital. But I also contend, that capital is only useful and re-productive, when it is obtained by fair and honest industry; and that whenever it is created by legal coercions, the productiveness of the common stock of capital is diminished, just as it is diminished by the excessive expenses of a civil government. Every species of capital thus accumulated, by whatever name it is called, belongs to the same genus, diminishes the efficacy of the common stock of capital, enriches individuals, impoverishes a nation, and all operating in the same mode deserve to be equally odious.

I will endeavour to exhibit an old idea in a new form, for the purpose of explaining how it has happened, that the policy of creating a monied interest has become so lamentably interwoven with the continuance of the union.

The federal is not a national government; it is a league between nations. By this league, a limited power only over persons and property was given to the representatives of the united nations. This power cannot be further extended, under the pretext of *national* good, because the league does not create a national government. Either this word "national" can or cannot enlarge the limited powers bestowed by the constitution over persons and property, upon the federal government. If it can, it expunges all its limitations and restrictions, and leaves to the constitution only the simple office of organizing a government, invested with an absolute power of providing for

the national good, equivalent to the power of the British government, organized by events, without being subjected to constitutional laws. If it cannot, the term can never be fairly
used in any discussion whatsoever, for defining the powers of
congress. If the federal league creates a government for exercising specified powers, as to those cases only, wherein the
united nations have a common interest; and contains no clause
for investing it with the great power of acting upon persons and
property, or of transferring property from man to man, or from
state to state, or from the states to individuals, by donations,
or by exclusive privileges; it can never be imagined, that a
power so enormous and tyrannical could have been given without using a single word expressive of such an intention. The
exercise of these powers, even by a government really national,
and absolutely sovereign, has uniformly resulted in oppression,
although the persons thus legislated out of natural rights, are
actually represented; but under the federal government, in
which local and personal interests are not, and cannot be represented, an exercise of these powers, utterly unnecessary to a
fair and free government, must produce mischiefs of ten-fold
magnitude. These local and personal interests were therefore left as politically and geographically arranged, into distinct compartments; and a federal was preferred to a national
government, because that commixture of local interests, and
inextricable sympathetick cohesion, which infuse into election
and representation their substantial value, was stopt by nature
at the state governments, and could not be extended to a national government, by melting up the states into one vast empire. A federal government was therefore adopted to provide
for the interests of states as separate nations, as to those cases,
and those cases only, in which a similar commixture would produce a mutual sympathy, and federal cohesion would infuse
into election and representation their substantial value. It
was intended by this federal policy to prevent a geographical
majority from dispensing injustice, oppression or ruin, to geographical interests; but if a geographical majority in congress,
under cover of misconstrued or interpolated words, such as
sovereign, supreme, national, paramount, necessary and convenient, may still exercise a power so enormous, the precaution is
defeated, and the essence of a federal government is already

lost. Even the members of congress and the president of the United States do not take an oath to protect local or personal interests; and that frivolous security does not exist in their favour, however little its absence is to be deplored, after the loss of a genuine representation. If these ideas, though badly expressed, are sound, they furnish a very plain rule, by which to determine the extent of federal legislative power. It was never intended to become an instrument of geographical partialities, or personal privileges, or an illegitimate offspring of the principle of representation.

We felt with great resentment the usurpations of internal powers over this country by Great Britain. We hear with indignation of the interferences of one European state with the internal affairs of another. We viewed with disapprobation, the interferences of other states with the internal affairs of France, under the pretence that a European nation existed; and that therefore some of these states had a right to meddle with the internal affairs of others, for the general good of Europe. Even an emperor has protested against this doctrine, and we applaud his opinion. And at this very time, judging disinterestedly, and guided by the principles of justice, we deprecate any interference by other states, with the internal affairs of Spain. Is there any difference between these cases, and an interference by congress with the internal affairs of the states? A majority of states in congress are as much a foreign power, as to the internal affairs of each state, as was a majority of European states to France. If such a majority can transfer to themselves by their own laws the property of any one state, they are not less inimical to the injured state, because they do not effect their purpose by armies; and may as justly be resisted, as Poland resisted the impositions of monarchs legislating for their own benefit.

Let these observations be a telescope, through which to view the continuance of the union. Something has suggested to the members of congress the policy of acquiring geographical majorities. This is a very direct step towards disunion, and must foster those geographical enmities by which alone it can be effected. This something must undoubtedly be, a contemplation of particular advantages to be derived from such majorities. If we can discover what these are, and can also remove the temptation, we shall destroy the most dangerous enemy to the best system of government, which ever existed. And is it not notorious, that they can consist of nothing else but usurpations of internal powers over persons and property, by which they can regulate the internal wealth and prosperity of states and individuals ? This was the sole cause, which has rendered the possession of a geographical preponderance in congress of so much importance, as to have suggested sundry pernicious artifices to obtain it, and to have produced sundry battles with pens, the precursors of battles with swords. To this motive the Missouri controversy itself is ascribable. It was really at the bottom of all the ingenuity and zeal lavished upon that subject. The true case may be shortly stated thus. Congress has no power to bestow exclusive privileges, or to arrange property between states or individuals ; therefore, no motive exists for obtaining a geographical majority in congress. Congress has a power to bestow exclusive privileges and to arrange property between states and individuals ; therefore, a powerful motive exists for obtaining a geographical majority in congress. Had the motive for the pernicious Missouri discussion never existed, the discussion itself would never have existed ; but if the same cause continues, more fatal controversies may be expected. It is therefore evident, that if the people in any state should be deluded into an opinion, that they will be enriched by an exclusive privilege for enriching a few capitalists, they ought very seriously to consider the risque to which the union will be exposed, by a power in congress to regulate wealth and poverty internally, so well calculated to generate the most exasperated geographical parties. If the neighbours to a courtier should wish him to receive extravagant douceurs, from a hope of admiring the palace he might build, or of tasting occasionally the luxuries of his table, yet, should these partialities be likely to excite a civil war, they would hardly be so infatuated by these frivolous considerations, as to bring upon themselves the worst of evils, by becoming advocates for the partiality by which it may be caused.

The weighty authority of congress has affirmed the truth of this reasoning, by changing the sales of publick lands from credit to cash, because the creation of a considerable pecuniary interest by credit sales might produce a combination of a pernicious political tendency. If a pecuniary combination, which feeds upon a wilderness, would endanger our form of government, what may be expected from such combinations, which feed upon the profits of labour? If a combination of a small band of land-speculators, united in one interest by a small capital, might shake the union; what may be done by the mighty combination of banking and manufacturing capitalists, stronger in number, in influence, and united by an enormous annual income? And if a policy which must have vanished, when the uncultivated lands were exhausted, was yet an object of apprehension, ought not the same policy, which may last as long as land is cultivated and labour is exerted, to suggest some degree of foresight?

But suppose, that all these objections to the protecting-duty system are unfounded; and that, surrendering the freedom of labour, the federalism of the constitution, and the safety of the union, its policy should be settled by a maxim, canonized by capitalists: "Get money; fairly if you can, but get money." The only difficulty is to ascertain those to whom this maxim is addressed by the protecting-duty system; to the capitalists or to the community. If to the capitalists, they may avail themselves of its whole doctrine; if to the community, it can only avail itself of the two first words. The scope and design of this treatise, is to maintain the right of every body to get money, and I only differ with the capitalists, by proceeding to assert, that every one has a further right to use it for his own benefit, because he has earned it. This every body composes the community, and if it shall consider the two first words of the protecting-duty maxim, as applicable to itself, the question only is, whether it will be made richer by each of its members employing his own capital for his own benefit, or by yielding up annually a portion of it to rich capitalists. There is nothing which excites an ardour for getting money, more than a right to use it; and nothing which damps that ardour more, than its being annually taken from us. To effect the object of getting money, the policy of transferring the ardour to a few capitalists, and applying the refrigerator to the community, is as if a nation having ten millions of hands should diminish the industry of nine millions nine hundred and ninety-nine thousand, to excite a money-getting temper in one thousand. The pecuniary loss to the community will therefore not be limited by what the one thousand may gain, but will be incomputably aggravated by a general discouragement of industry.

A dislocation of capital by laws has no other object but to effect its accumulation in a few hands, by diminishing it in those of all others ; an effect, comprising the essence of oppression, in every form hitherto experienced. The real question, therefore, is, whether nations are richer, unexposed to the essential instrument of tyranny, than when suffering under it. If free nations are more prosperous than enslaved, free capital will be more productive, than capital deprived of its liberty. It would be a strange anomaly, if the freedom of other human rights advance the wealth and happiness of nations, that the freedom of labour or capital should produce poverty and misery. And it would be an evident contradiction in economists to assert, that cultivation by personal slavery is unthrifty, but that the subjection of capital to legislative dislocation, will make it more productive. I perceive no consistency in patronizing the rights of slaves, and anathematizing the rights of capital. The freedom of labour must supply the arguments in both cases, since there is no difference between constraints imposed upon the body, and constraints imposed upon the acquisitions of the body.

After capital is dislocated by law, is the law still to pursue it in its accumulated state, and to prescribe its future destination ; or are the receivers to hold and use it, according to their own free will and judgment ? The law it is said transfers it, that it may be employed in a mode more productive, than if it had remained with its owners ; but if these new occupants are left at liberty to use it as they please, its productiveness must continue to depend, not upon the law, but upon the freedom of individual will. If the principle of free will in the use of capital be a good one, applied to the acquirers of capital by law, it cannot be a bad one, appl   to the acquirers of capital by labour ; nor can it cause capital to be productive in one case, and unproductive in the other.

Let us consider some other established facts, and apply them to the point of national wealth. No fact is better established, than that commerce is a source of wealth. Such is its effect from its powerful capacity to excite industry. The examples of Venice and Holland are modern ; that of Carthage is less explicit from its antiquity. In the former cases, and probably in the latter also, the national wealth obtained by commerce did not arise from prohibitory duties imposed upon the importations of foreign manufactures, but from the freedom of importations and exchanges, combined with the skill and industry, produced by this freedom. Holland long flourished in the midst of Europe, under very unfavourable circumstances, tottering on the brink of some political precipice, by importing the manufactures of all countries within her reach.

The case of Britain differs from these in the protecting-duty item ; but her commercial system, considered in its essential characters, is substantially the same. She imports *whatever she wants or can advantageously exchange*, and does not import what she does not want nor can exchange with other nations ; taking care that her ships shall return with valuable cargoes. How far these cargoes are composed of articles ready for consumption, or requiring labour to be prepared for it, is a point, difficult and not material to decide. Her importations from the east are chiefly of the former description ; those from the west remain doubtful, as to their comparative value. Among the articles ready for consumption are bread-stuff, fish, rice, indigo, and others ; even tobacco may be considered as belonging to this description of her importations, as she re-exports the most of it, in the state received, and as it employs an inconsiderable portion of manufacturing labour. These are manufactured articles of the United States, imported by Britain and her dependencies to a great amount, to be consumed or exchanged ; and probably equal in value to the raw materials she also imports to manufacture ; but taking her whole commerce into contemplation, there can be no doubt that her importations of manufactures to be consumed or exchanged, greatly exceed in value her importations of raw materials to be manufactured. Such is the general character of her commerce ; she has prohibited the importation of those particular kinds of manufactures only, which she does not want, and cannot advantageously exchange, because she is overstocked with them ; but this is a particular exception suggested by a particular circumstance, and not extending to the general character of her commercial system. And yet, by adverting to the recent suspicions in Britian itself, as to its wisdom, and combining with its policy her debt and taxes, far exceeding the debt and taxes of any other European nation, a doubt of its effect, and a fear of its adoption, ought to be inspired.

Instead of teasing ourselves in a perplexing endeavour to disentangle the convolutions of a tissue, made of shavings from these facts, let us apply the plain facts themselves to the United States. Venice and Holland became rich, by importing manufactures ; and had they prohibited this importation, their commerce must have dwindled and perished. Will not the commerce of the United States be more flourishing, by following, than by rejecting these brilliant examples? England imports a great variety of manufactures, which she either consumes or exchanges ; may not the commerce of the United States be nourished by the same means ? England only prohibits the importation of those manufactures in which she abounds, and begins to doubt whether even this prohibition is a wise one ; does this example recommend here a prohibition of the manufactures which we want, whilst England encourages the importation of such as she wants ? The prohibition of those manufactures in which England overflows, causes no monopoly, and inflicts no tax upon consumers for the benefit of capitalists ; but the prohibition of the importation of those wanted here, causes a tax and bestows a bounty, locally and individually partial.

In all these cases the soul of commerce shews itself at its eyes, to be compounded of full freights, rich cargoes, and free exchanges. The facility and freedom of exchanges is as essential to commercial prosperity, as to civilization and happiness. Abolish it entirely, commerce is destroyed, and savageness and misery restored. Domestick, as well as foreign commerce all over Europe is restrained of its freedom, and avarice has erected toll gates for cities, just as it purposes to do it here for whole states, by the protecting-duty project ; not for the sake of increasing the comforts of those within, but merely to get money for itself. The English protecting-duty system does not impair the facility and freedom of exchanges, as to internal or domestick commerce, in any degree ; ours destroys it ; nor does the English system impair this freedom and facility in relation to foreign commerce, beyond what we should do by duties to prohibit the importation of cotton, flour and tobacco, as articles are chiefly prohibited, which could not be imported to any advantage if they were not prohibited. The domestick commerce of England is left quite free ; the foreign nearly so. And to procure the commercial prosperity she is supposed to have obtained by this policy, we are rapidly subjecting both domestick and foreign commerce, to strangling restrictions.

We are blinded to the rights of domestick commerce, by clouds of dust brushed from foreign practices, of which we cannot form a judgment by the help of those honest intelligencers, the senses ; but surely we may be permitted to take a glance at it, through this dusky medium.

Suppose the nations, composing what is very incorrectly called the non-manufacturing district of the United States, (for they are probably as great manufacturers as their sisters,) should believe the arguments and adopt the policy recommended by the protecting-duty system. If the policy be wise and good between the United States and England, it must also be wise and good between the nations composing our union. If it be injurious to the United States, to admit the importation and use of foreign manufactures, subject to competition, it must be more injurious to the southern states, to suffer the use of northern manufactures, enhanced by a monopoly. It cannot be proved, that a policy, chastened by competition and a freedom of exchanges, is bad, but that it may be made good by poisoning it with monopoly. It cannot be proved, that foreign nations draw wealth from the United States, unjustly, by selling them manufactures cheap ; and that one state may draw wealth from another, justly, by selling to it manufactures, dear. Nor is it possible, that so enlightened a body of men as congress should be able to discern any species of injustice or loss in one case, which is not aggravated in the other. Therefore, if the capitalists can prove that a prohibiting policy is wise and just for the United States in reference to other nations, they have also proved that it would be wise and just for particular states in relation to themselves. Its wisdom and justice in relation to the southern states, called non-manufacturing, being proved by the capitalists, it only remains to consider whether they have a right to do that which is necessary for the preservation of their internal wealth and prosperity. Have congress a right to inflict upon some nations composing the union, local and internal evils of impoverishing severity? This question has been discussed in a former section. But it may be added, that if congress can effect this, by a circuitous mode of internal taxation, the complete concurrency of that power between the states and congress, in every case, invests, or rather leaves to the states, a constitutional right of resistance. The states may tax every species of internal property; and by internal prohibitory excises, prevent the use of any manufactures of pernicious internal consequences. This idea will again be adverted to; now I shall only observe, that every state in the union has exercised the right in a multitude of instances. If then congress assumes a power of dealing out the same partialities, in an aggravated form, between states and manufacturing capitalists ; said to be ruinous between the United States and the English manufacturing capitalists, though of a milder type; the old contest arises (so common among mankind) between a power to oppress and a right to resist; and it would not be very important to decide, whether the right was both natural and constitutional, or natural only. But this contest between power and power, or power and right, or injury and resistance, will never occur, provided the principle of the freedom and fairness of exchanges between the individuals composing the several states, is adhered to, as a principle of the union, uncontaminated by a capitalist monopoly.

This principle, internally just, has universally been also considered as wise, by all commercial nations. This principle, and not prohibition, was the basis of Carthaginian, Venetian and Dutch commercial prosperity; and is in fact the basis also of the British. It brings home merchandise and not ballast, either for consumption or re-exportation. Both descriptions of merchandise constitute the sustenance of commerce; and of course commerce will languish, if its sustenance be diminished. I am no merchant, but it seems to me, that by diminishing the business of commerce in any way, we must unavoidably diminish its wealth, and also the naval power of the United States. I have endeavoured to prove, that the distinction between raw materials and manufactures is verbal and unsubstantial, as labour is the source of both. Whenever ships bring home the products of labour, they bring home solid wealth, and by bringing home wealth, they add to the wealth both of the mercantile class and of the community. This truth is universally assented to, except when it is contested by the design of enriching some home monopoly or exclusive privilege. Thus we import the manufacture called tea, both to supply our own wants and to re-export, because a manufacture brought from a foreign country is an acquisition of so much wealth; and we prohibit the importation of other manufactures, only because the nourishment of a monopoly is preferred to the nourishment of commerce, and the acquisition of national wealth. Had no such combination as manufacturing capitalists existed, the policy of encouraging commerce by leaving its importations free would never have been doubted; and the cause of the doubt affords no argument in favour of its confirmation.

What are importations? Money. They are something better; they are a universal currency. They are the substance, of which money is only a representative; and are of more universal value, than money itself. And they inspire more skill and industry than money, because they give employment to more labour. Commerce is supposed to flourish, and a nation to be rich, when they abound in money or currency; but this is only a sign of probability, and not a positive truth, as Spain has proved by a metallick, and the United States by a paper currency. On the other hand it is a positive truth, that nations abounding in things represented by currency or money, whether imported for use or exchanges, or fabricated by itself, is wealthy; and that commerce abounding in the same things, is prosperous and flourishing. This abundance can never be effected except by importations, and no nation nor commerce can therefore be rich and prosperous, if these are excluded. A total exclusion is death to commerce; a partial, sickening. I do not believe that either nations or commerce are benefitted by confining their importations to things in their least valuable form, or what are commonly called raw materials; on the contrary, it seems to me, that the richer the cargoes, the greater will be the prosperity both of the nation and its commerce. Would it be better for us to import from Mexico the ore, than the manufactured dollar? This might possibly be answered in the affirmative, if our country was so overflowed with people, that the loss in freight and labour occasioned by importing only as much wealth in fifty or an hundred ships, as could be brought in one, would be compensated by the employment of manufacturing the ore into money ; but under our circumstances, it would enrich us more to receive one cargo of dollars, as valuable as an hundred or ore, because it would be a great saving of capital and labour, capable of being beneficially employed otherwise. For the same reason, it is better for us to import English cloth than English wool.

The Dutch were extremely wealthy, whilst their warehouses groaned with the most valuable manufactures of all nations. They preferred rich cargoes to those of little value, because fine manufactures were a currency of gold, and raw materials, like the iron money of Sparta. An abundance of universal currency brought wealth to the Dutch through the instrumentality of exchanges ; but it will bring wealth to us through an additional and important channel. The Dutch had few or no domestick articles for sale and exportation ; the United States abound in them. An abundance of currency enhances prices. Manufactures are a substantial and universal currency, and of course the more of this currency is brought to us by commerce, the better will be the price of every article we have for sale. By a diminution of this currency, the prices of all articles we have for sale must be correspondently diminished. Such is the effect of embargoes and restrictions upon commerce, because they expel from the market a portion of the currency, foreign manufactures, by which the prices of our own are upheld. If barter was practised without the intervention of money, the more manufactures were brought to us by foreign nations, to exchange for ours, the more we should get for ours ; and the fewer they brought, the less we should receive. Thus it is better, that a foreign merchant should come to us full than empty-handed, because we shall get more for our commodities in the first than in the latter case ; and though we receive payment in a currency called manufactures, yet as it is universal, and we live in the commercial world, it is real wealth to us. Indeed it often happens, that the enhanced price for our commodities, arising from an abundance of manufacturing currency, will enable us to rival or undersell in other countries the fabricators themselves. Accordingly, those who have observed the fluctuations of prices since our revolution, must have seen, that they have been distinctly influenced by the plenty or scarcity of imported universal currency, and that the wealth and prosperity of the United States has been visibly increased by its abundance, and diminished by its expulsion. In fact, it is exactly the case of a plenty or scarcity of money.

The protecting-duty system advocates a scarcity of currency, and gravely informs agriculture, commerce, the fisheries and all other occupations, except one, that by expelling the abundance of imported currency, and substituting one about twenty fold less in amount, these occupations will get as good or better prices than ever. But do we not know, that as currency becomes scarce, its value increases; and must it not of course follow, if ninety-five per centum of it is driven away, that the holder of the remaining five would be made very rich? The policy of this project therefore is, to deprive commerce of that branch of her business, consisting of importations, re-exportations, and free exchanges by which the Dutch grew rich, and English commerce is now flourishing; and moreover to deprive agriculture and all other occupations except one, of good prices for their labours, by expelling a great portion of the currency by which these prices are enhanced, and granting to a few individuals an exclusive privilege to coin the very same kind of currency proposed to be expelled. They do not pretend that they can coin as much as they propose to expel, but they propose by way of some compensation for the deficiency, to make each half dollar, pass for a whole one.

Neal, in his history of the puritans, vol. 2. p. 223, speaking of the government of Charles the first, remarks, that "he levied "the duties of tonnage and poundage, and laid what other "*duties he thought proper upon merchandise,* which he let out "to farm to private persons; *the number of monopolies was* "*incredible; there was no part of the subjects' property that* "*ministry could dispose of, but was bought and sold.* They "raised above a million a year by taxes on soap, salt, candles, "wine, cards, pins, leather, coals, &c. *even to the sole gather-* "*ing of rags.* Grants were given out for weighing hay and "straw, for gauging red herring barrels and butter casks; for "marking iron and sealing lace; and a great many others; "which being purchased of the crown, *must be paid for by the* "*subject.* His majesty claimed a right, *in cases of necessity,* "(of which necessity himself was the sole judge) to raise mo-

" ney by ship-writs for the maintenance of the royal navy.
" The like was demanded for the royal army, by the name of
" coat and conduct money; the men were billeted upon pri-
" vate houses. Large sums of money were raised by the fines
" of the star-chamber and high commission court, and the *ex-*
" *traordinary projects* of loans, benevolences and free gifts."
We have imposed duties, not for the exclusive purpose of
defraying the expenses of government, but also *to enrich private persons.* The number of monopolies thus created *is incredible.* They extend to clothes of all kinds, iron, furniture,
carriages, and a multitude of manufactures, and even to the
conversion of rags into money. The profit reaped from all
these monopolies *must be paid by the citizen. Every citizen's
property* is reached by them to a great extent, and as far as it
is reached, *transferred* to other citizens. Thus it is bought and
sold by a traffick between laws and courtiers and speculators.
Charters to collect money of the people are openly sold, under
the pretexts of *necessity or convenience,* and in virtue of the
power of sovereignty, according to the maxims and policy of
Charles. Much larger sums of money are annually taken from
free citizens by charter-bounties and monopolies, than were
taken from Charles's subjects by the star-chamber and high
commission courts. Charles extorted money from the people,
and then squandered it among his favourites; we squander it,
and then extort it from the people; as in the cases of the
grants to certificate-holders and revolutionary soldiers. Charles
sometimes, by granting monopolies, enabled his favourites to
collect great sums of money from the people themselves; we
follow his example by banking and protecting-duty monopolies.
I shall not attempt to try either the conduct of a Stuart, or
our own by the principles of civil liberty, in order to discern
the preference. The most material differences between them
are, that our banking and protecting-duty monopolies cover
every thing; whereas by selecting particular articles, acute as
he was in the science of monopoly, Charles might have overlooked a few. His monopolies were always sold; ours are
sometimes given away. Publick revenue was the pretext of
his; private emolument the design of ours. He pleaded necessity; we plead speculation. He used force; we delusion.

" Tax luxuries," is sometimes the cry. " Tax necessaries,"
at others. But "tax both" is at all times the creed of fraud
and avarice. What are these luxuries and necessaries? Are
the products of agriculture assignable to the former class, and
those of manufacturing to the latter? Is food a luxury, and
clothing a necessary? Is iron a luxury? Are wine, rum, whiskey, sugar, coffee, tea, spices, salt and physick, all luxuries?
God saw that all his works were good, and avarice impiously
prohibits the divine benevolence. It taxes comforts, by calling
them luxuries, and it taxes necessaries, by pretending that they
are politically pernicious, with the design of introducing those
very abuses, to which the term luxury is most correctly applied.
A legislative distribution of wealth begets the luxury which is
pernicious, and the poverty which is miserable; but the freedom of industry diffuses the pleasures which the creator has
provided for man, and softens the evils by which they are attended.

But avarice pursues industry in all her recesses, and computes her earnings with the eye of a master. Self-interest is
capable of any estimates, however false, for its own gratification. Thus we have seen the wages of labour in the agricultural occupation, enhanced beyond those in the mechanical,
merely because it was necessary to make the only accessible
victim of a pecuniary combination, rich, and the soldiers by
whom they were to conquer, poor; although it is notorious that
mechanicks, white or black, freemen or slaves, earn much higher
daily wages than agricultural labourers can gain; and that
slaves, having a good trade, sell for double the price they would
do if they had none. The capitalists, whilst they deny or
obscure this fact, confide in it for the success of the protecting-
duty project in conveying to their own pockets whatever it
shall extort from those of the community; for it demonstrates,
that the present disproportion between mechanical and agricultural wages is sufficiently great to secure to them a supply of
workmen, without the least necessity for argumenting the temptation by suffering their labourers to participate of the bounty.
Truth is every where truth, but imposture, stimulated by
avarice, every where attends her; thus benevolence to workmen is the exterior of the protecting-duty system, as beautiful

as the skin of the tiger, which nevertheless covers a rapacious animal.

The art of cutting up nations into sects, or creating combinations, is the work-shop of avarice and ambition, the wares of which are never offered to nations without being varnished. The framers of our governments, impressed with the danger of this art, which had been unexceptionably pernicious to human happiness, endeavoured to destroy it by establishing religious freedom, by forbidding noble orders, by denouncing exclusive privileges, and by limiting the powers of governments to prevent its introduction, and equalize the rights of property, knowing it to be a Trojan horse, either to be disembowelled, or to become the vehicle of destruction. We have rejected tithes as highly oppressive, though paid for the blessings of religion, and established a five-fold tithe, paid for the curse of a capitalist sect.

The advocates of the protecting-duty system assume the title of "friends to national industry," formed their reasonings upon the maxim, that "the productiveness of labour is increased in "proportion as it is directed by *intelligence*," and endeavour to sweep away all the arguments which are adverse to the system, by asserting that the " miseries of labourers in Britain and " China result, not from manufactures, but from the *nature of* " *these governments*."

A maxim, theoretically sound, may be erroneously applied; and its obvious truth is often plausibly used to recommend practical conclusions, at enmity with the real principle of the maxim itself. The position "that intelligence will increase the productiveness of labour" is unquestionably true; but an inference, " that combinations ought therefore to possess a power " of taxing labour by a monopoly acting upon labour," may yet be unquestionably false. A monopoly of intelligence by any class or combination would be a tyranny, if it could be effected; but a monopoly of any means for obtaining wealth from a community, by a class or combination, unpossessed of an unnatural superiority of intelligence, prevents the increase and diminishes the stock of national intelligence; because it is only cunning, associated with avarice, which resorts to means for the gratification of self-interest, unfavourable to the increase of intelligence itself. The productiveness of virtue by religion is at least as desirable as the productiveness of labour; but monopolies of intelligence by combinations have assumed its direction, and overspread mankind with vice. The productiveness of civil liberty by government is of the next importance; but monopolies of intelligence by combinations have assumed its direction, and overspread mankind with oppression. The productiveness of labour is the third great source of human happiness; but monopolies of intelligence by combinations have also assumed the direction of labour, and overspread mankind with fraud and poverty. The evils resulting from the usurpations of a power of direction, founded in the false assumption of superior intelligence, in these three cases which decide the temporal destiny of nations, admit of no remedy, except that of the freedom of intelligence. It is this freedom which makes both religion and civil government more productive of benefits to mankind, than when intelligence is monopolised by combinations, and exerted by exclusive privileges. And if the freedom of intelligence both produces it and makes it more productive in these two cases, it must have the same effect in the case of labour. The three cases make up but one political system, and that system, to be consistent, must adhere to one principle; it must either prefer the national intelligence to the intelligence of combinations, or the intelligence of combinations to that of the nation; and having made an election, it must embrace all three cases, or the system will be incomplete and internally contradictory. Can the freedom of intelligence or intellect be productive of good in the two first cases, and of evil in the third? Can the freedom of religion and of civil government be preserved, if the freedom of labour be surrendered to the *intelligence* of combinations? Are slaves free, because their labour is made more productive, (if such be the fact,) by the intelligence of their masters? Is the white population of the world justified in converting to its own use the labour of Africa, on account of a superiority of intellect? Would the intelligence of the negroes in Africa be diminished by a freedom of labour? In short, the whole reasoning upon which the advocates for the protecting-duty system rely, is at the threshold, dependent upon a preference between national intelligence, and the intelligence of a self-interested combination for the object of generating productiveness, moral and physical, as the means of national prosperity and happiness; and having made an election between

these competitors, a further examination of the argument becomes superfluous.

The "miseries of labourers in China and Britain results, not
" from *manufactures*, but from the *nature of their govern-*
" *ments.*" Here again the position is true, and the inference
false. A position, that the "miseries of labourers in China and
" Britain results, not from *agriculture*, but from the nature of
" their governments," would have been equally true, and the
inference, "that therefore agriculture ought to be directed by
" the intelligence of a mercenary combination here, to increase
" its productiveness," would equally follow. I am not reasoning against manufactures, but for the freedom of labour, and
against combinations and exclusive privileges destructive of
that freedom; believing that the general intelligence of labour
will be increased, and its general productiveness encouraged
by its freedom. The same principle embraces manufacturing,
agricultural, and every other species of labour. If the maxim
advanced by the advocates of the protecting-duty system will
justify congress in assuming, or rather in empowering a few
capitalists to assume the direction of manufacturing labour, it
also invests that body with a power of legislating for the direction of every other species of labour, and assigning all occupations whatsoever to the care of the *intelligence* of mercenary
combinations. This is the very power which constitutes the
nature of the Chinese and British governments, enables them
to place labour under the *intelligent direction* of mercenary
combinations, and causes the *miseries of labourers* in those
countries. To admit the deplorable consequences of a cause,
and immediately to propose the introduction of the same cause,
discloses a latitude of reasoning, which evinces no small degree
of confidence in a deficiency of intelligence in those who are
thus addressed. The reliance expressed to avert the evils
said to be caused by the nature of the British government, is
in the nature of our own government; and the nature of our
own government is proposed to be changed, by infecting it with
the identical principles which constitute the nature of the British government, and have caused the *miseries of labourers.*

A recurrence to sundry of the objections which have been
urged against the protecting-duty system will enable us both
to estimate the extent of these English interpolations, and also

to discern that the system here will considerably exceed, in malignity, its criminality in England.

It destroys the division of powers between the federal and state governments, by investing the former with a sweeping, internal power over persons and things. In England, it does nothing so bad.

It violates the principles of representation, because local and personal interests are not represented in congress. Not so in England.

It recognizes a sovereign power over property, and consequently over persons, according to the political principles of England and China.

It destroys the freedom of labour, and enables government to subject it to the cupidity of combinations or individuals; as is practised in England.

It taxes the great mass of capital and labour, to enrich a favoured few; as in England.

It increases the burden upon the people by this operation, in the same degree as if a correspondent addition had been made by law to the salaries of the officers of government; as in England.

It subjects the poor to this burden of raising capital for the rich, and thereby increases the mass of poverty; as in England.

It impoverishes workmen and enriches employers; as in England.

It increases the expenses of government, and entices it into prodigality; as in England.

It leaves to one occupation free will in exchanges, and takes it away from all others. Not so bad in England.

It is a system of pains and penalties, by contracting the natural right to provide for subsistence, comfort and pleasure, and leaving so much of this right as it does not take away, dependent upon a precarious toleration, like the freedom of religion; as in England

It deprives commerce of the freedom of exchanges, and prohibits it from bringing home universal currency, so as to diminish its profits, depreciate native commodities, and obstruct naval prosperity. Not so in England.

It corrupts congress and endangers the union, by making a geographical majority an object of solicitude, for the purpose of obtaining geographical advantages. This enormous evil is not attached to the system in England.

And it generates the extremes of luxury and poverty; as in England. Most of these lineaments identify the visage of this policy, both here and in England; but there are several of such local hideousness and exclusive deformity, under our particular circumstances, that I cannot see a better motive for its adoption, than that which induced some uncivilized nations to become enraptured with their idols.

The subject of bounties or pensions has been anticipated. As it regards all our legislatures, their constitutionality depends upon the truth of the doctrines I have advanced concerning sovereignty, and the natural rights of labour. If our legislatures are not sovereigns, they have no power to give away one state or its property to another, or one man's person or his property to another man. In regard to congress, their constitutionality depends also upon the limitations of the powers of that body over persons and things.

I discern no difference between pension, and alien and sedition laws, in principle. All depend upon the doctrine, that congress have a mysterious power, to act upon persons and things, beyond the definitions of the constitution. If such had been the opinion of its framers, a special power to legislate concerning counterfeiters, pirates and traitors, would have been unnecessary. The coincidence in the powers bestowed, between persons and lands, demonstrates an intention that the restrictions resulting from specification should not be destroyed by inferences from sovereignty. A limited internal power over land is given to congress, similar to the limited power over persons; as in the cases of public lands, forts, dock-yards, and the ten miles square. A state cannot constitutionally make a cession of either persons or lands to congress, beyond the constitutional permission. Maryland and Virginia could not have conveyed to congress twenty miles square, because congress is only permitted to receive and govern ten. If a state cannot convey all its territory to congress, it cannot convey an inch, beyond the permission of the constitution; because the powers bestowed by the federal compact cannot be extended in the smallest degree by unfederal means. Now, if no bargains of any kind between congress and a state can constitutionally alter the federal compact by diminishing the state powers reserved, or increasing the federal powers delegated, it follows more strongly, that congress cannot extend its sphere of action without the consent of the states. And as the specification of a limited power over land was intended to be restrictive by the terms of its definition, so the specification of a limited power over persons was intended to prohibit every other power over persons, not therein contained. Hence congress cannot gradually disembowel a state of its citizens or property by incorporations, alien or sedition laws, or protecting duties.

Does the constitution empower congress to act without limitation over persons and property by bestowing pensions on patriots or paupers, at the expense of the community? It must be admitted that no such power is delegated. It can then only be inferred from the recondite sovereign power supposed to reside in that department of government; and if such a power does exist, it will cover the alien, sedition and protecting-duty laws, as well as the pension laws. Of the whole catalogue, the last is the most dangerous, and is most capable of disordering the division and limitations of power, so assiduously contemplated by the constitution. Kings by pensions strengthen and extend their power; congress may do the same. It is an unlimited power over persons and property, and therefore liable to be abused; the federal constitution delegates limited powers over both, to prevent abuses. The alien and sedition laws acted only on a few persons by penalties; pension laws upon a great number, by douceurs and taxes to pay them. The protecting-duty laws are called bounties, because they contemplate some compensation to the publick; pension laws are gratuitous. The strong objection to the protecting-duty laws arises from their effect in transferring the private property of one man to another; pension laws do the same thing. Both violate the natural freedom of labour, and the latter are more illimitable than the former. The sovereign power of disregarding the rights of property by congress, as to pensions, is as dangerous as it is comprehensive. Not only individuals, not only corporations, but whole states may become pensioners of congress; and by the instrumentality of this power, all the constitutional restrictions, for securing the equality of taxes, and their destination to federal purposes, may be effectually defeated. As an unlimited power, it may be exercised upon whatever persons it shall please congress to select; and the ministers of a particular sect, or of all sects, are as much within its scope, as any other persons. The history of pensions would be a history of frauds and abuses; and their consequences to society are universally agreed to be demoralizing and oppressive. These consequences will be aggravated here by the great number of patrons, the facility with which they are approached, and the variety of causes for invigorating their solicitude, for the success of their clients. The effects of these causes are already severely felt both by the people and our governments; and much as pensions have been complained of as a grievance in other countries, and reprobated in this when contemplated at a distance, they have already come home to us in an extent exceeding the semblance of justice, and making even benevolence ridiculous. The multitude of pensions granted by congress and the state governments, and the increase of legislative expenses occasioned by this extensive business, would probably compound a sum of money far exceeding whatever any other community has ever paid on the same score, and constitute a very considerable item in accounting for the publick distresses; but, if we exclude from the computation all these expenses, and the whole catalogue of pensions, except those bestowed by a single law, the astonishment and indignation of beholding a capital of fifty millions devoted at a blow by a temporary fanaticism, as a gratuity to actual fraud or hypothetical merit, would sufficiently demonstrate the magnitude of a sovereign power over property, and the danger of its abuse when usurped by legislative departments.

I have never heard the law alluded to, or the loose mode of bestowing pensions approved of; and probably at this time that law is more generally reprobated, both by congress and their constituents, than the alien and sedition laws ever were at any period; but, it remains as a monument of the falsehood of the common assertion, that the continuance of a law, is an evidence of publick approbation; and as an evidence in favour of the common observation, that mankind are more fickle in practising what is right, than in adhering to what is wrong.

" Nolumus leges Angliæ mutare," we are unwilling to
change the laws of England, is a maxim borrowed from our an-
cestors, which we reverence so far as it is foolish and bad ; and
despise so far as it is wise and good. In multiplying laws and
changing constitutional principles, no people ever disclosed
more mutability ; in adhering to laws unconstitutional or
grievous, more perseverance. This English maxim sustains
bad principles in their form of government, and bad laws here ;
and though it is rejected when constitutions are violated, it is
quoted with veneration, if it be proposed to abolish such viola-
lations. Pecuniary combinations have the address to persuade
us to reject it, in granting them an introduction, and to adhère
to it as a sufficient counterpoise to their impositions after they
are detected.

I shall presently advert to the evils resulting from an assumption of judicial powers by legislatures, and from legislative
patronage ; but the mischiefs arising even from these unjust and
prodigal practices, are inconsiderable, compared with those of
a power to bestow exclusive pecuniary advantages upon chartered companies, sectarian combinations, entire states, or particular districts. As nations like individuals are often tempted
to imitate other nations with whom they associate, instead of
considering the evils which have been produced in England, as
an admonition to avoid a baleful system, we have been seduced
by avaricious combinations to imitate the pernicious example,
at the expense of our republican policy, and contrary to our constitutional principles. Publick good is invariably the plea of
all such combinations, and publick distress as invariably the
fruit. The specious pretext of encouraging manufactures has
caused the United States to shut their eyes upon two maxims
of Mr. Jefferson's (when shall we see his like again ?) contained
in his messages to congress of 1801 and 1802, then received
with general applause, and now buried in the tomb of forget-
fulness. " Let economy be substituted for taxation, and indus-
" try be free." Against these maxims, wise, benevolent, honest
and republican, combinations have successfully urged the following arguments. " Manufacturing is more profitable than
" agriculture ; therefore, give it a bounty. It is less so ; there-
" fore, give it a bounty. Navigation is a blessing ; therefore, open

"canals and shut up the ocean. One portion of the union is
"afflicted by negro slavery; therefore, make it tributary to
"capitalists. Cultivation by slaves is unprofitable; there-
"fore, make it tributary to capitalists. The freedom of labour
"deprives it of the benefit of being directed by intelligence;
"therefore, subject it to capitalists. Taxation is preferable to
"economy; therefore, enhance it for the nourishment of capi-
"talists, and the gratification of avarice." Such reasoning depends upon the position, that it is better to raise oranges in a
hot house, than to import them from a warm climate. The
structure of the terraqueous globe seems to have forbidden a
policy for enhancing prices, breeding scarcity, diminishing comforts, and excluding pleasures. It seems to have intended to
equalize the means of acquiring happiness among mankind, nor
can I discern a stronger reason than that of retaliation and ven-
geance for frustrating the beneficent design. England has
already revenged itself upon the feudal aristocracy by creating
a monied one. But a landed aristocracy in Russia at this time
holds the manufacturing interest in a tributary state. Let us,
therefore, revenge the injury by making the landed interest
here, though it asks for no exclusive rights or privileges, tributary to the owners of manufactories, and create one species of
aristocracy, because the other still exists in Russia. Is the
British and Bonapartean policy of commercial restrictions
recommended by his being in St. Helena, and the heaviest taxation in the world being in England?

SECTION 13.

ASSUMPTION OF JUDICIAL POWERS AND PATRONAGE BY LEGISLATURES.

The usurper, Augustus, could never be persuaded to re-establish the Roman republick. What hope is there, if one man was thus inexorable, that three thousand should be persuaded to renounce the unconstitutional powers which they have assumed? With ten times his honesty, they have ten times as much of that invigorating aliment of a love of power, called conscious integrity ; and our strongest ally may therefore become our strongest adversary. Augustus no doubt persuaded himself, that his government would make Rome happier, than the restoration of the republick ; and our legislatures undoubtedly have as good reasons for believing, that their usurpations will be better for the community, than our constitutional divison of powers ; but both he and they in such reasoning look only at themselves, without weighing their successors in the scales of probability. He did not anticipate a Caligula, nor do they a French revolutionary assembly. The solid value of representation is a plausible and seducing argument in favour of usurpations, and yet nothing has been more fatal to science in general, and especially to political science, than the art of extracting erroneous conclusions from sound principles. The framers of all our constitutions, sensible of this truth, have laboured to enforce it, by limiting the powers of legislative representatives, to prevent an accumulation of power, which is invariably overwhelming. Their chief precaution has been to take care, that they should none of them be *representatives* of any judicial power, by assigning judicial power to other trustees ; and, therefore, representation in exercising judicial powers acts exactly as the judges would do, by exercising legislative power. Through inattention, however, to a very visible constitutional distinction, all our legislatures have fallen into an error, which all would condemn if committed by the judges.

The delicacy of the proposed subjects is as deterring, as their importance is imperative. The difficulty of writing in a style, vigorous enough to convince, and yet polished enough to please the very gentlemen, who must either be censured, or the proposed reformation abandoned, becomes extremely formidable when we reflect, that the reformation to be recommended depends entirely upon the persons, so likely to be offended. I have no reliance upon myself for getting over this risque ; but I have great reliance upon the consideration, that patriotism and integrity do yet greatly preponderate in our legislative bodies ; and that these qualities would view with scorn a sacrifice of truth at the shrine of power, and will pardon arguments enjoined by loyalty to her dictates. Besides, our representatives are themselves governed the greater part of their lives, and their families and friends belong entirely to the governed class. For this reason they would prefer a rough pleader in favour of constitutional principles, to the smoothest flatterer of temporary power. My apprehensions, therefore, are gone, and I will consider the subjects with the same integrity, by which the representatives of the people are themselves actuated.

Let us take a glance at the origin and progress of judicial power in England. It was at first considered as an attribute of sovereignty, and whilst that was supposed to reside in the king, he either exercised it himself, or delegated it to judges, dependant on his pleasure, and guided by his will.

The judicial power of the house of lords is a remnant of the feudal power of the barons. The caprices, the passions and the partialities of feudal kings and barons, in the administration of justice, had scourged England for centuries, and long called for remedies in vain. At length the king was deprived of his sovereign judicial power, and the house of lords moulded into a jurisdiction less objectionable. Had that house exercised the power of receiving original suits, and deciding upon exparte testimony, the zeal, address or eloquence of individual members would have directed each decision ; and innumerable fraudulent individuals would have taken tickets which cost nothing, in a lottery which might yield prizes.

The progress of intellectual improvement gradually introduced several remedies for these evils. The original jurisdiction of the barons became appellate, so as to exclude the discussion of facts, and the frauds of ex-parte affidavit testimony. But the house of lords, still conscious of the inadequate nature of a numerous assembly for dispensing justice in particular cases, have been invested with a power of requiring the assistance of the judges; so that this appellate jurisdiction is practically exercised by twelve men of the best legal knowledge. By providing thus against fluctuating and inconsistent decisions and by subjecting the parties to costs, the incitement to try luck by frivolous suits has been suppressed.

The expenses of the English government were for a long time chiefly defrayed by lands appropriated to kings, but which soon came to be considered as national property, and when squandered by regal donations, were frequently as such reclaimed. The disposition of this national property, by the will, caprice, or favour of the sovereign, without any judicial interposition, guided by established laws and rules of evidence, was naturally infected with the taints of waste, and injury to the publick, so incurable, that in spite of the occasional resumptions of this landed national property, that resource for sustaining the government was at length exhausted, and taxation was necessarily substituted for it. At first, the king or sovereign claimed and exercised an absolute power of disposing of the national property in the shape of taxes, according to his pleasure; but, it was soon discovered that this pretended sovereign right over the national property operated upon taxes, just as it had done upon lands; and produced the same capricious misapplications and prodigality. After various struggles between the kings and the commons; by the first to retain, and by the second to destroy the royal sovereignty over the national property; the evil was at length imperfectly corrected by the establishment of a treasury department, under the superintendence of a court of exchequer, both subject to known laws, and fixed rules of evidence. The parliament, however, retained the sovereignty over the property of the nation, of which the king had been so justly deprived; and the innate viciousness of this political principle has produced in their hands, the same profusion which it caused in the hands of the king. Still howe-

ver, it deserves the praise of having established a court to prevent its own time from being diverted from great national concerns, and expended in the trial of trivial private suits. It
may perhaps be thought, that the English lords and commons
deserve no eulogy for a regulation, so wise, economical and just,
because they receive no wages; and that, had they been paid
by the day, at a rate fixed by themselves, each house would
have entertained all private suits for publick property, and
would long since have grown into courts of exchequer, the most
whimsical, burdensome and inconsistent which can be imagined;
and that as judges, whose income depends on their business,
will draw before them as many suits as they can, a perpetual
session of these two numerous courts, would long since have
been the consequence. I confess that all men, and particularly
the lords and commons of England, have disclosed sufficient
indications of a respect for money, to justify a supposition, that
if they could have acquired comfortable annuities by assuming
a judicial power over the property of the nation, it is not impossible that they would have yielded to the temptation.

But, besides the want of daily pay by these lords and commons, there was another obstacle to their trying suits and rendering judgments. The king had long been considered as the
fountain of justice, and they had laboured to deprive him of a
power to render it personally, or by *during-pleasure* judges. It
would have been an awkward business therefore for them to
practice that, which they had forbidden to the king as tyrannical, after they had gotten *during-good-behaviour* judges. The
king would forcibly have retorted upon them their own arguments. "You," he might have said, " have successfully proved
" in my case the mischiefs arising from a judicial power in one
" man, neither subject to impeachment or any appellate juris-
" diction. You have proved, that judges ought to hold their
" offices during good behaviour, without being subject to be
" dismissed from office, should I dislike their judgments. Are
" you subject to impeachment as judges, and removal from
" office; or to an appellate jurisdiction? Do you hold your
" places during good behaviour, as you say all judges ought to
" do? May not you be influenced by electors, as during-pleasure
" judges were by kings? If these judges would buy the vote or
" good will of the king by giving him the property and even

" the lives of individuals, in order to keep their offices; may
" not you be tempted to buy the votes or good will of electors,
" by giving to them the property of the nation? And are not
" you moreover exposed to the great influence of private friend-
" ship and family connexions, in acting as exchequer judges, or
" exercising an arbitrary power over the national property, from
" which my during-pleasure judges were free?" The English
lords and commons have avoided much of this retort, by for-
bearing in a considerable degree to meddle with judicial business.

The habit, which prevails in all the legislatures of the United
States, of trying individual suits or claims for publick property
evidently bears a strong resemblance to the old feudal modes
of dispensing justice and expending the publick property. Testimony is ex-parte. Evidence is not weighed by any rules. Ora-
tory and influence generally supply its place. No witnesses
are examined or confronted. The trial by jury is excluded.
Decisions are never directed by law, but always dictated by
policy, influence, selfish views or benevolence, except when
they are the result of accident, inattention, fluctuation of the
judges, ignorance of the truth, or some species of cunning management. In short, our exchequer legislative judgments are
generally rendered in the same mode, that legislative attainders
and confiscations were enacted during the most tyrannical
periods of the British histories.

It may however be objected, that looser principles are justi-
fiable in the disposition of the property of a nation, than that
of one man; and that what would be robbery in one case, is
munificence in the other; just as the killing of a single person
is murder, and the extirpation of a nation, heroism. Supposing
this reasoning to be sound in general, (and it must be admitted
to be so, if usage makes moral rectitude,) I think that it may be
controuled by national constitutions. It is admitted that all
civil powers are appendages of sovereignty, and that sovereignty may of course bestow them as it pleases. If a sovereign
monarch should appoint one set of men to form a code of laws,
and another to execute them, neither would think of discharging the functions of the other, nor would he suffer it. If we
were to select the plainest intention disclosed by the sovereignty of the people, none could be preferred to the separation

of legislative and judicial power; nor can I see how the legislatures of the state or federal governments can have acquired any judicial powers, except they can shew, that the sovereignty of the people is dead, having devised its estate, with all the appurtenances, privileges and emoluments, to the legislative department. Though no such will has been produced, yet the fact of the death of the sovereignty of the people seems to be presumable, from the sundry law suits about the division of the estate. All civil powers being appendages of sovereignty, if legislatures can assume judicial powers, they are undoubtedly entitled to the rest. The federal court has indeed made a division of the intestate's estate, among a family of political spheres, nominally upon principles of distribution, but essentially according to those of primogeniture, except that it is difficult to determine whether congress or itself is heir at law; or rather, according to the tenure called borough English, by which the youngest son gets all the estate. But this distribution, however it may reserve to the court something like legislative and even constituent powers, by no means invests legislatures with judicial, and menaces such a usurpation, by hurling a gauntlet at unconstitutional laws.

If the sovereignty of the people be however still alive, and we look into the commissions to make laws, we shall find no trace of a power to try suits. The law-makers take no judicial oath. They have no power to enforce the attendance of witnesses; nor does a single precaution exist for obtaining from legislators upright judgments, because they were not empowered to try any suits at all. In fact, the sovereignty of the people established a judicial power distinct from and independent of all other political spheres, for the purpose of securing property; and improved upon the principles of the English system of government in relation to it, by the identical maxim, considered among us as the only solid security for that and all other civil rights. Our maxim is, that a government is not a sovereign, but a trustee of the sovereignty of the people, invested only with limited powers and composed of co-ordinate departments established to discharge specified duties. This maxim withholds from these departments all the appendages of sovereignty, and only entitles them to exercise the powers bestowed. It deprives them of the absolute power over the lives and property of the people, claimed and exercised by every other species of sovereignty. Hence the creation of a judicial sphere became necessary, which would have been useless had legislative power possessed a sovereignty over property ; since, it could in that case have moulded courts according to its will, so as to make them subservient to its wishes. This corrects that principle of the English government, which has produced the greatest evils, " that the parliament is invested with an " absolute sovereignty over property and all other rights."

Whilst I contend that it is true in theory, that our legislatures do not possess a power of giving away the national property according to their caprices, or even from motives of benevolence; because, they are not invested with a sovereignty, but only with a trust in regard to it ; I admit that an adherence to this undoubted principle must, in a great measure, depend upon themselves. If, however, the men who compose them should turn their attention to this subject, and be convinced of the truth of the doctrine advanced, this dependance is far from being insecure. Our system of government is happily contrived to unite interest and patriotism ; and deviations from its principles, which may inadvertently arise, will therefore be corrected as they are discovered, so long as the system itself remains uncorrupted.

The practice of transferring the property of one man, or of one class of men to another, directly and unequivocally, gradually became unsafe even to despotism itself, and therefore it has been abandoned by the best of those governments which yet retain a sovereignty over property. But, although this species of tyranny has become too atrocious to be borne by any of the Europeans except those subject to the Turk, when inflicted without disguise, yet it is still pursued to a most oppressive extent by their governments, concealed behind exclusive privileges, pensions, and a variety of abuses, by which the evil is disseminated over a whole nation, and every individual, except the objects of its bounty, is injured.

Between the declaration of independence and the establishment of our present federal constitution, sundry legislative exertions of sovereign power had occurred, which displayed some of the evils deposited in that principle. Laws of attainder had past, and many partial confiscations of private property had been made, by laws of tender, and for suspending the administration of justice. The injustice and tyranny of these legislative usurpations, under pretence of being invested with a sovereign power over persons and property, induced the states to apply a remedy, by prohibiting themselves "from making "any thing but gold and silver a tender, from passing any bill of "attainder or ex post facto law, or any law impairing the obli- "gation of contracts." These appendages of sovereignty, prohibited to the states, are not delegated to congress. This constitutional fact proves, that none of our governments is invested with sovereign powers, and is particularly adverse to the novel idea of spherical sovereignties; for, if the union of all our political spheres will not constitute a sovereignty, surely it is not constituted by their separation. If neither of our departments constituted by the sovereignty of the people, nor all of them united, are a sovereignty, then they can only be co- ordinate deputies entrusted with appropriate powers. As no one is a sovereign, neither can suppress another. The legisla- tive department cannot suppress the judicial, nor the judicial the legislative. The former cannot prohibit the latter from rendering judgments according to law, nor the latter prohibit the former from legislating. In short, no department can con- stitutionally suspend the functions of another, because all de- rive their authority from the sovereignty of the people.

What then is the obligation of a contract, how is it to be en- forced, and how may it be impaired? The obligation of a con- tract arises from the consent of the parties, entered into under the sanction of the existing laws; and the constitutions under which we live, are a notification to them, that it is to be enforced by the judicial department having a jurisdiction of the case. The prohibition to impair contracts is directed to that quarter from whence only the impediments can proceed. This is le- gislative power. From hence the impediments which produced a positive vindication of the true spirit of our constitutions proceeded; and if the remedy be so construed, as to permit the very evil it designed to remove, both its reason and its end must be disregarded.

Every suspension of the payment of debts by law is an actual sequestration, which almost invariably terminates in a partial confiscation for the benefit of the debtor. If our legislatures do not possess a sovereign power to take away directly the property of one man, and give it to another, they have no power to do the same thing indirectly. Their office is to pass laws for establishing rules by which property is to be distributed; but when the right is vested under those laws, so long as they exist, it is beyond the cognizance of legislative, and appertains to judicial power. Laws cannot constitutionally transfer the property of debtors to creditors, nor of creditors to debtors, any more than they can transfer that of the rich to the poor or of the poor to the rich. It is our policy, that property should be divided by industry and not by any species of sovereign power; and our judicial departments were established for the preservation of that policy against whomsoever should molest or impair it; and particularly against executive and legislative power, by which the principle has been generally overturned.

A suspension of debts by replevy or any other laws, not only impairs contracts, by defeating the mutual risque, as to the fluctuation of money, voluntarily incurred by the contracting parties; but is always intended to operate, and generally does operate, as a confiscation of a portion of the property of the one, for the benefit of the other. In contemplation of this effect only are such laws either solicited or past. Besides this unconstitutional character, such laws are highly penal upon innocence, ex post facto, and participate largely of the nature of legislative attainders. Man cannot live over again the days he has past, nor postpone his wants until his incarcerated property is liberated. Though robbed of it but for a year, it is still a robbery in the proportion that year bears to his chance for life. He may starve, he may suffer, or he may be forced to sell his deferred stock at a loss, to get the necessaries of life. When the prison doors are unlocked, some is always found to have perished in jail, and all returns impaired by confinement, in its value. But such laws have effected their intention, though they violate the constitution; for the depreciation they produce in debts, by the fear and distress they inflict upon creditors, never fails to diminish their value, and to enable debtors to obliterate them by modes, incorrectly called payments. What species of patronage can be more unjust?

The evil of bad examples by governments is often greater, than the immediate mischiefs arising from the act itself. The replevy laws which have conferred on many individuals the use of property belonging to others, and invented easy modes of getting rid of debts, have induced the bankers also to exercise the power prohibited to the states; and taught them to refuse to pay their debts, in order to make money by sequestering the property of others, or to take time for effecting a confiscation, by becoming insolvent. The same example solicited individuals to seek for wealth by speculation in preference to industry, from a reliance on legislative shelter against payment. The catastrophe arising from the excitement to incur debt, happened in a year of exuberant plenty, as a providential demonstration of the inveterate malignity, contained in the principle of a sovereignty over property and its exercise by *impairing contracts*, to human happiness. The year 1818 produced unexampled abundance and unexampled complaints in the United States. The fields teemed with crops, and the newspapers with lamentations. All the comforts of life were plenty and cheap, but the United States resounded with distress. The beneficence of the Deity was insufficient to remedy or to satisfy the speculations of avarice. Disappointed in the hope of amassing wealth by cunning, it asserts, that the patronage of industry by providence ought to be countervailed by a patronage of speculation by legislatures. Despising constitutions from its innate depravity, it proposes to invest congress and the state legislatures with a common power of suspending specie payments in favour of banks, and the latter with a power of impairing all other private contracts. Banks stand at the head of the faction, which pretends to a degree of merit so transcendant, as to require the sacrifice of the second best principle of our political system. Their character defines that of their progeny. They have caused the nation to divide its money among swindlers, and those who have gotten it, request that the remnant of justice left to the injured may be converted into an additional reward for the guilty. The banking projects of England, exhibited in all the finery of fancy, are said to be worthy of our imitation; whilst the squalid legions they have helped to generate, the misery only controulable by a great army, and our own experience, are passed over as proving nothing. A sovereignty over private property is the European principle of government, to which I ascribe most of the European oppressions. An essential principle of our policy is, that private property cannot be constitutionally transferred by law to others, except for national purposes. To a deviation from this principle I ascribe many of our own sufferings.

A legislative sovereignty over the national property seems to me to have been unconstitutionally exercised to a great extent, and in a mode highly pernicious by what I shall call legislative patronage. It is true that in a few cases of a particular kind, the state legislatures are wisely invested with the power of making appointments; but with respect to the federal government completely, and to the state governments generally, the legislature raises the money, whilst some other department designates the person who shall receive it. The framers of all our constitutions must therefore have seen a distinction between legislation and patronage, and have conceived that our free form of government would be destroyed by their union in one body of men, if we may draw a conclusion from their efforts to keep them disunited. Personal calculations constitute the chief danger to be avoided in legislative bodies. If these can tax, bestow, and designate the receivers of publick money, personal calculations to a countless extent must be awakened. The advantages and gratifications resulting to ourselves from pecuniary favours to our friends, relations and partisans, influence most the minds of the ambitious and dangerous; and there is but little difference in the degree of corruption between patron and client. Kings and popes, who could corrupt civil and religious principles by patronage, could never remain virtuous themselves. The senate of Rome was converted into a despicable body of men by uniting legislation and patronage. The legislative assemblies of France owed both their crimes and their fate, to an honest opinion, that their conscious integrity and representative character might safely exercise both legislation and patronage. But the experiment terminated in a despotism. A division of the powers to raise and appropriate money for publick use, and to nominate the receivers of that money, is our constitutional precaution for sustaining a frugal and honest system of legislation; and for excluding stratagems for purchasing votes, providing for friends and gratifying vanity and avarice, from those bodies of men, upon whose purity and patriotism the continuance of a free and easy government depends. Even commiseration will be successfully implored to weep over the calamities of individuals, and easily persuaded to gratify its feelings *at the publick expense*; and to overlook the wounds it is inflicting on the constitution of its country, by assuming a sovereign power over its property.

It was an object of our constitutions to secure a common feeling between legislators and constituents under the operation of laws, whether good or bad. This is confessed to be a wise and just, and some think, an indispensable security for good laws. Can a legislator, who gives away the publick money to his friends, his clients, or his partisans; who is interested in the traffick of corporations, to be created and nurtured by his laws, or who can increase his own wages by protracting a session in trying private suits, be any other than a representative of himself?

Congress has already enlisted state governments among its clients, and these, like the Roman provinces, are reduced to the necessity of providing patrons in the senate. An union between legislation and patronage will enlist an assortment of suitors, composed of individuals who ask for dollars, of companies who ask for millions, and of states which ask for bounties, roads and canals. Patronage begets clientship. States will soon vociferously demand local favours, to balance other local favours. Why should not congress endow schools in the old, as well as the new states? I see no end to the parties, intrigues and animosities, by an usurpation on the part of the federal government of internal and local powers, and of unlimited patronage. These will not be less dangerous, for being geographical. Federal favours are at first silken fetters to the states, which will gradually be converted into iron by the menstruum of precedents, as soft stones exposed to the atmosphere become hard. Yes, I do see an end to this baleful policy, and I write only as a humble assistant to abler advocates of our constitution, towards obstructing its arrival. I see a nation dissected into pecuniary and political corporations; legislation dabbling in the frauds it fosters, and sharing in the spoils it bestows; representation converted into personal motives, incapable of detection; legislatures sinking into exchequer spendthrifts; hordes of speculators gambling with legislative judicial patronage, for private and publick property; the recommendations of frugality as indispensable to the continuance of our free form of government, so often recommended, and so steadily practised by two of the wisest and most virtuous patriots who ever blessed a nation (Washington and Jefferson) derided; in short, I see a picture bespangled with noxious meteors, gliding between our eyes and the admired system of government, under which we have enjoyed so much happiness.

The judicial mode of patronizing individuals has been assumed by legislatures, under a garb apparently innocent and lovely, nor have they perceived the corruption and unconstitutionality which it covered. It is the right of the people to petition, and the duty of the representatives to redress grievances. But no individual has a right to petition legislatures to perform judicial functions, or to expect that a constitutional division of powers and duties should be confounded for his benefit. Legislatures are well qualified to ascertain general principles, and utterly incompetent to ascertain particular facts. The first comprise the field of their power, and the second object, with the means for effecting it, is committed to the courts of justice. Can that be a legitimate jurisdiction, which is unable to come at truth, and of course, to do justice? A court of this character, which can only decide in favour of the plaintiffs; which cannot subject him to costs; which cannot give a final decision, nor prevent the most vexatious reiteration; which is annual or duennial, and also subject to influence in various ways; and where the judges must act as solicitors or attornies; is certainly a judicial monster. If this court should assume a power of trying suits between individuals, its incapacity would be instantly discerned even by itself; and yet it is better calculated for rendering justice in suits between these, than between individuals and the publick, because it would not be influenced by a notion of a sovereign power or right over the money in dispute, nor by ambition or a love of popularity. A judge between individuals could not benefit himself or a partisan to any great extent. If this be true, how can it be imagined, that our constitutions designed to exclude legislatures from a power to try suits between individuals, and yet to invest them with a right of trying suits between an individual and the publick? Is it to be imagined, that in the establishment of a judicial department, the security of the property of the whole nation was not at all regarded, whilst that of the poorest individual was protected by a salutary division of power ?

The federal constitution includes within the jurisdiction of the federal courts " *controversies to which the United States* " *shall be a party.*" How then can congress try them ? It enables congress to tax, not as having a sovereignty over property, but " to pay the debts, and provide for the *common defence and* " *general welfare.* of the United States." How then can it indulge a patronage in favour of individuals, or impose taxes for conferring local benefits ? The courts of all the states are open against the government; therefore, the state legislatures by exercising this judicial legislative patronage exercise a concurrent jurisdiction with these courts ; and it is often a reason for entertaining a cause, that the courts would decide against the claimant. Nothing has been more oppressive to nations, than the practice of kings, to buy popularity at their expense. Should this practice become established here, as we shall have three or four thousand kings, exercising sovereignty over the property of the nation, one need not be a conjurer to foresee the consequences. If the annual docket of all our legislative bodies were published, reasoning would be superfluous. It would account to a great extent, for our deviation so rapidly from that frugality, deemed essential to the preservation of liberty by almost all the real patriots who have ever appeared. Or, if our pension list were compared with the pension list of Great Britain, I believe we should be found to have already outstript her in the application of the maxim, "that governments are sove- " reigns over national property." The reason I suppose to be, that she has only one sovereign, whereas, according to the new opinions, we have at least two, each of which possesses an unlimited spherical sovereignty over property ; and these, instead of being units like those of Lacedemon, are above ten times as numerous as were the sovereign conscript fathers of Rome. If legislators are publick servants, their numerosity will be our salvation; but if they are sovereigns over our property, and exercise without controul judicial legislative patronage, the same numerosity must be our ruin. Avarice and ambition deride political restrictions, and talk of estimating how much liberty a people can bear ; but the fact is, that governments by their own morals mould them into a capacity to be free or to be enslaved. The French nation was soon moulded by the patronage and judicial usurpations of legislatures, into a fitness even for a military despotism; and then the sophistry which inflicted the evil, under pretence that the nation could not bear good government, prevailed; but these legislative errors were in fact the stepping-stones of fraud, the corrupters of the nation, and the ladders of ambition.

The reason why a nation is oppressed and enslaved, whenever one man, or any body of men, though elected by the people, shall absorb and exercise a sovereign power over property, is obvious. It disorders all balances, and overturns all checks, and establishes an irresistible authority. The framers of our excellent system of government, sensible that election and representation, however inestimable, were yet insufficient, alone, to prevent an evil which has frequently proved fatal to republican governments, called in divisions of power, checks and balances as auxiliaries. They divided legislation between local and internal objects, and those of an external or general nature; they excluded legislation from judicial functions; and they denied to every department of government the appendages of sovereignty. All were only fiduciaries, and the duties of each trustee were defined and limited. But if the congress, one of these departments, can pass local and internal laws; if it can give away the publick money by no rule but its own pleasure; and if it can exercise judicial functions, it cannot be in conformity with those principles upon which our system of government was established.

I recollect but two classes of claims, which can be offered to legislatures by individuals or corporations; the gratuitous, and the just. As to the first, if legislatures are only trustees, and do not possess a sovereign power over property, they have no right to exercise benevolence at the expense of its owners. As to the second, they are constitutionally prohibited, and internally disabled from dispensing justice to individuals. Particular laws for rendering individual justice, instead of general laws extending to all similar cases, are substantially judgments and decrees. Their character resembles a scheme of jurisprudence, which should exclude general rules of inheritance, and leave it to legislation to provide for each case. They are exactly the same in principle with the mode of rendering justice, adopted in Turkey. A fluctuating will and pleasure decides upon an imperfect enquiry after facts, instead of a general law, to be executed by judicial investigation. If the individual grievance be real, it ought to be the basis of a general law extending the remedy to all similar cases ; and if such a law would be an evil to the community, the supposed individual grievance cannot exist. The multitude of suits for publick property, instituted before legislatures, evinces that such claims are not solitary, but similar to a great extent; and that there would be no great difficulty in framing a law, by which the just might be reached, and the unjust excluded. Thus fixed rules of decision would be commuted for fluctuating, truth might be discovered, and our legislative bodies might avoid a waste of time, in trying frivolous claims in an imperfect manner, which no other legislatures that I know of have ever incurred.

We have not lost sight of our great question of internal legislation by congress, in considering this subject. On the contrary I contend, admitting the state legislatures to possess a sovereignty over property, and a right to bestow the publick money upon objects of benevolence, that it is a subject for internal and local legislation, not comprised within the powers of the federal government. It is true, that the federal constitution invests congress with a limited and special power in relation to persons, but it cannot act upon persons beyond the power bestowed. By referring to the constitution it will be found, that all the powers over persons given to congress are intended to effect some general federal end, and not to confer any right to legislate over persons, except for such a purpose. As for instance ; the power over persons in the imposition of taxes is given for the purpose of providing a revenue. No power to lavish the revenue thus obtained, in donations to individuals, is bestowed ; on the contrary, it is limited to the use of the United States. If this reasoning be correct, the donation to the remnant of the revolutionary army, (a remnant more numerous than the army itself at the end of the war, after an interval of above thirty years,) was unconstitutional. Whether this donation was constitutional or not, it is a monument of what is to be expected from the principle of a legislative sovereignty over the national property, and the effects of a casual humoursome enthusiasm, which had slept for near forty years, and was awakened, not by reason or justice, but by the sound of a drum.

President Adams has somewhere said, I believe, that liberty consisted in an equality of laws. The definition is good, as far as it goes; but it is imperfect in being only one ingredient of liberty. An equality of oppression, which may exist with an equality of laws, cannot constitute liberty. It would be a better maxim to say, that liberty cannot subsist under an inequality of laws, by which one portion of the society or associators is endowed with exclusive benefits. Upon this maxim the union of the states was founded. The states were the associators, and in their compact laboured to prevent congress from being able to distribute among the members of the association, by the instrumentality of exercising local or internal powers over persons or things, unequal advantages; because, an inequality of laws would destroy the equality of rights among the associators, intended by their compact to be established. Hence that body was only invested to legislate upon subjects common to all. Suppose that a body of guardians were appointed to take care of an estate held in common by twenty-three virgins, each of whom held also a particular estate, over which these guardians were not invested with any power. If these guardians should endeavour to corrupt and seduce some of these virgins by using the profits of the estate held in common, to improve several of the particular estates, by cutting canals or making roads; by granting bounties or exclusive privileges to some of the tenants of the particular estates, to be paid by the tenants of other particular estates; or by bestowing pensions on others of these tenants, to be paid out of the profits of the common estate; what maxim of equality, of justice, or of liberty, would they fulfil?

The constitution of the union prohibits to the state governments a power of regulating currency, and limits the power of congress to the establishment of a metallick currency. These restrictions of power, in relation to the representative of property, do not recognize in either government an absolute power over property itself. On the contrary, it was idle and vain to limit the powers of government as to the sign of the thing, if the government possessed a despotick power over the thing itself. Where is the difference in principle between giving away fifty millions of the national property in pensions, and in giving away the whole? And what power over property can be more despotick, than a power thus to dispose of it? The restrictions as to currency, combined with the division of legislative and judicial powers, evince, that this sovereign power over property did not exist under our principles of government.

The restrictions as to taxing property, imposed upon both the federal and state governments, also recognize only a limited power over it in either; and as to the application of taxes, it is, in the case of the former, expressly limited to the execution of the powers delegated, for which purpose and no other the power of taxation was bestowed. Among the powers delegated, there is none to grant pensions, or to dispose of the public money according to the dictates of caprice, or benevolence, as the English kings claimed a right to do. As to the state governments, the same principle, which is the only sound security for civil liberty, ought also to be a security for property. As trustees, they have no better right to give away one than the other. If they cannot take away the property of A to give it to B, what right have they to take away property from the whole alphabet, to give it to B?

Societies are not instituted for the purpose of enabling governments to destroy natural rights; and as no man possesses a natural, or necessary, or convenient power over the natural rights of another, a majority of men cannot have a right to surrender to a government an absolute power over these natural rights. I have previously endeavoured to prove, that the freedom of conscience and of labour are essentially natural rights. If it be the intention of a society to erect a government for the purpose of protecting both, an invasion of either is a deviation from that intention; and nothing can be more unconstitutional than a stab at the vital part of our political system. Neither nature, nor necessity, nor convenience, has invested the people, or their representatives, with an absolute power over private property, or over conscience; and though mankind were long deluded by fraud into an opinion, that civil government could not subsist without one species of tyranny, this imposition is so thoroughly exploded, that it ought to suggest a strict examination of the other. The same orators, whose eloquence so long suppressed the rights of conscience, now plead, that civil government cannot subsist without regulating property by charters, establishments, corporations, exclusive privileges, bounties and pensions; the same instruments by which they contended that conscience ought to be regulated; for they say, that free opinion as to the use of property will be as pernicious to the publick, as free opinion in relation to religion was, according to their exploded doctrines. Luxury is now made the heresy, by which the new order of apparent zealots, but cool calculators of dollars and cents, advance their designs. Wealth and power to priests was the pretended cure of heresy; wealth and power to corporations and combinations and pensioners, is the pretended cure of luxury. The orators long persuaded mankind, that they would damn themselves by heresy, if they enjoyed a freedom of opinion as to religion; they now endeavour to persuade them that they will ruin themselves by luxury, if they enjoy a freedom of opinion as to property.

In selecting general principles, we ought to be guided by general effects, and not by particular cases. Several devout ministers undoubtedly deserved the salaries derived from an absolute power in a government over the freedom of conscience; and several worthy pensioners undoubtedly deserve also the pensions derived from an absolute power in governments over the freedom of property; but both powers are so incurably exposed to abuses, and an exercise of judicial powers and legislative patronage so incurably infected with qualities of irreconcilable enmity with the virtue, happiness and interest of a community, that the policy of being led astray from the general good, by particular cases, is simply that of preferring an oppressive to a free and moderate government.

It is an error to suppose, that the people approve of bad measures, because they are silent. In all nations, the majority approve of political morality; and they are silent, both from the influence of government and a want of time or information to detect its infraction. Therefore, they are seldom roused into resistance, except by the extremity of the evil. Our governments are so happily contrived to influence those in power in favour of truth and justice, as to infuse into the people a reliance on their structure, which yet farther disposes them to be inattentive to the laws. But, this reliance dictates a cautious watchfulness against the introduction of any new principles, by means of laws or legislative patronage, undermining the basis of the reliance itself, by having the effect of exchanging an influence in favour of truth and justice, designed to be estab-

lished by the structure of our governments, for an influence in
favour of partiality, exclusive privileges and erroneous principles. It is impossible to convince the suitors of legislative
tribunals, the feeders upon legislative patronage, or the receivers
of exclusive privileges, bestowed, not by constitutions, but by
laws; that legislative bodies ought not to possess the unholy
power of converting publick property into private donations:
but, if the question was propounded to the people, silent as
they have been upon the subject, " whether legislatures had not
" better employ the portion of their sessions, worse than wasted
" in trying and deciding cases of cupidity, in a thorough ex-
" amination of treasuries, and an annual disentanglement of
" the destinations of the taxes," would the answer of their
moral sense and common sense accord with the practice, to
which they have indiscreetly submitted? Do they really approve
of the new policy of sacrificing the general good to private interest?

When the human mind receives a strong impulse towards
either truth or error, it is difficult to check the current of conviction or prejudice, and to give it a new direction. The impulse derived from our revolutionary principles was strongly
adverse to legislative sovereignty and exclusive privileges, and
a counter-current in their favour has been gradually introduced.
One flows from truth, and the other from error. Being opposed,
they are of different characters. In which are we to look for
that mercenary temper which has notoriously generated for the
few last years an unusual number of instances of moral turpi-
tude, and materially affected the national character? Morals
are regulated by religion or by laws. Our religion will not be
accused of imperfection. A love of money or of property,
nurtured by fraud, becomes sordid and base; but nurtured by
justice, it is a source of civilization, of virtue, of happiness, and
the bond of society. If it could be destroyed, civilized society
would perish. But the value of property is a temptation to
fraud, and the end of government is to restrain and correct this
temptation. If then, governments themselves shall yield to it
by contriving means to transfer property from the community
to individuals, each culprit in contemplating their example will
conclude, that if this be right in relation to a whole nation, it
cannot be wrong in relation to one man; and so the national
character is changed.

SECTION 14.

THE LAWS OF NATIONS.

This formidable phalanx has with great ingenuity been impressed into the service of spherical sovereignty. The philosophers
who invented them, were actuated by the benevolent intention
of civilizing the intercourse between nations, and softening the
evils of war ; and not by the wicked design, of increasing domestick oppression, by dissolving restrictions imposed for the
security of civil liberty. They did not intend by restraining
the ravages of avarice and ambition, when exercised against nations, to turn them loose upon individuals. Little would be gained from these laws by mankind, at the expense of opening those
sluices at home, through which they have so often been flooded
with misery ; and if the laws invented by one set of benevolent
philosophers, to civilize nations in their commerce with each
other, should demolish those contrived by another set of benevolent philosophers, to procure internal national happiness, the
former will evidently produce more evil than good. The self-
constituted legislators, who compiled the laws of nations, drew
their conclusions from the then established principle "that
"governments were invested with sovereignty ;" but our constitutions, framed by legitimate legislators, are founded upon the
principle "that there is no sovereignty among men, except
"that species which resides in the people or society." The
question therefore is, whether a false principle shall destroy
a true one ; or whether rules recommended without authority
ought to supersede those established in the most perfect mode.
The old principle placed nations in a state of vassalage to governments ; the new one places governments in a state of dependance upon nations. Without launching into the ocean of
despotism, created by the old principle, it will suffice to observe,
that governments could sell or give away the people, or their
property, and alter or abolish the form of the government

itself. The power of treating away a part of the community, and transferring them to any degree of tyranny, far transcends that of taxing them without their consent. The cortes of Spain saw the enormity of this power, and endeavoured to moderate it, by prohibiting its exercise, without the concurrence of a representative assembly : but we have gone farther ; and by withholding from our governments the powers of sovereignty of which this was one, abolished it entirely, by rooting out the error from which it sprouted up. The rights of declaring war, and of creating corporations or granting exclusive privileges, as considered by the writers upon the laws of nations, were rights of sovereignty ; but the case of war is specially provided for by the federal constitution, because the federal government, as having no sovereignty, could not otherwise have declared it; whilst no provision is made for the cases of corporations and exclusive privileges, because none was necessary ; these, therefore, were abolished, as being powers derived from the old doctrine of a sovereignty in governments. As the powers of making war and peace were necessary, it became necessary also to provide for them, not as emanations from the principle of a sovereignty in governments, but as delegated powers conferred by the social sovereignty, or natural right of self-government. Several conclusions result from this reasoning. No powers in relation to war are derived from the old doctrine of a sovereignty in governments under our system ; and none can be justly inferred from the conclusions of the writers upon the laws of nations, deduced from that old doctrine. As it was thought necessary to delegate powers in relation to war to the federal government, it is plain that without such a delegation, the framers of the constitution did not conceive that the federal government would possess any powers at all in relation to war. If the federal government would have possessed no powers at all in relation to war, had none been delegated to it by the states, because it has no sovereignty, either innate or conventional ; the conclusion amounts to a demonstration, that it has no power to create corporations, or grant exclusive privileges, because such powers must either flow from an innate sovereignty, or from an express delegation, and neither of these sources of power exists in the cases of corporations, pensions and exclusive privileges.

But this reasoning is endeavoured to be overthrown, by inferring the powers of sovereignty from a delegated power; as the power of establishing banks, from the power of taxation; the power of granting exclusive privileges and pensions, from the power of regulating commerce and appropriating publick money; and the power of making roads and canals, from the power of declaring war. To deduce the powers of sovereignty from the delegated powers, the greater powers from the lesser, undefined and unlimited powers from defined and limited; is an evident inversion of reasoning, which terminates in the conclusion, that the limited powers substituted for the unlimited powers of sovereignty, supposed to have been abolished, furnish inferences which revive these same unlimited powers of sovereignty.

But in the case of war, this mode of reasoning was not foreseen. When two nations are at war, a third may subject itself to a legitimate attack from either, by certain actions; yet even in this case, which calls for a prompt decision, the constitution pays no regard to the idea of a spherical sovereignty; and disregarding the language of the laws of nations, assigns the power, as in every other case where a declaration of war may be necessary, to a department, not as being sovereign, but as being a trustee of the sovereign power. This trustee alone possesses a right to involve the United States in war; and no other department, nor any individual, has a better right to do so, than a constable has to bring the same calamity upon England. As the laws of nations cannot deprive congress of any power with which it is invested by the constitution, so they cannot invest congress or any other department, with any power not bestowed by the constitution. If the laws of nations could bestow any powers under our system, there would be great difficulty in ascertaining the department which should receive them. They contemplate the powers of declaring war and making peace, as residing in an executive department; but the constitution divides them, and does not intrust the president with either. Which then of these three departments shall receive the new powers, drawn from the law of nations? As to these, the constitution is silent, except that so far from recognizing any sovereignty in either, it rejects the idea entirely by a division of powers allotted to sovereignty by the laws of nations. As these laws cannot find a sovereignty to receive their bounty, is it to be bestowed according to their recognition of executive power as the recipient ; or can there be any recipient at all under the federal constitution, which only creates departments with limited powers, and does not create any species of sovereignty ? If congress does receive the powers of sovereignty from the laws of nations, then it may create corporations, because being invested with sovereignty, these laws have an object to act upon, and to endow with powers ; but, if these laws cannot give sovereignty to congress, they can give it nothing. Upon this hinge the right of creating corporations turns, as belonging to the powers of sovereignty. If the power of creating corporations results from a paramount spherical sovereignty, all other powers allowed to sovereignty by the laws of nations follow it, and henceforward, considering the liberality of the laws of nations to sovereignty, the difficulty will not be, to discover what powers congress has, but what it has not. The question, therefore, is, whether these laws of nations or our constitutions have delegated powers to our political departments. If it should be decided in favour of the constitutions, sovereignty and the laws of nations united cannot create corporations, nor confer any power whatsoever ; if against them, these allies can convey every other power, as well as one to create corporations.

It was wholly unnecessary to the advocates of a power in congress to make corporations, roads and canals, to append the two latter among the wide spreading branches of the war-making power, if a paramount spherical power to remove obstacles, by setting aside the state power of internal taxation, existed ; because this species of sovereignty would as easily be made to reach internal things, as persons : but still there is much ingenuity in the habit of allowing limitations to this prolifick source of power, whenever one is drawn from it, because this language is less alarming to the nation, than an undisguised claim of power in virtue of spherical sovereignty, construed by the laws of nations. It is agreed, that the powers of congress, inferred from the paramount sovereign power of declaring war, are limited to things useful in war, and only roads and canals are as yet specified as among these useful things. Now mark the united effect of the concession, and its example ; and it instantly appears, that they cover all the ground which the most absolute sovereignty can occupy, or at least enough to satisfy the utmost greediness for power. Men, food, agriculture, manufactures, clothes, horses, iron, leather, powder, lead, liquors, and many other things, are more useful in war than roads and canals ; and are not of a more local, and internal nature. It would be ridiculous to say, that a flourishing state of agriculture would be a less useful preparation for war, than a power in congress to make roads and canals. If the powers of congress are impliedly extended to means useful in war, they must embrace such as are important, as well as those which are trifling. Insignificant as these roads and canals are in themselves, they cover a boundless political space. They carry the powers of congress, to be exerted according to its own will, to every thing at least, equally useful in war. By this doctrine, congress may create corporations to provide food, clothes, horses, iron, powder, lead, liquors, and even men for war; or to manage agriculture and manufactures ; for, these are undoubtedly as convenient and necessary for war, as banks are for taxation. The doctrine by which this construction is asserted, collected and condensed, is this : "The federal constitution "has not prohibited implied powers ; whatever is useful, neces-"sary or convenient in the execution of the delegated powers, "constitutes an implied power ; the receiver of the expressed "power is the sole judge of the extent of the implied power, "in two cases only ; those of congress and the supreme court "of the United States; congress in virtue of a paramount "spherical sovereignty may remove every obstacle to its action "from subordinate spheres ; the states are subordinate spheres, "and congress may restrict their right of internal taxation, if "it obstructs the execution of any implied power in the opinion "of the federal court; but this court is not a subordinate "sphere to congress, and it has the exclusive power of obstruct-"ing the action of congress by setting aside laws as unconsti-"tutional." This medley of conclusions is collected indiscriminately from the constitution, the idea of sovereignty, and the explanations of that idea scattered in the laws of nations ; but there is no confusion in their design. They unequivocally tend to the destruction of the state governments, and the erection of some non-descript federal government upon their ruins.

The road precedent is enough to justify congress in a restriction of the state right of taxation, to a demolishing extent, according to the decision of the federal court in the bank case; as it might legislate upon every other object useful in war, and the court would determine that the states could not tax those objects. I can recollect nothing which might not, according to the doctrines advanced, be made an object of exclusive legislation by congress. It might abolish slavery as useful for war. It might legislate over the class of free blacks, for some useful war purpose. Let war be the propositum, and all means useful to prepare for, or prosecute it, are considered as its legitimate progeny of powers, and the federal judges must have erred, in admitting the federal government to be a limited one. It would resemble the praying wheel of some Russian hordes, patched round with prayers, from which the Deity may pick and choose as he pleases.

To me this new notion of a constitution by implication is, I confess, exactly like no constitution at all; nor has it been proved to my satisfaction, that principles ought to be lost in verbal definitions, or property crushed in the jaws of sovereignty by its prerogatives, to create corporations, exclusive privileges and pensions, bestowed upon it by the laws of nations. I have not the least doubt that the United States, though they thought the federal government highly trust-worthy, as is proved by the great powers with which they invested it, thought themselves trust-worthy also, in relation to the inferior powers retained; nor was it presumptuous, whilst they were granting a power to raise armies, to imagine that they might be confided in for making roads. If they cannot, with what right affecting the publick good, can they be trusted? and if this pitiful suspicion is sufficient to deprive them of a power so inconsiderable, ought not the mistrust to swell as a power becomes greater, and the reason for an assumption of local powers by congress, to reach every case of more importance than roads?

I think the constitution contains internal evidence, adverse to that construction, which, taking its stand upon a supposed paramount spherical sovereignty, and armed with mining tools by the laws of nations, endeavours to work out a new division of powers between the federal and state governments, by the pioneer implication. Where was the necessity of adding the power of raising armies to that of declaring war, if this pioneer could dig new powers out of those expressed? Surely the raising of armies was as much an appurtenance of declaring war, as making roads. Arguments of this kind might be greatly multiplied, but I will endeavour to include them in a general observation. Supposing all means convenient or necessary for the execution of an expressed power to pass with it by implication, the powers of taxing and declaring war would include, with less violence than one is made to include banks and the other roads, many of the powers also actually given to congress, together with so many more, as to obliterate to a great extent, or entirely, from the constitution, the idea of a limited government. Now, as means which would have been included by the implication-mode of defining powers, are yet expressed, does it not follow, that other means not expressed are not delegated by implication, since otherwise the expression of any was a mere tautology? It was bestowing powers by a specification, which, as this mode of construction supposes, had before passed, along with the mother power, by implication. There is no such incongruity in that mode of construction, which supposes, that a division of internal and external means, as well as of internal and external powers between the federal and state governments, was intended to be established by the constitution. The publick confidence does not seem to have been exclusively extended to either of these governments in the division of powers; was it suddenly withdrawn from one, in the case of means? In this view, as means are powers, their division between governments intended as checks upon each other was as necessary as a division of any other powers; and the local or internal rule, applied to powers expressed, was equally called for by implications of new powers under the disguised name of means.

It is obvious, that this word "means" is only a tautology of the words "necessity and convenience," and therefore I will illustrate the nature of the coalition by another quotation. In the famous trial of Hampden in the case of ship-money, the decision of all the judges of England, except Crook and Hutton, was in these words: "That the king might *levy taxes* " without grant of parliament in *cases of necessity*, or when the

" kingdom was in *danger; of which danger and necessity his*
" *majesty was the sole and final judge.*" Lord Clarendon, though
a court-writer and partial to the king, makes the following observation upon this decision : " The damage and mischief can-
" not be expressed, that the crown sustained by the deserved
" reproach and infamy that attended this behaviour of the
" judges, who out of their courtship, submitted the grand ques-
" tion of law to be *measured by* what they called the *standard*
" *of general reason and necessity.*" And, says another histo-
rian, " the people by this decision were struck with despair,
" and *concluded very justly, that magna charta and the old*
" *English constitution were at an end.*" How nearly related are
this " general reason" and " the laws of nations !"

Means being only necessities or conveniences, the application of this precedent to our subject is obvious. To measure
the grand question of the parliamentary right of taxation by
the standard of general reason and necessity, was the same
thing, as to measure the state right of taxation by the same
standard. In both cases, a plain positive right would be subverted by necessary or convenient means. The king's claim
of an exclusive right of judging as to his means, was equivalent
to an exclusive right by congress of judging as to their means.
If this spherical power in the king was sufficient to destroy
magna charta, and the old constitution of England ; it is sufficient to destroy the new constitution of the United States.
The destruction in England would have been effected by anni-
hilating the balancing powers of the lords and commons ; the
destruction it will effect here, will arise from the annihilation
of the balancing powers of the state governments. This decision in England was bottomed upon the words paramount and
sovereignty as construed by the laws of nations. Had the
judges considered the principle of co-ordination as applicable
to king, lords and commons, they could never have decided
that one sphere might resort to means for taking away powers
from the others. But by endowing one sphere with a paramount sovereignty, and then enquiring of the laws of nations
what was meant by a paramount sovereignty in the king, it
was discovered, that it was something which had a right to remove all obstacles to its action, proceeding from subordinate
spheres (as the lords and commons were supposed to be,) out of

the way. So here, by rejecting the principle of co-ordination as inapplicable to the federal and state governments, and endowing the former with a paramount sovereignty, and then enquiring of the laws of nations what a paramount sovereignty is, the conclusion also follows, that it is something which has a right to remove all obstacles out of its way. The judges decided, that the royal sphere was only limited by spherical sovereignty, supremacy, necessity, convenience, and means of which the king was to be the sole judge; but the nation considered the decision as destructive of its constitution. If our congressional sphere be only limited by spherical sovereignty, supremacy, necessity, convenience, and means of which it is the sole judge, can the nation believe that it will preserve the constitution of the United States?

The security, arising from representation, is so repeatedly urged to defeat the force of these observations, that it must be repeatedly noticed. The undeniable fact, that sovereignty expounded by the laws of nations has in every form oppressed mankind, suggested to them the idea of dividing it, before they had conceived the idea of a government throughout responsible, and subservient to the interest of the community. In these divisions, representation has been subjected to restraints; but if it cannot be restrained because it is representation; if it can destroy the checks imposed upon itself, then no government can admit of checks, balances, or divisions of power, in which representation is an ingredient; and mankind after a long travail have returned to the very doctrine they have been trying to abolish, namely, that they must inevitably elect between a despotism in one, a few, or in many, because representation may be trusted with unlimited power. Confined to such a choice, they have generally agreed that the last species of sovereignty is the worst of its bad associates.

But we have encountered the doctrine of sovereignty in representation, because it is representation, by a great variety of constitutional limitations and restrictions upon representation; thus expressing a publick opinion, that, invested with sovereign power, it could not be confided in. We have made executive power a representative of the people; shall this, like legislative, extract sovereignty from representation? But, as if to puzzle inextricably the extractors of sovereignty from representation,

we have made both the federal and state governments representative, and given to each the quality said to absorb sovereignty;
nor is there any way of getting over this unlucky moral equality,
but by asserting that representation is paramount to representation.

An interlude was played off many years ago between the
treaty-making power and the house of representatives of congress, applicable to this idea of a spherical sovereignty. The
treaty-making power contended, that the house of representatives had no right to contravene the means it had resorted to
within its sphere of action, but were obliged, in obedience to
its paramount spherical sovereignty, to appropriate money for
carrying a treaty into execution. But it being a case at which
the federal court could not get, there was no tribunal able to
remove the obstruction of a refusal to surrender a constitutional
discretion, as to appropriating money by the house of representatives; and they arrayed the positive powers conferred by
the constitution, against the implied powers and paramount
means claimed by the treaty-making power, though defended by
many quotations from the laws of nations. The positive power,
of taxation reserved to the states, has not been so fortunate in
its controversy with the implied power in congress to create a
bank, merely because a powerful ally of the latter has inter-
posed; for I cannot discern any distinction between the cases.
The doctrines of a paramount spherical sovereignty, of means,
of convenience and of necessity, drawn from the laws of nations, were the pillars which sustained the pretensions of the
treaty-making powers over the house of representatives, as they
are now repeated, to deprive the states of a power as expressly
reserved to them by the federal constitution, as the power of
appropriating was to congress. But, co-ordinacy kept its ground
in one case, and subordination is imposed in the other.

I think this concubinage between these words and the laws
of nations is very fairly detected, by observing that the 8th,
9th and 10th sections of the constitution comprise a system of
delegated and prohibited powers, by which some are *expressly*
prohibited to the states, and others *expressly* delegated to congress. Delegation is a species of prohibition, which begins
where delegation ends. The objects in view were, to bestow
exclusive powers on a federal government, to retain exclusive

powers to the state governments, and to invest both with concurrent powers. This third class was the least numerous, and consisted chiefly of taxation and promoting arts and sciences. If a specification of the concurrent powers bestowed on congress was not intended as a limitation of this class of powers, congress may exercise any power which the state governments can exercise; if it was, congress cannot exercise concurrently with the state governments, any power not contained within the specification of that class. If the specification of the exclusive powers given to congress be a limitation of that class of powers, the specification of the concurrent powers given to congress must be a limitation of that class also; because candid reasoning does not admit of a different construction of the same cases in the same instrument. The specification of both classes of power, the exclusive and concurrent, must therefore prohibit congress in both cases from extending the powers delegated, or in neither. Yet, as if the principles by which these two classes of delegated powers are limited were not the same, the catalogue of exclusive powers has received no addition that I recollect, whilst that of concurrent powers, originally much the shortest, is daily growing. The precedents of the alien and sedition laws, and of the bank corporation, recognize a concurrent power in congress with the state governments, over persons; and that as to roads, a concurrent power over every thing useful in war. Under the operation of these precedents, which have arisen merely from selecting six or eight very comprehensive words, and making a glossary of the laws of nations, the federal constitution is rapidly becoming an instrument, by which sundry very great powers are exclusively bestowed upon congress, and by which nearly all other powers are consigned to the concurrent class, so as to leave very few exclusive powers to the state governments, except those which go to the organization of the federal government.

SECTION 15.

THE MISSOURI QUESTION.

It is with great reluctance that I consider a question, which has been so ably discussed with so little edification; but it constitutes a proof so forcible, in favour of the construction of the federal constitution for which I have contended, that it cannot be neglected.

The idea of a balance of power between two combinations of states, and not the existence of slavery, gave rise to this unfortunate, and as I shall endeavour to prove, absurd controversy. What is the political attitude of nations towards each other, supposed by a balance of power? Hostility. What is the effect of hostility? War. A balance of power is therefore the most complete invention imaginable for involving one combination of states, in a war with another. It is in its nature, and will be in its consequences, equivalent to the balance of power between England and France; and after a series of bargains and contrivances to stunt or pilfer each other, the party worsted in the warfare, disguised by these bargains and contrivances, will be driven by interest or resentment to use more destructive arms.

But can this happen, when congress itself is to hold the scales, make the bargains, and adjust the balance? If it would discharge this business fairly, a balance of power would be worth nothing, nor would a preponderance be so fiercely contended for. The extreme anxiety to obtain a preponderance acknowledges a thorough conviction on both sides, that a majority in congress will not make fair bargains; and that it will sacrifice the interest of some states and individuals to advance that of others. The very first debate under the influence of this new balance of power has ascertained, that it will destroy the old federal principles, founded in similar and sympathetick interests, and transform congress into a body, merely diplomatick. The new confederation to be substituted for the old one, ought to be stated without disguise, that it may be duly estimated, and compared with its rival. It proposes to draw a geographical line between slavery and no-slavery; to train the people on each side of it, into an inveterate habit of squirting noisome provocations at each other through the press; and to create a degree of animosity as an ally to ambition and avarice, quite sufficient to induce a preponderating balance to exert its whole energy, in obtaining exclusive advantages. Thus every vestige of the federal union, according to the existing compact, would be gradually destroyed, because the two bands of congressional negotiators would be employed in making successive bargains in relation to the balance of power, or in triumphantly exercising an acquired preponderance over a vanquished adversary; and every new bargain like the one already made, and every new partiality, would be an alteration of the federal constitution. Congress would be converted by the new federal scheme of a balance of power, between two combinations of states, into a convention, meeting annually to make new bargains for obtaining a preponderance, and local advantages over each other; or in fact to make annually a new federal constitution. To those who saw the difficulty of making that we now have, the consequences of this species of policy will be quite plain.

It will very much resemble the whig and tory policy of England. By that, two parties were artificially created, whose whole business it was to get money and power, without any regard to the publick good. The parliament retained its representative and debating qualities, but the intention of discussion and deliberation was wholly defeated. The most conclusive reasoning ceased to make any impression, and every decision, almost every individual vote, is certainly foreseen before a deliberation. But there is one very material difference between this new project for a balance of power in the United States, and the English balance between whigs and tories. Ours will superadd to the disgusting moral deformities of theirs, the hideous feature of being geographical.

Our idea of a balance of power contemplates two spacious territories, with the population of each separately integral, as conglomerated by an adverse interest; and though substantially federal in themselves, substantially anti-federal with respect to each other. It is absurd to imagine that slavery is the real con-glutinator of these conglomerations, (hard words will be par-doned on this hard subject,) because one party cannot want slaves, now that the slave trade is abolished; would not keep them; and a rape, like that of the Sabine women, is by no means to be apprehended; and because, should any disposition exist to take them away, the other party are quite willing to part with them.

A political balance of power, and a crusade against slavery, through the bowels of the constitution, are two things so very distinct, that a thousand reasons might be urged against their supposed consanguinity; I shall, however, only trouble the reader with six. First, the crusade would certainly destroy the union; now the conviction of both parties, that it is their interest to preserve it, causes a profession on the part of our balance-mongers, that this new division is intended to cement it. Secondly, zeal to abolish slavery may find ample food, without hazarding the union upon the experiment. The Bra-zils, Cuba, or Africa itself, would supply it with ample employ-ment for the furor liberandi. Thirdly, a little matter of trade might be mingled with crusades to these countries; and if in Africa for instance, things should not be found ripe for chivalry, a consolation for the disappointment might be found in lucra-tive return cargoes for the other two countries. Fourthly, the honour of a crusade against foreigners, and in one case hea-thens, would be as great as the honour of a crusade against brethren and christians, and the danger would be less. Fifthly, it is prudent, when a resolution is taken to set fire to some body's house, to go far from home, lest the flames may reach our own, as the wind is apt to change. Sixthly, if our consciences tell us that we ought to enslave freemen, to make slaves free, and to cause the destruction of a million or two of people, white and black, in the good work, nature tells us to give the prefer-ence in such favours, to those who need them most; and not to destroy the rights and lives of those whom we love and who love us, because they are suffering a misfortune imposed on them by others. My imagination seizing upon this suggestion went to work, and conjured up a set of witches before my eyes, who seemed to be pouring into a huge cauldron called the

United States, a collection of poisonous ingredients, all labelled at top "slavery," and to be singing,

> " Double, double, toil and trouble,
> " Fire burn, and cauldron bubble."

But upon looking at the underside of the labels, I invariably discerned the words " ambition, avarice, exclusive privileges, bounties, pensions and corporations."

The subject of internal slavery was definitively disposed of by the federal compact, and it would be a fraud to open it again. To violate the compact as to a local internal affair, would destroy it. For above thirty years since the last union, this subject, unstirred, has given the United States no trouble. No reflecting man can hesitate to believe, that our experience has ascertained, that let alone, it will be harmless to the union; and that if it be used to excite hostile feelings between two great divisions of states, its mischiefs may exceed the most apprehensive anticipation. Besides, all politicians agree that a reformation of long standing evils is best effected by slow remedies, and the progress made by the states themselves towards diminishing this, shews that they may be trusted with confidence in an affair of their own, of which they are the rightful and best judges.

When I was at college in 1775, a shoemaker sometimes made speeches to the students to invigorate them in the patriotism so necessary at that period. Being intoxicated upon one of these occasions, he was obliged to sustain himself by a post in the street whilst he delivered his harangue, which he demonstrated by concluding with the maxim "united we stand, divided I fall," and letting go the post, down he tumbled. The post, it is true, kept its ground; but if the union be lost, no divination is necessary to foresee, that every state will get a fall. If the United States are intoxicated by the word "slavery" not only to let go, but to dig up the post, by which they are supported, how will the comparison stand between them and the drunken shoemaker?

I have said that this new policy is absurd, and I will attempt to prove it. A permanent balance of power can only be founded in natural causes, and slavery has no connexion with geographical circumstances. Climate, proximity and navigation, can only beget combinations between states, sufficient to create the baleful idea of a geographical balance of power. Maine can never be united with Ohio, nor Maryland with Missouri, in form- ing a balance of power composed of two divisions of states. But, if a balance of power is attempted to be established by the line of slavery, it will introduce a natural, instead of an unnatural geographical division, and a line between eastern and western states will very soon be substituted for this whimsical species of geography. The experiment will produce great disorder and confusion, and afford a temporary gratification to individual avarice and ambition; but it will soon be discovered that natu- ral, local and lasting interests are more conglutinating than a temporary, flagging and crusading enthusiasm; and if the states must be divided and arrayed against each other, they will take refuge from the sway of a fanatick, within lines marked out by nature.

The boundaries of the states were respected, and the right of internal self-government reserved to them by the federal constitution, to remove the temptations arising from a natural dissimilarity of circumstances, which might seduce them into the ruinous system of partial combinations; and congress were only invested with powers reaching interests which were com- mon to all the states, to prevent a possibility of geographical partialities, which would certainly operate as provocations towards the chief danger which menaced the glory and hap- piness of the United States. From this policy, intended to avert the greatest misfortune the United States can sustain, the policy of an interference by congress with an interest not common among all the states, of exciting local feelings and manufacturing mutual provocations, and of establishing two great combinations of states, is a complete departure; and it cannot therefore produce the effects, which the policy of the constitution laboured to accomplish. In pursuance of its great object to prevent combinations between states, the constitution, after having distributed powers between the federal and state governments, with a view to supersede all the means having a tendency towards the deprecated calamity, closes the subject by a positive prohibition upon a state "to enter into any agree- " ment or compact with another state." Now, is not the Mis- souri *agreement or compact*, a positive violation of this plain prohibition, and supposing no other argument existed, clearly unconstitutional from this single consideration ? It is a compact or agreement by one half of the states with the other half, and from its magnitude, and the power of the parties, infinitely more dangerous than the attempt by the Hartford convention to conglomerate a few states into a separate interest, adverse to that general interest, comprised by the powers delegated to the federal government. The Missouri compact or agreement was made by negotiators elected by the states to sustain the existing federal union, and not to form two new confederations of states, and to make a new compact between them; in doing so, the negotiators therefore exceeded their representative powers, and their compact was void. The members of the Hartford convention had better powers; they were chosen for the purpose of making a new compact between a few states, and though it would have been against the constitution, and a subversion of the union to do so, they would yet have acted by a representative authority. But, supposing that the members of congress should be considered as genuine representatives of the states, clothed with a power to make a new compact between them, yet no such compact could constitutionally be made, by delegates or representatives, or the Hartford convention was not reprehensible. The attempts, therefore, of this convention and of congress were equally unconstitutional, because the old compact of union prohibits any new compact between the states, except in the modes pointed out by the constitution itself, in which modes both are equally deficient.

Slavery being an absurd motive for establishing the proposed geographical division and balance of power, so positively forbidden, and so sedulously counteracted by the federal constitution, because it cannot be permanent, and would destroy the union; we are forced to look for some other, to unriddle the sudden enthusiasm, ardently cultivated at this juncture; and to consider whether the true motive is more favourable to a lasting union and to good government, than the spurious one. Considered only an instrument to effect ends, the real question to be considered is, whether these ends are good. The ends to be effected are, a monopoly of the offices of government, and of the partialities of congress, by the means of this artificial and fanciful geographical balance of power. This must ensue, unless the balance be kept perfectly even, and if it was kept even, the federal machine could not move at all ; but it cannot be kept even, because it will be disordered by a single vote, and the votes will be influenced by avarice, ambition and local calculations. If we find it extremely difficult to sustain a division of power between the federal and state governments, defined by the federal constitution ; what hope can exist of sustaining an undefined balance, dependant upon the caprices and selfishness of fluctuating individuals ? Let us suppose, that one of these balances should acquire a preponderance, which would be certain, and contemplate the consequences. It would absorb the offices of government, and the favours of congress. Well, what good would this do to the inhabitants of the preponderating balance ? It might indeed gratify the avarice and ambition of a few individuals among them for a short space; but the people would have the same sum to pay for the support of government, and in the end much more, because by substituting personal avarice and ambition for general good, an oppressive political principle is introduced, of the bitterness of which, the people of the preponderating balance would very soon taste. It would also tend strongly towards the dissolution of the union, in the effects of which the people of both balances would share. It is therefore very plain, that the interest of the people in every state of the union will be more advanced, by leaving appointments to be made by a labyrinth of interests and opinions, as at present, than by transferring them to a preponderating balance for the purpose of gratifying personal avarice and ambition.

The end of monopolizing the favours of congress, wounds more deeply the true principles of the union. These were intended to disable congress from granting internal favours, and committing internal partialities; but the design of obtaining them by means of a preponderating balance, positively expresses an opinion, that congress has a power of exercising internal partialities; and this opinion expunges from the federal constitution the distinction between delegated and reserved powers, for which the construction I have endeavoured to support, contends. The opposite construction, by its baleful success, has already established the doctrine, that congress does possess this power, and suggested the idea of a preponderating balance, not to correct it, but to aggravate its operation ; and to gather from

it the fruits it can yield, without controul. The policy clearly
meditates an extension of internal usurpations, and is itself
one. If a lust of power, natural to man, has been sufficient to
induce congress, unmoulded into two diplomatick bodies, to
assume internal powers over persons and property, what will
be the consequence, when a preponderating geographical balance shall be able to play the whole game, and win of the light-
est, even by a single vote, under no restraint but that of its
own conscience? Is there no difference between constitutional
restraints upon the frailties of human nature, and the boundless
liberty they will derive from commuting these restraints for
the contemplated preponderating balance? Let us recite the
succession of events. The great pecuniary favour granted by
congress to certificate-holders, begat banking; banking begat
bounties to manufacturing capitalists; bounties to manufacturing capitalists begat an oppressive pension list; these partialities united to beget the Missouri project; that project begat
the idea of using slavery as an instrument for effecting a balance of power; when it is put in operation, it will beget new
usurpations of internal powers over persons and property, and
these will beget a dissolution of the union. The genealogy is
strictly consanguineous, and the prolificacy of the family obviously natural. It furnishes complete materials for a comparison between the construction of the federal constitution,
which excludes congress from exercising internal powers over
persons and property, not expressly delegated; and one which
lets it into this boundless field by inferences at enmity with the
meditated division and limitation of powers. A field, thick set
with modes of transferring money from balance to balance,
from states to states, and from persons to persons, cannot be
entered at all by congress, without provoking those feelings
which never fail to embroil nations with each other. The federal constitution proposed to shut out both the federal and state
governments from this perilous field, by excluding the former
from a power of bestowing money on some states and individuals at the expense of others, and the latter from a power of
exercising any stratagems to get money from a sister state. It
contemplated a political garden of Eden, planted with principles yielding fruit nourishing to the community, and did not
design to invest either the federal or state governments with a

power to eradicate them, and substitute a parasitical shrubbery, enfeebling the good principles, and only nourishing serpents. If the division of powers between the state and federal governments be rooted out of the federal constitution, and the freedom of labour or of property should be lost, by the temptations of the two devils, avarice and ambition, to induce legislatures to meddle with forbidden fruit, the essence of our political system will be destroyed, and with it our vaunted residence in a region of political felicity.

The scheme for creating the proposed balance of power, considered as addressed to the states, evidently required some stupifying preparative to induce them to swallow it. Their inclination and interest to keep their reserved powers was too manifest to venture upon a proposition in direct terms, advising them to surrender to congress a power of distributing internal partialities; and to divide themselves into two combinations, to try which should be able to get the most of these partialities. It was too absurd plainly to say to the states, "yield to con-" gress your internal rights, for the sake of a chance to get " some of them back." The spectacle of slavery was therefore a cunning device to draw their attention from home; but let them remember, that those who forget their own pockets in a fray, often lose their money.

I might stop here, and rest the constitutionality of the Missouri question upon the positive prohibition of compacts or agreements between the states; and its policy, upon the very visible consequences which would follow the notion of the proposed balance of power between two great combinations of states: but I will proceed with the subject, because it ought to be considered in all its bearings, by a great community, the happiness of which it will materially affect.

The extremities of the union can never be made by law, to think alike upon the subject of slavery, because the evidence respectively contemplated is entirely different in different states; and therefore the idea of consolidating the union by coercions of opinion as to this affair, is as preposterous as the exploded idea of consolidating religion, by legal coercions upon conscience. Compulsion in both cases is so evidently tyrannical, that it never fails to be met by resistance, whenever it is practicable. Missouri has no right to compel Maine to admit of slavery, nor Maine any right to compel Missouri to prohibit it, because each state has a right to think for itself. A southern majority in congress has no right to compel the northern states to permit slavery, nor a northern majority to compel the southern states to abolish it, because it is a subject of internal state regulation prohibited to congress, and reserved to the states. One and the same principle applies to the two rights of suffering or abolishing slavery, and to assert and deny its efficacy, will never operate any conviction upon the party whose rights under it are invaded, by a party who claims and uses its protection. It has been handled as a religious question, and zeal, even in these modern times, has forgotten the freedom of conscience, and adopted the antiquated plan of effecting conversion by violence. The French nation, actuated at first by an honest but intemperate enthusiasm, attempted to compel the other nations of Europe to be free and happy; and the events produced by the fanatical undertaking were such as may be expected, should a combination of states attempt to administer by force the same medicines to another combination of states. Nothing can be more offensive than such attempts, because they assail natural rights ; nor more presumptuous, because the dictators are infinitely worse informed upon the subject, than those who have the right of determination. To prevent this dictatorial and absurd exercise of power by a majority of states, as being an infallible cause of civil war and disunion, congress was not made a representation of any internal powers, those few excepted necessary for common safety; and all internal powers, except a few specified prohibitions, were reserved to the states. The reasons for this policy which then existed, still exist, and will exist forever. The members of congress could never be well informed of local concerns, and therefore could never decide upon them correctly. Vanity cannot supply the place of knowledge. They would not feel the effects of their local laws, and therefore congress as to local subjects would not possess the best quality of a representative body. Above all, they would not decide like local representatives ; this is so true, that if all the members of congress now opposed to slavery in Missouri, should emigrate to that state, there is no doubt but that most of them would soon change their opinion. Indeed, this is the reason of the difference of opinion between the eastern and southern states upon the question; and if either placed in the circumstances of the others, would have adopted opinions the reverse of those now held, it forcibly displays the injustice of a dictatorial power to be exercised by either party.

It is highly edifying, in computing probable consequences, to recollect similar cases. The society of Amis des Noirs in France, zealous for amending the condition of the free people of colour, and believing that a conscious philanthrophy was local information, invested them with unqualified citizenship, wrote the slaves into rebellion, finally liberated them, and these friends of the blacks turned out to be the real murderers of the whites. An intemperate zeal, united with an ignorance of local circumstances, had to bewail the massacre of about forty thousand white men, women or children, of about thirty thousand mulattoes, after they had united with the blacks in that atrocity, of about one hundred thousand of the blacks themselves, and of dividing the residue into tyrants, and slaves to tyrannical laws, always more oppressive than any other species of slavery. These friends of the blacks in France disavowed at first the design of emancipation; but yet their speeches and writings gradually awakened the discontents of the slaves, and excited efforts which terminated in a catastrophe proving them to have been the worst enemies of the whites. This awful history engraves in the moral code the consequences of a legislation exercised by those who are ignorant of local circumstances, and the wisdom of our distinction between internal and external powers. The people of St. Domingo pressed upon the general assembly of France, its ignorance of local circumstances, and consequent incapacity to judge of the case; but as St. Domingo had representatives in that assembly, it persisted in its fanatical philanthrophy, and lost the finest island in the world of its size. The eastern states have as little knowledge of the Mississippi states, as the general assembly of France had of St. Domingo, and therefore the writings of the friends of the blacks in the United States are almost exactly the same, with those which they uttered in France.

The next case is the memorable controversy between Great Britain and her colonies. She insisted upon legislating for them locally and internally. They replied, that her parliament had not a sufficient knowledge of their local circumstances, to do this with any propriety, and that they were not represented in that body. She at length proposed to remove the last objection, and offered them a representation. But they declined it upon the ground, that the same species of ignorance, so obviously objectionable, would still prevail over a majority of the members. And the disunion between Great Britain and her colonies was caused by a claim of internal legislation for a body of men, whose internal knowledge of the countries, which were to suffer it, was too imperfect to produce good laws. But there was another cogent reason for rejecting a compromise with England, upon the condition of a representation in parliament. It was impossible that the essential qualities of representation could ever be annexed to it by that project. These are, as we all agree, that the representative should feel his own laws, and that those, upon whom those laws operate, should have a periodical power to remove him. Now, the people of the colonies would have had no power to remove a member of parliament, elected in Great Britain ; nor would the laws passed by a majority in that country, but operating exclusively in this, affect any individual of that majority. Such a representation was therefore viewed as a mere mockery of representation, and credulity itself laughed at the clumsiness of the device. These projects, however, of Great Britain suggested our distinction between internal and external powers, and the necessity of a genuine representation for the exercise of each class, impressively illustrated by the question of slavery, although it is equally applicable to roads, canals, the encouragement of manufactures, and other laws operating locally, passed by congress. The proposed law as to slavery was to operate exclusively upon Missouri. She had no representation in congress. If she had, it would be nugatory ; for, the majority necessary to pass the law, would neither feel it, nor would it have been liable to be rejected at any time, by the electors who did feel it. Such is the case with respect to all local laws passed by congress. The majorities which pass them, must be insensible of their operation. The 8th section of the federal constitution is both an illustration of this reasoning, and a test which forcibly confirms the construction for which I have contended. All the powers, bestowed upon congress, are such as will, in their execution, operate *generally* both upon the members of that body, and also upon the people of all the states. Thus the legislators would feel their own laws, the electors will be influenced by a common interest, and the essential principles of representation are preserved. If the principles of representation are thus carefully preserved, by the nature of the powers delegated, a construction which supposes that they are destroyed by a tacit permission of means, inconsistent with the design expressed, is, in my view, both literally and morally incorrect; literally, by the care to delegate such powers only as would operate equally upon all the members of the union; morally, by the equal care taken to preserve the essential principles of representation. Some years ago, much was said about virtual representation. Under this idea, it has even been contended, that hereditary kings and nobles were national representatives. And it must be admitted, that they participate more largely of that character, than a body of legislators elected by one of our states, whilst making local regulations to be imposed upon another; because, kings and nobles of the same state may feel their own laws to a great extent. We have however an exact parallel of the local powers claimed on behalf of our congress, in the recent congress of European kings for settling the affairs of that quarter of the globe, hardly larger than our share of this. These kings, as representatives of some states, undertake to make local regulations for others, which, far from feeling themselves, were dictated by their avarice and ambition. If our congress can also make local regulations, which may gratify the avarice or ambition of particular states at the expense of others, I do not discern any difference between the cases.

But, though the exercise of local legislation by congress may be evidently inconsistent with reason, with the essential characters of representation, and with the principles deemed by us indispensably necessary for the preservation of liberty, yet in this slave question, as in some others, the pure and invigorating spirit of the constitution has been assailed by the science of construction; and its words are turned into worms for eating up its vitals. A sect called Pharisees, by preferring ceremony to essentials, and signs to substance, contributed largely towards the corruption and ruin even of a theocracy; and therefore this species of sophistry demands all the attention, which its capacity to do mischief deserves.

"*New states* may be admitted by congress into this union." Such is the whole power. But then this power is a spherical sovereignty, and it is an appendage of sovereignty to annex conditions to its *grants*. Such is the recent construction of the words quoted. The meaning of the word "state" is first to be settled. We have understood it to mean "a po- "litical association of people, able to confederate with similar " associations." It was never before imagined, that congress could make a state. The power is to *admit*, not to *make*. If congress cannot mould, it cannot modify a state. It must be the work of the sovereignty of the people, associating by their title to self-government. Do congress participate of this sovereignty with the people of Missouri, or is its supposed spherical sovereignty paramount to the sovereignty of nature? The parties to the association composing a state, are the individuals by whom it is formed. By what principle can a body of men, neither collectively nor individually parties to this association, dictate its terms, except that of arbitrary power? The constitution abounds with instances to prove, that it did not mean by the term "states," a moral being capable of being created or modelled by congress, but we will confine ourselves to the special power under consideration. "*New* states." *Old* being the relative to *new*, both words are predicates of the same subject. A new state was, therefore, literally contemplated by the constitution, as exactly the same moral being, created and moulded by the same right to self-government, with the old. There was a good reason, why congress should be only entrusted with the naked power "to admit." Had it been empowered to annex conditions to this admission, it might easily have enlarged its own powers, and obtained an authority dangerous to the thirteen original states. It was foreseen, that the new would in time exceed the old states, in number and population ; and the old states, therefore, for their own security, withheld from congress the dangerous power of modifying the new, by conditions ; as such a power might easily be brought to bear upon themselves, and might be used materially to alter the constitution. Suppose the naked power of admission had been given to the president. Would he also have had the power of annexing conditions, by virtue of executive spherical sovereignty? If it would have been in his hands a mere personal power of rejection or admission, without conveying to him a power of annexing to admission a local law for the government of the state, it must be the same in the hands of congress; for the nature of a trust is not changed by the name of the trustee. Congress have frequently conferred upon the president certain trusts. Could he have annexed conditions not warranted by these laws? As in the cases of his being empowered by proclamation to abrogate a law, upon the performance of some specified act by a foreign nation. Could he have enacted a new law, by annexing a condition to the execution of this trust? The power of appointment or nomination is exactly similar to the power of admitting new states into the union. No conditions can be annexed to the execution of such trusts. Congress are intrusted eventually with appointing a president, as well as with admitting states into the union. Does the power involve a right to annex conditions, in one, in both or in neither of these cases?

The reason for intrusting congress with the power of admitting new states, was not to enlarge the powers of that body, nor to bestow on it a species of legislation, purely local, but to avoid the inconveniences which would have resulted from the reservation of the right by the parties who held it. Hence, as a mere naked power or trust was conferred, there exists a precise description in a few words, of the body politick to be admitted, and also of the compact of which it was to become a member. *New states* were to be admitted into "*this union.*" I do not discern any words which could more exactly have described parties and rights. The new parties were to be the same as the old, and the rights received were to be those conferred or secured by "this union." If, therefore, "this union" does not empower congress to legislate exclusively in relation to the internal civil government of each old state, it cannot so legislate as to those admitted. In fact, "this union" would never have existed, had such a power been proposed by the constitution. The people of no one state claimed any power of local regulation over another. They neither thought of, nor does there exist any compact, conveying such a power to a majority of states. There existed no primitive power by which one state or several possessed a right to form a constitution, or to enact internal laws for the government of another state ; and it is a sound principle, that a delegated power cannot exceed the power from which it was derived.

A power in congress of annexing conditions to the admission of states into the union would be in its nature monarchical, and analogous to the feudal system. Chiefs established that system upon the principle, that conquests were made for them ; and thus obtained the right of annexing conditions to grants. But with us, conquests are made for the community, and not for congress ; and the principle which sustained the right of annexing conditions, in the case of feudal chiefs, fails in the case of congress. The community, therefore, prescribed the rule by which conquered lands were to be erected into states, in doing which they have not invested congress with a power of annexing feudal conditions to this disposition.

But, this feudal power of annexing conditions to the settlement of a conquered or acquired territory, by the government of the country making the acquisition, has even been exploded as tyrannical both here and in England. One of our principles in the colonial state was, that emigrants to such territories carried with them their native rights. The colonies claimed the rights of Englishmen, and not only obtained them, but have I hope greatly extended them. But this would not be the case, if our emigrants should be subjected to a diminution of their native rights, by the pleasure of congress. All of them enjoyed the right of forming local constitutions and laws before their emigration. If congress cannot legislate over the states from whence they removed, and may do so by annexing conditions to a trust, over that which the emigrants from these states may create, it is obvious that these citizens must have lost some very important native rights, by an emigration from one part of our country to another. If the colonists emigrating from England were correct in asserting by force of arms, that they brought with them all the rights conferred by the English system of government, our emigrants may also contend, that they carry with them all the rights conferred by our system. Among these, the unconditional right to make their own local constitutions and laws, without being subject to any conditions imposed by an extraneous authority, has been the most important ; and universally exercised by every state in the union.

The same principle has been judicially decided in England. Some of the kings of England (of the Stuart family I believe,) in admitting several West India islands to establish representative governments, annexed the condition to their grants, that these islands should pay to the crown a perpetual revenue of four and a half per centum on all exports; and several of the legislatures were so weak as to pass laws confirming the condition, which soon became excessively oppressive, and greatly impeded the prosperity of the islands upon which it was inflicted. Grenada alone both claimed a right to representative government, and disputed the validity of the condition. And an English judge, even lord Mansfield, no enthusiast for liberty, no enemy to the crown, decided in favour of the island, which retained its government, annulled the condition, and prospered far beyond its paler-livered comrades. This decision was founded upon the rights of Englishmen, which adhered to these emigrants, and which being rights, could not be subjected to conditions.

In answer to a precedent, so fully up to the point, it is supposed that congress possess an arbitrary power to refuse the admission of new states into the union, the language being permissive and not imperative. I consider even this objection as only literally plausible, and as substantially flimsy. Had congress attempted to retain our wide-spreading new states under its government, it would have been an enormous grasp at power, not intended to be bestowed upon that body, but intended to be prevented by the provision for multiplying states, as territories extended. The old states would, by an attempt on the part of congress, so flagrantly adverse to the principles of the constitution, have been instantaneously excited; and have united with the new territories in preserving their own rights, and vindicating those of their fellow citizens. Whilst the constitution limited the local powers of congress to ten miles square, it hardly intended to invest that body with perpetual and unlimited local powers over a country more extensive, and likely to become more numerous, than the thirteen states which adopted it. The reason of the case was considered as sufficiently mandatory, and has hitherto proved to be so; and if the constitution has not provided for a violation of the trust, it must have been upon the same ground, that the laws of Rome provided no punishment for a son who should murder his father.

But, the decision of Lord Mansfield discloses a sufficient reason, why the framers of the constitution thought it unnecessary to subjoin to the trust, a prohibition upon congress to annex conditions. They knew that the execution of the trust would be valid, and that all conditions would be void. An affirmative power does not require any prohibition against its being exceeded. Suppose then Missouri should have been admitted into the union upon the condition proposed. Her membership would be perfect, and the condition would be void. She might at any time adopt a new constitution. Every state retains that right; and may, in that mode, abolish or re-establish slavery at its own pleasure. The proposal of this condition was therefore an invitation to congress to rush over rocks and precipices in pursuit of a phantom.

The conditions, annexed to the grants of kings, were founded on the fictions of an absolute sovereignty over persons and property. If a similar power here can be engrafted upon our new stems, called spherical sovereignty, no restraints would exist upon its exercise, as in the case of kings. Congress, by conditions, might mould states into as many varieties as it chose, as kings did colonies; and render one as little like another, as an eagle is like a buzzard. It might create forfeitures of lands by annexing conditions to patents, or even forfeitures of membership in the union, and revive the principles of the Boston port bill, enacted by the English parliament. And indeed, feudal might be substituted for allodial principles to an incomputable extent. If a trustee for the sale and conveyance of lands should annex conditions to the deed, suggested either by his interest or benevolence, and not specified by the trust, it must be admitted that the title of the purchaser would be good, and the conditions void; because it would be derived from the principal, by whom no such conditions were required. But if the conditions annexed should be prejudicial to the interest of the principal, the case would become infinitely stronger; as no power to perform a special act for his benefit was ever construed either in law or equity, as an unlimited or general power, to do that which was injurious to him. Now a power in congress of exercising a concurrent right with the states, both as to their constitutions and laws, is obviously injurious to all the states in the union, from which, as principals, the trust of admitting new states is derived.

Ramsay's United States, vol. 3, p. 8, " In these arrangements " the difference between American and European principles in " colonizing is strongly marked. In the latter, the object has " been pre-eminently the benefit of the parent state: In the " former, the joint benefit of both, *by a free communication of* " *equal rights and common privileges.* In the one case, some " commercial advantages of the mother state has been pursued ; " in the other, the good of mankind, by extending the benefits " of civil government, on terms of *equality and independence.* " Congress give no *charters* to their colonies ; but *sell* lands in " absolute property to settlers, who, *from the gift of God, were* " *in the actual possession of the rights of man,* and invite them " as such to join in a common, equal, social compact. The " sovereigns of Europe *gave* lands to their colonists ; *but re-* " *served by charters a right to controul their property, privi-* " *leges and liberties.*" This quotation is too explicit to need much comment. It is however remarkable, that the power claimed for congress of colonizing by conditional charters, exceeds the similar power exercised by the kings of England. The kings *gave* away the lands as their own absolute property. Congress *sells* the lands, not as an owner, but as a trustee for the proprietors ; a power of annexing conditions to the *sale* of property belonging to the United States far exceeds a power of annexing conditions to a *gift* of property belonging to the king. The trustee by the first power might depreciate the value to the injury of the owner. The receiver under the second may reject the donation, if he dislikes the conditions. When the doctrines of spherical sovereignty and law charter shall have reached an entire state, and comprised more than the charters of the king of England could do in the case of Grenada, it will be impossible to foresee how far they may be extended.

The last argument, (for I exclude declamations addressed to our passions or prejudices,) in favour of the proposed condition to the admission of Missouri into the union, is deduced from the fourth section of the fourth article of the constitution, which is this : " The United States shall guarantee to every state in

" this union, a republican form of government; and shall pro-
" tect each of them against invasion, and *on application of the*
" *legislature,* or *of the executive,* (when the legislature cannot
" be convened,) against domestick violence." It has been contended, that this duty to guarantee a republican form of government to each state is by this section imposed upon congress;
that to discharge it, that body must determine what is a republican form; and that this obligation comprises a power of imposing conditions on a new state, necessary to fulfil the guarantee. Admitting this construction, the argument either fails, or
proves too much. It fails, if negro slavery does not destroy a
republican form of government. And it proves too much, supposing that it does, by investing congress under the powers of
a guarantee, with a power to emancipate all the slaves in the
union. All the states in the first confederation were slave-
holding states, when they formed their constitutions. If slave-
holding states possessed the contemplated republican forms of
government, then that circumstance is not inconsistent with
such forms, and if not, it cannot justify an imposition of conditions upon Missouri under the authority of the section quoted,
though it shall be so construed as to invest congress with the
guarantee expressed. But even this in my view is an evident
misconstruction. The 8th section of the first article is devoted
to the enumeration of the powers bestowed upon Congress;
and the fourth article is chiefly employed in stipulating duties
to be performed *by states to states.* Among these, the fourth
section declares, that the *United States* shall guarantee to every
state in the union a republican form of government. The terms
"United States" are frequently used in the constitution, to
convey a different idea from "congress." "We the people of
"the United States." "A constitution for the United States."
"A congress of the United States." "The senate of the United
"States." "A citizen of the United States." "A president
"of the United States." And in the section immediately preceding, "United States" is twice used. A substitution of
"congress" for the "United States" in all these instances
would be manifestly absurd, and, therefore, I am unable to discern how it can be consistently done in that under consideration. But the section is internally unequivocal. The plural
and the singular are grammatically of the same genus. One

arrow in the talons of our emblematical eagle represents one state, and nobody ever suspected that all the arrows were emblematical of congress. "The *United States* shall protect each "*of them* against invasion." "Each" is singular and relative, and "them" is plural and antecedent. The relative and antecedent are "every state and the United States," unequivocally recognizing the stipulation of guarantee, as entered into by the contracting parties for the preservation of their mutual liberty. What is a guarantee? Undoubtedly a compact or undertaking. Now how could congress, neither in existence nor a party to the compact between the states, enter into any engagement whatsoever to preform a guarantee for the mutual safety of these States? It is by no means rare or useless, for independent states to enter into engagements for the sake of individual safety; but, if the United States of America, by endeavouring to guard themselves against arbitrary power, with the bulwark of a mutual guarantee, have conveyed to congress an absolute power over the forms of their governments, they have not only committed a mistake which is rare, but one, which is, I think, solitary in the annals of mankind. The article proceeds, "and shall protect each of them against invasion, "and on *application* of the legislature or of the executive (when "the legislature cannot be convened) against domestick vio-"lence." "Legislature and executive," terms applicable to states, are used because the whole section is speaking in reference to states. And "congress and president," terms applicable to the federal government, are not used, because the section has no reference to that government. The mutual protection here stipulated for, is by an assistance to be rendered by states to states upon such emergencies, as would make contiguity and dispatch important. General powers for defending the whole union had been previously bestowed upon congress. It was empowered to declare war, to raise armies and navies, to call forth the militia, *to suppress insurrections and repel invasions.* These powers are not subjected to any special restriction, and the two last cases, "insurrection and invasion" are entirely tantamount to "invasion and domestick violence," mentioned in the section containing the guarantee. Now, it would have been absurd, after bestowing an unrestricted power on congress in the first article of the constitution, to have conferred the same power upon it, to be exercised only "*on application* "*of the legislature, or of the executive.*" The reasons are obvious, why congress are not to withhold assistance in all cases of invasion and insurrection, until applied to by the legislature or executive of the suffering state, and why the states are. It is the duty of the federal government to provide for the common defence of the whole union, but it would not have been the duty of particular states to defend an invaded state, except for this stipulation; and a previous application for assistance is required, to prevent one state from obtruding itself into the affairs of another. "*The United States shall guarantee and protect on application.*" The same power was to do both, and if I have proved that the latter undertaking referred to states, it follows that the former has no reference to, nor confers any power on congress, as to the constitution or form of government of any state. It would have been a tremendous power, considering the scope given by the unsettled signification of the word "republican," and quite sufficient to lash any state into an humble subserviency to the will of congress. Between the states themselves, an agreement in interest rendered such a power both safe and useful; but between congress and the states, who would be often in collision, it would be a scourge in the hands of a rival. The *United States* must be the parties, both to the guarantee and to the union, or to neither, as the *United States* constituted both.

But it is not in this particular case very important, whether the guarantee is a duty imposed upon the states, which contracted to perform, or upon congress, which did not contract to perform. Its end is "a republican form of government." The meaning of this expression is not so unsettled here as in other countries, because we agree in one descriptive character, as essential to the existence of a *republican form of government.* This is representation. We do not admit a government to be even in its origin republican, unless it is instituted by representation, nor do we allow it to be so, unless its legislation is also founded upon representation. Now, this condition prohibiting slavery, both as constitutional and legislative, destroys these radical and necessary qualities, without which no government can be republican. Congress is not a representation of Missouri, either for legislation or forming a constitution. If, therefore, the guarantee be imposed on the states, it is the duty of all to resist an obvious violence to republican principles ; if on congress, it can never be its duty, or its right, to commit an act, which the guarantee was intended to prevent.

One other argument remains, apparently sufficiently strong of itself to settle the question. Even allowing to congress a degree of sovereignty, equal to the regal, yet the plenary sovereignty of kings did not empower them to annex conditions subsequent to gifts or grants of land, much less to sales for a pecuniary consideration. Such arbitrary attempts have been frequently adjudged to be void in the English courts. Had the English kings, after having granted or sold lands upon specified terms, prescribed new conditions as to the mode of their cultivation, their own courts would have decided it to be an unwarrantable imposition. Does congress possess a higher species of sovereignty than the kings of England, able subsequently to controul the mode of cultivating lands previously sold, and to diminish their value to the purchaser, after having received the price ? Whatever may be the power of a state legislature in this case, the same power does not extend to congress. The power given to it by the constitution is " to dispose of the ter- " ritory of the United States." Having disposed of it by sales, the power is at an end, because it is executed ; and no power remains with congress in relation to the lands sold, beyond what they possess over the lands, or the mode of their cultivation in the oldest state of the union. Ex post facto laws, and laws impairing contracts, are recognized as contrary to republican principles, because they are inconsistent with the freedom of property or of labour, the preservation of which is an essential object of those principles ; and thence arose the positive prohibition upon both the federal and state governments to enact them. Thence also the powers delegated to congress are all prospective. I cannot, therefore, believe, that it will persevere in legislating retrospectively, locally, and contrary to the genuine principles of representation, as preferable to that republican moderation, which never withholds from others the rights enjoyed by itself.

In contending for political liberty, I have not meddled with the subjects of slavery and emancipation, because it was sufficient to prove, that they belong to the local powers reserved to the states, and have been so considered by every state in the union. Inheritances and the regulation of property are not powers more local than slavery, and if congress can legislate as to the last, and also regulate property by corporations, it may as correctly insist, that an uniform system of inheritances, and for distributing wealth, is comprised within the scope of its powers. But, although the absurd enthusiasm as to the subjects of slavery and emancipation, recently excited, needs no fuel, an endeavour to abate it is not reprehensible ; and for this purpose it would be well for moderate men to consider, whether emancipation in the slave-holding states does not appear by the census to be proceeding as fast as their circumstances will justify, and as the general interest of the community of states can require.

There remains a right, anterior to every political power whatsoever, and alone sufficient to put the subject of slavery at rest; the natural right of self-defence. Under this right, societies imprison and put to death. By this right, nations are justified in attacking other nations, which may league with their foes to do them an injury. And by this right, they are justified, if they see danger at a distance, to anticipate it by precautions. It is allowed on all hands, that danger to the slave-holding states lurks in their existing situation, however it has been produced ; and it must be admitted, that the right of self-defence applies to that situation, of the necessity for which the parties exposed to the danger are the natural judges : Otherwise this right, the most sacred of all possessed by men, would be no right at all. I leave to the reader the application of these observations.

SECTION 16.

THE DISTRESSES OF THE UNITED STATES.

The previous attempts to ascertain the principles and construction of our constitutions have been made with a view of unfolding the ultimate causes of the distresses experienced by the United States. If they have flowed from false constructions, and real violations of constitutional principles, the remedy must lie in a return to those principles, and no where else; because good principles are useless, without practical extracts; and indeed pernicious, if they inspire a confidence, which serves as a cloak for abuses.

Let us previously take a glance at the causes which have produced the existing distress in Britain, as a mirror by which those which have operated here, will be visibly reflected. I premise, that the distresses of Britain cannot have been caused by a deficiency of manufactures, because she makes a superfluity of them, beyond the demands of home consumption, and a surplus for exportation. The best authority for facts within my reach, is the Edinburgh Review. It states, that the publick burdens of that country amount to the annual sum of £ 106,084,203 sterling. This total is compounded of taxes, £ 64,506,203. Poor rates and county levies, £ 12,000,000. Tithes, £ 5,000,000. And an enhancement of grain by the protecting corn-laws, £ 24,578,000. But the acquisitions by banking, and by all other exclusive privileges, are left out of the computation; and the total of the national burden is therefore stated at considerably less than it ought to be. Nevertheless, from this reduced total, the distresses of Britain are very clearly deduced. Estimating the profits of capital at three per centum, somewhat under the interest of money, but about the rate at which land sells, it requires a capital of three thousand millions of pounds sterling, to supply ninety millions annually, being about sixteen millions less than the annual expenditure;

and the conclusion is irresistible, that the distresses of Britain arise from the condemnation of this vast mass of national capital to eleemosynary purposes. As I shall make some use of the corn prohibition when I come home, it, is necessary to borrow a reason from the Review, to prove that it is a tax of this character. This tax arises from an enhancement of the price of bread beyond what it would cost, if importation was free. Now the Reviewers prove, that which is indeed obvious, that this tax is paid by consumers, and received by landlords; because, by increasing the value of agricultural products, or to speak more correctly, of agricultural manufactures, rents will be correspondently increased, and thus the protecting corn-laws must augment the income of capitalist land-owners. This transfer, though indirect, of the profits of labour to those who do not labour, is strictly of the eleemosynary character, and the tendency of every eleemosynary measure to produce national distress, in whatever garb it appears, is well established, both by the existing state of England, and also by all experience. We have universally seen national distress graduated by mortgaging national capital, for the gratuitous benefit of idle or unproductive individuals. Though some people are rich enough to be idle, it is an evil both corrected and more than counterbalanced, by the great productive right of the freedom of labour or of property; but when a nation is robbed by laws of this productive right, and forced to buy idleness, the best corrective of idleness is destroyed, and its prolifick procreator is created. Idleness is encouraged by being pensioned. Industry is discouraged by being subjected to the payment of these pensions. Capital becomes less productive by being taken away from its owners. And therefore, every increase of the eleemosynary family produces a correspondent degree of national distress, as in the case of England.

The United States, by associating themselves with several of this family, have found a degree of national distress, which they are gravely told was caused by futurity; for this is the amount of the doctrine, that our distresses have been caused by our having neglected to make our protecting duties high enough. If the affairs of a merchant, a farmer, or a mechanick, go on badly, he looks back for the cause, should he be a man of good understanding; but if he be a weak man, he rejects the evidence of experience, and trusts to some future speculation for amending his circumstances. This mode of discovering the causes of distress, that is, by shutting our eyes upon them, and taking a new leap in the dark, to cure the wounds already sustained from such chivalry, is constantly recommended by all abuses; because they abhor the prudence of looking back, as it would lead to detection; and therefore they assure us, that although we have hitherto felt nothing but thorns in the eleemosynary road, a-head it is strewed with flowers.

It is really wonderful that the most lively imagination should be persuaded, that our distresses have been produced by what we have not done; or that the effect has preceded the cause. This, however, is the doctrine of the protecting-duty panacea. We are ruined, it says, for want of more protecting duties and obstructions to commerce: but as causes precede effects, it is more probable that we have had too many. Instead, therefore, of ascribing the distresses of the United States to things which they have not done, I shall look for them in things which they have done; to which I am induced by considering, that the national distresses of Britain and of the United States could not both have been caused by the manufacturing occupation, because abundance and scarcity could not have produced the same effects; and a similarity in the distresses does not indicate a contrariety in their causes.

The creation of a nest-egg for rearing an eleemosynary family was almost the first act of the federal government. It received the people of the states with the pre-existing relations produced by a paper-currency intercourse, prescribed by unavoidable necessity. This currency was called by two names, "certificates" and "paper money," both offsprings of the same necessity, both sanctioned by publick faith, and both transferable; but one species had been collected into a few hands, and the other was more equally distributed among the people. These currencies, whilst passing, had gradually depreciated; and each temporary occupant had sustained the losses thereby occasioned during his occupation. In this state of things, justice called for some consistent remedy, equally applicable to all the currency and to all the sufferers. Either all the intermediate losses sustained between the emission and termination of the whole currency, or none, should have been reimbursed.

Both the currencies should have been redeemed at their nominal value, or neither; or both should have been redeemed at their depreciated value. The last rule would have perfectly corresponded with the right of free will in contracts or exchanges, to risque gain or loss; but it was directly adverse to legislative interferences with this right, for the introduction of the eleemosynary system, to get rid of which the states had recently passed through a long war. Instead of an equal and consistent rule, according with the publick interest, and recommended by justice, an exclusive eleemosynary capitalist interest was created by a partiality, unjust as it regarded individuals, and highly impolitick as it regarded the United States, if such an interest be oppressive and dangerous to liberty. No recompense was made to those who had sustained losses of property and labour by depreciation, during the circulation of these credit papers. If the right of free will in exchanges be sound, no recompense was due or practicable, and each individual ought to sustain its consequences; but by no principle could it be right, that these losses, instead of being thus merged into the national capital, should have been seized by law, and bestowed upon a selected class, in order to introduce the eleemosynary system. The losses inflicted upon individuals by depreciation, during the circulation of these currencies, were either property or not property. As property, they were either transferred with the paper, or not transferred. If they were transferred, they passed with both the paper certificates and the paper money, to the last holder of each species of credit paper; and the right of all such holders to the value of the paper, when issued, was the same. But if these intermediate losses did neither pass, nor constitute a just claim to compensation on the part of the last holders, both the certificate and paper-money holders were equally excluded from advancing such a demand against the publick. However, disregarding consistency, the partiality was committed, of considering certificates as carrying to the last holder all intermediate losses, and paper money as carrying none. One sect of holders being a minority and influential, obtained the value of its paper when issued, with interest; and the other sect, including the body of the people, was put off with depreciated value without interest. This was the more glaringly unjust, as the receipt of depreciated paper money was enforced by tender laws highly penal, and the receipt of depreciated certificates was free and voluntary. By this management, a certificate which had passed from A to Z, depreciating as it travelled, and purchased by Z for a twentieth part of its nominal value, resuscitated the intermediate losses for the benefit of Z, and subjected the actual sufferers to taxes for paying to Z what they had themselves lost, with interest; whilst the certificate holders escaped the burden of contributing for making good to the paper money holder a claim of the same nature with his own. This exclusive partiality transferred about one hundred millions of capital, from the people of the United States to a capitalist sect artificially created, and became the source of a stream of taxation, which may perhaps run and increase down to another revolution. The wealth of this sect was not derived from fair industry, but from an unfair law [for what law can be fair which creates what industry never does, a rich eleemosynary sect?] which, under cover of a sovereign legislative power over property, contrived to gratify the personal interest of a few members of congress, and a sect of certificate holders, by slicing off one hundred millions from the national capital ; a paltry sum indeed compared with subsequent speculations, but at that time considered as so very formidable, that it generated two animated parties. The certificate sect happened chiefly to reside in particular states, and had the address to persuade these states, that the trivial and transitory circumstance of personal residence was a sufficient reason to induce them to put upon their own necks an interminable eleemosynary system, to be transmitted with their other legacies to their children.

A greater speculation upon the national capital soon grew out of the hundred millions of capital thus created by law. The artificial capitalist sect wanted more profit than funding interest, and taking into partnership members of legislative bodies, it convinced the states collectively and individually, that they would be enriched, by enabling certificate, now funded debt holders, to convert their fictitious capital into bank stock, without changing its capacity as funded stock. Thus, the same paper transferred national capital to an eleemosynary sect, in two characters ; and the first acquisition of one hundred millions became comparatively inconsiderable. The locality of artificial capital soon disappeared, as if providence designed to give all the states a taste of the eleemosynary policy, to enable them to decide, whether the residence of its disciples would make that policy a publick good. Let us consider whether it can be so in the form of banking.

To determine this question, I shall urge a new argument to prove, that banks, both state and federal, destroy a principle essential to all our constitutions, and essential also to every conceivable free form of government; and that this vital desolation has caused many of the publick distresses. The people, by all our constitutions, have delegated to their representatives a power of legislation; but by none have they delegated to their representatives a power to delegate legislative powers to persons, not elected by the people, nor indeed by themselves. Legitimate legislatures have no power to appoint deputy or attorney legislatures, and if they had, they must do it themselves, and not depute others to do it both for their constituents and themselves. These positions bring to a fair test the doctrine of legislative sovereignty. If it be true, I admit that our legislatures may create deputy legislatures, or enable stockholders or whomsoever they please to elect deputy legislatures, and invest them when elected with legislative powers; but if it be not true, then our legislatures cannot directly or indirectly invest bank directors with legislative power, formal or substantial. Now I ask, if a power of regulating the national currency, and increasing or diminishing its quantity at pleasure, is not both a formal and substantial legislative power? What is legislative power? Something able to dispense good or harm to a community. Cannot bank directors do this? Some body has said that money *governs* the world. Have those who govern money no governing powers? If they have any, are they legislative, executive or judicial? The idea, that banking was an aristocratical institution, has been hitherto inferred from its privilege of getting money in an exclusive mode; but it is far better founded. It establishes a great body of directors, invested with an absolute power of pecuniary legislation, and in no degree responsible to the people. If this be not a formal and complete aristocratical power, I am unable to conceive one. The house of lords in England is an imperfect aristocratical power, because it can pass no law without the concurrence of

the commons; but if it could regulate the currency of the country without the concurrence of the representatives of the people, is there any one who can believe, that it would be less aristocratical and less legislative than it now is? In that case it
would be an exact portrait of our bank directors.

I ask every candid man, whether the community has not
suffered a great variety of calamities from the doings of bank
directors, in the exercise of their powers over currency. What
are these doings? Are they not powers, able to hurt very materially the whole United States? If they are powers, do they
belong neither to the civil nor political classes of powers? But
if they belong to either, is not a body of men constituted as
bank directors are, and exercising powers either civil or political, affecting a whole community, an aristocratical department,
as formal and as complete as can be imagined, and infinitely
more so than the British house of lords?

Need we go searching about for the causes of the publick
distress, after we have found a perfect aristocracy, exercising
an absolute power over the national currency? If there be any
object of legislation, through which a nation can receive deeper
wounds, I hope it will never be discovered; as those which
this can inflict, seem sufficient to punish us for all our political
sins. The secret, as to the distresses of the United States, lies
in the difference between republican and aristocratical legislation, upon the important subject of money. It is a power probably equal in its capacity of doing harm, to all other legislative powers united. It can derange the fairness of all
exchanges between man and man; it can tempt by legislating
an abundance of currency, and ruin by legislating a scarcity;
it can raise and diminish prices according to its interest, its
caprices or its partialities, without controul, detection or responsibility; it can refuse when it suits its interest, to redeem its
own paper, and terrify the people and the government into
acquiescence, by a fear of losing their debts and salaries, and
by the inconveniences of wanting a circulating medium; and
when it does not choose to pay its debts, it can put its funds in
its pocket, say that it has got nothing, and enjoy the fruits of
fraud beyond the reach of justice. Can any republican legislature remedy these evils except by removing the cause? Dare
any republican legislature to produce the distresses, which have

for years been mere sport, however cruel, in the hands of their aristocratical deputies? It is wonderful, after mankind have discovered the folly and mischief of a single legislative maximum of price, to see them quietly submit to an eternal alternation between maximum and minimum, and bear injuries from the aristocracy by which they are imposed, which would be indignantly resisted if imposed by a republican legislature. I do not compute the power of an aristocratical legislation, without responsibility, over national morals; it is sufficiently seen and felt, and it unfortunately operates most upon those classes of society, whose integrity and patriotism are perhaps the only hostages for the continuance of a republican form of government. These aristocratical legislatures have even been able to prescribe, not a test oath, but a test of honesty, to most or all of our republican legislatures, by furnishing them first with a pretext for raising their salaries, and then with a correspondent reason for reducing them; thus directly legislating upon that whole order of men, upon whose honesty and patriotism a free and fair government immediately depends.

For this aristocratical legislation, the state and federal governments have appropriated a portion of the capital of the community, far exceeding that appropriated for all our republican legislatures. It is probable, that the dividends of banks have sometimes amounted to twelve millions of dollars annually, requiring a capital of four hundred millions to supply; but as these dividends have sustained an occasional diminution preparatory to an augmentation, nine millions only may now constitute the total of the dividends received by all the banks; yet in contemplation of a prospective augmentation, twelve may be assumed as a future probable amount, and four hundred millions of national capital as appropriated to the use of bankers. It would have been correct to have charged banking with a great augmentation of salaries, expenses and taxation, which it has bestowed upon the community, but this enormous item is left out, because the community possess the means of throwing it off; until it does so, however, it ought to be considered as nearly or quite equal to the other.

The thirdele emosynary appropriation of national capital was effected by the protecting-duty laws. There is more difficulty in computing its amount, than in the similar instances of the same system we have passed over, because we cannot ascertain the portion of the tax they inflict, which gets into the pockets of owners of manufactories. But, as these laws create a species of aristocratical legislature over manufactures, exactly of the same character with that created to regulate currency, there will undoubtedly be a great similitude in their proceedings. Behold then a great community, industrious, at peace, and in distress. What an enigma? But behold its currency consigned to the regulation of bank directors, and its consumptions to the regulation of manufacturing capitalists, and you will confess that there is no enigma in the case.

The corn laws of England are equivalent to our protecting-duty laws, with respect to that portion of the tax, which goes into the pockets of capitalists. The prohibition of the importation of grain, until wheat gets to the price of eighty shillings sterling a quarter, is a tax upon the nation for augmenting the rents of landed capitalists. Whatever is carried by our protecting-duty laws into the pockets of manufacturing capitalists, is a tax upon the community for augmenting their wealth. Bread and manufactures being both necessaries, both these taxes are direct and unavoidable. By the corn laws of England, the manufacturers are compelled to pay about one-third more for home made bread, than they would have paid, if importation had been free. At this time, the price of wheat in England is about nine shillings sterling, and about eighty cents here. By our protecting-duty laws, agriculturists and all other occupations are compelled to pay for home made manufactures, about one third more, than if importations were free. The corn law tax falls most heavily on the poor, whence arises much of the distress of the working manufacturers. Our protecting-duty tax must also fall most heavily on the poor, because every tax upon necessary consumptions operates as a poll tax. A protecting-duty system exists in England in favour of manufacturing, but it inflicts no tax upon the nation, because the surplus of manufactures, beyond the wants of home consumption, renders their monopoly impossible, and makes the law internally, nominal; but the land capitalists have used this inoperative law as a pretext, to inflict an impoverishing tax upon manufacturers by the corn laws. Protecting-duty laws have been passed here in favour of several agricultural manufactures, but they are wholly unbeneficial to agriculturists, and inflict no tax upon any other occupation, because of the abundance of agricultural manufactures beyond the home demand. Yet the manufacturing capitalists here, in imitation of the land capitalists in England, have seized upon these inert laws as a pretext, for inflicting an impoverishing tax upon all other occupations for their own benefit. The appropriation of English national capital to the use of land capitalists is a heavy item of an eleemosynary system in favour of the rich, which requires a great standing army to maintain. The appropriation of a large portion of the capital of the United States to the use of the same system, has only caused hitherto such distresses, as suggested a necessity for the English army. An important distinction, however, exists between their corn laws, and our protecting-duty laws. Corn possesses few or none of the qualities of a general or universal currency. Being too perishable to bear repeated voyages, and of universal growth, it is unsuitable for a re-exportation and exchange; and would not act as circulating currency upon English manufactures, or increase their value in any considerable degree. But manufactures possess most of the qualities of an universal currency. They are susceptible of long preservation, and can endure repeated voyages, and are every where in demand. They are in short a better currency than any local paper. A surplus imported, beyond the wants of internal consumption, is therefore an accession of mercantile currency as valuable as coin, and will have a similar effect in raising the value of products in the country so fortunate as to obtain it. We hear continually of the balance of trade; but we err, if we compute this balance only by money, and reject those things which money represents. A nation would have the balance of trade in its favour if it never brought home money, and only more valuable things than it carried out; nor would it be difficult to prove, that it would be better to receive a balance of trade in commodities, than in coin. Many cities have derived great prosperity from being depots of commodities, because they are the most valuable species of universal currency; and if all the manufactures of England could be circulated by way of the United States, it would undoubtedly add to our wealth. Whatever portion can be so circulated, will have a comparative effect. Nor is it a sufficient answer to this observation to say, that protecting-duties do not prohibit importations for exportation, because by diminishing the home market, and changing an alluring invitation into a scowling prohibition, the adventures of commerce will be dispirited, and the sources of a surplus for re-exportation dried up. However this may be, it is evident that the English corn laws, bad as they are, may be defended by one argument, of which our protecting-duty laws cannot avail themselves ; namely, that an importation of corn is not an acquisition of an universal currency, and an accession of wealth.

But there is another material distinction between corn, and the whole compass of manufactures. The consumption of manufactures excites the effort and industry, which are better sources of national wealth, than exclusive privileges and commercial prohibitions. It converts numberless feelings of human nature into productive labourers, and constructs comfort, taste, pride, luxury and self-love into a machinery, worked by the steam of our passions, which compared with the sluggishness caused by suppressing gratifications, or with the animation inspired by consuming corn, will manifest the true character of the intervening gradations. Freedom in the enjoyment of the comforts and elegancies of life is the parent of that activity which reimburses a nation, both with intelligence and re-productions for its consumptions, by enlarging the capacities of the mind and body. By copying the English corn laws, we are therefore cultivating two supernumerary evils, with which those laws are not chargeable, in expelling from our shores a general and valuable currency, and in suppressing some of the strongest motives for bodily industry and mental improvement.

In computing the evil inflicted by our protecting-duty laws, that inflicted by the English corn laws will reflect much probability upon our conjectures. The corn laws, says the Edinburg Review, inflict an annual tax amounting to £ 24,580,000. This, at three per centum profit, is a dislocation of above £ 800,500,000 of national capital for the benefit of land capitalists. The enhanced price obtained by manufactory capitalists upon their annual sales constitutes the tax here, and when we consider that a man consumes a far greater value in manufactures than he does in corn, it is obvious that a tax upon so many commodities either is, or will soon become more oppressive and distressing than a tax upon one. Its present amount might be nearly ascertained by finding the difference between former and existing importations, and debiting the capitalists with the consumptions resulting from their diminution, as well as those arising from an increase of population. I conjecture that home manufactures may be annually sold to the amount of fifteen or twenty millions, and that their price may be enhanced by the protecting-duty laws about six millions. But I think that these laws ought also to be charged with a dead loss of three millions more, sustained by the mercantile, agricultural and maritime employments, by the expulsion from our ports of a great number of commodities, which would have increased profit, price and employment to that amount at least. These sums dislocate three hundred millions of national capital.

The fourth great trespass upon this capital is compounded of pensions and legislative waste of time and money by doing judicial business. It is probable, that these items have absorbed about three hundred millions of national capital, but as they are included in the item of taxation, it is unnecessary to estimate their amount for the condensed view to which I am advancing, however important it may be in considering the remedies for the publick distress.

Taxation is the last heavy item of the system for transferring national capital from its owners, to eleemosynary uses. Exact vouchers to ascertain its total amount in the United States are not attainable, but I suppose the expenses of the federal government to be about twenty-six millions, and those of all the state governments to be about thirteen millions. Dollars are meant in reference to the United States, and sterling money in reference to England. I have understood that the revenue of Virginia, exclusive of county taxes and poor rates, exceeded a million, and these taxes generally amount to nearly as much more. All the taxes of every kind in Virginia being about two millions annually, as that state only contains about one tenth of the whole population of the union, it would follow from this rule, that the taxes of all the states amount to twenty millions; but as I have no vouchers, seven are deducted as a sufficient precaution against error. We shall not, therefore, be very much mistaken, by supposing that the people of the United States are paying to all their governments at this time about thirty-nine millions. Estimating the profit of capital at three per centum, this item transfers from the use of owners to eleemosynary uses, thirteen hundred millions of national capital.

It is of no consequence whether the term " eleemosynary" be correctly or incorrectly applied to taxes, or whether governments be classed as productive or unproductive, if the facts be admitted, that governments may become oppressive by taxation, and that taxation, light or heavy, transfers capital by absorbing profit. Nor is it very important, that the estimate of three per centum as the average nett profit of all the taxable capital of the country, should be exactly correct. When an evil is felt with sufficient severity to suggest a remedy, it is losing time to be computing its amount in drachms and scruples. It is the amount of national capital, whatever that amount may be, transferred by laws from the conventional and natural owners to eleemosynary uses, which is the true cause of the publick distresses ; but considering the dead surplus of land in the United States, for want of labour to cultivate it, the general poorness of the soil, and the high price of labour, my conviction is, that the whole capital of the country, subject to taxation, does not average a nett profit even of three per centum.

Thirty-nine millions of taxes absorb of national capital, - - - -		$ 1,300,000,000
Twelve millions received by banks	do.	400,000,000
Nine millions received by capitalists, or lost by a depreciation of native commodities do.		300,000,000
		$ 2,000,000,000

In Great Britain, three thousand millions of pounds of national capital are mortgaged to eleemosynary uses, and in the United States, two thousand millions of dollars are mortgaged to the same uses. The difference is about six-fold. By computing the wealth and population of the whole British empire, and its great supplies from the four quarters of the globe, we should discover that it is able to raise six times more than we are, and thence we at once account for the existing similitude between the distresses of the two countries. It must be ascribed to causes common to both, and no other common cause can be found, except the system of appropriating national capital to eleemosynary uses.

In correspondence with this similarity between cause and effect, memory furnishes evidence which seems to be irresistible. The federal taxes in the time of Washington were three millions, and computing those of the states at half as much, one hundred and fifty millions of national capital sufficed to pay them. At that time, no national capital was mortgaged to manufacturing capitalists, and but little to bankers. Two great changes have taken place ; a great hypothecation of national capital to eleemosynary uses, and a great increase of publick distresses in a time of profound peace. Can any body believe that these fellow travellers have no connexion with each other?

There is another consideration of vast weight, to be estimated by the reader, and by all republican legislators, before we advert to the remedies for the publick distress. It is, that taxes, pensions, bounties, dividends and protecting duties, have been at least doubled by a rise in the value of money, and a fall in the value of produce and property, since they were imposed, without any legislative act by the representatives of the people. Madmen or tyrants only impose taxes without regarding the ability to pay. The legislatures, therefore, which imposed all our burdens, must have estimated the publick ability to sustain them, and have been governed by that estimate. When half this ability is gone, the taxes are obviously doubled, and the same estimate, by which they were imposed, requires that half of the taxes should be taken off. It is apparent that the old tariff, though unaltered in figures, is in fact doubled; together with all bounties, pensions, dividends and legislative wages, in their pressure upon the people. The notion of the manufacturing capitalists, that their bounties should be further increased, after their value to themselves, and their pressure upon the people, has been doubled by the appreciation of money, and the fall in the prices of produce and property, is founded in the same reasoning, which would justify legislatures in raising their wages, and pensioners in asking for an augmentation of pensions. Look at this reasoning. The taxes were imposed, the bounties and pensions bestowed, and the legislative wages increased, when the depreciation of money and the price of produce enabled the people to pay twice as much, as easily as they can now pay half as much ; therefore taxes, bounties, pensions and wages, all absorbers of national capital, ought to be

increased. Such is the reasoning of the whole sect of eleemosynarians, and it utterly precludes a redress of the evils under
which the United States are labouring.

There is another mode of reasoning, equally forcible, which
obstructs it. Admitting that the publick distresses arise from
legislative transfers of national capital to eleemosynary uses, it
would be cruel to restore this capital to the rightful owners.
Would a robber, who had, in a fit of generosity, divided a
purse he had taken, between a rich and poor man, be wrong in
reclaiming and restoring it to the owner? After repentance
has opened our eyes, can conscience be appeased without reformation? But, this is the great argument which pleads against
justice to the nation, and therefore requires some examination.

The legislative power over currency with which bank directors are invested, has been exercising, and is still exercising, so
as to produce many political evils, and countless individual
misfortunes. These have proved, that the prescriptions of an
interested aristocracy in relation to currency contribute neither to the health of society, nor the happiness of individuals.
They even render it impossible, that republican legislatures
should impose taxes by any correct estimate, because they can
diminish the ability to pay, by diminishing the currency; or
lessen the efficacy of the sum collected, by increasing it. These
are considerations sufficient to open our ears to the following
reasons opposed to the argument of cruelty. If legislatures are
sovereigns, they had a right to invest bank directors with a
legislative power of regulating currency; if not, more cruelty
is comprised in the breach of constitutions, by which the liberty
of a great people is endangered, and their happiness impaired,
than in their vindication. The retention of unconstitutional
and misery-inflicting acquisitions, will be a liberal compensation for the restoration of republican legislation over currency;
especially as bankers will receive the share of the benefits
which may flow from it. Patriotick bankers will find complete
consolation, by balancing publick good against aristocratical
legislation. Suppose we had blundered upon a king over currency; ought we to adhere to the error, after we had discovered,
that monarchy was as bad a principle of government in respect
to the representative of property, as to property itself? George
the third was recognized as their king for life by all the colo-

nies, and the recognition was rivetted by the word allegiance, the force of which these colonies admitted. Bank directors have been recognized by all the states as aristocracies to continue for years, and the recognition is attempted to be rivetted by the word charter, to deprive legislatures of the power of repeal by a misnomer, the force of which neither they, nor our constitutions allow. Shall the illegitimate word charter impose upon us an aristocracy for years, when the true word allegiance could not preserve a king for life? Brutus exclaimed, "virtue, "thou art but a name:" and it is now contended that liberty is only a word, subjected to another word of higher authority; but I do not see any possible mode of getting rid of monarchy or aristocracy, formal or substantial, except by their removal. George the third had only a negative upon our laws, and could not legislate over a dollar. Bank directors legislate over millions, and our governments have no negative upon their laws. Could the colonies have gotten rid of the royal negative, they would have acquired the independence enjoyed by our currency legislatures.

The cruelty of abolishing the protecting-duty system admits of the same answers, because that system is of the same character with banking. It invests a combination of capitalists with a legislative power over manufactures and exchanges. The nature of this power is illustrated by the article of cotton. Its price is universally diminished by an increased product in the East and West Indies, Brazil, Spanish America and the United States. The capitalists, by a partial monopoly of necessary commodities, have subjected our cotton planters and the rest of the community, to a considerable tax for their benefit. If this tax could raise the price of our cotton, it could no longer enter into competition with foreign cotton. If not, the tax paid by our cotton planters upon home made cotton goods, would be an addition to the expense of cultivation, to which their foreign competitors not being exposed, they would still enter into the competition under great disadvantages. If our prohibition of cotton goods could raise the price of cotton abroad, our cotton planters would derive no advantage, or a less advantage from it, than foreign cotton planters by the amount of the protecting-duty tax they paid to capitalists. If the tax could raise the price here and not abroad, it could only be momentary, as it could not be exported, and would be smuggled into this country ; nor could our cotton manufacturers ever export their work, whilst their rivals could buy cotton cheaper. If the protecting-duty system could raise the price of labour, justly and equally, it would do nothing, because its relative prices would remain the same ; but if it should disorder this relative value, it will cause such injuries to individuals as have been caused by banking. The cotton planters throughout the world are a community, or a species of United States, no section of which can tax other sections, or get bounties from them by taxing itself. The common law of this community is the natural right of free exchanges. It cannot choose a congress, with a power of granting exclusive privileges to favoured sections, nor can any section grant exclusive privileges to itself. Any section may, indeed, diminish or lose the benefits of this common law by taxing itself; but then it will be in a worse situation, than the sections which fully retain the right of free exchanges. Cotton manufacturers throughout the commercial world compose another community. It is said, that a tax upon our cotton planters will give them some advantage over foreign cotton planters. Would a tax upon our cotton manufacturers also give them an advantage over their competitors ? This is a mode of suppressing rivalry, which I never knew any interest to try willingly. It is said, that by taxing cotton planters for the benefit of cotton manufacturers, the capitalists may be bribed to sell cheap in some period, long or short ; but the first step towards obtaining cheap manufactures, is to get raw materials cheap ; and, therefore, the bounty ought evidently to have been given to the cotton planters, as the surest mode of effecting the promised good. But the wrong end is selected to begin at, because the right one would not bestow an accession of wealth upon capitalists. These gentlemen admit, and indeed warmly contend, that the country is cruelly distressed ; and call loudly for a remedy. They propose one, as they declare, out of mere patriotism ; and that of a nature so complete and effectual, that they all agree in opinion. It is simply an increase of the very eleemosynary system, which has brought us where we are, in their own favour. If this remedy will cure the publick distresses, it ought undoubtedly to be applied ; if not, the same remedy under which they have increased, ought to be renounced.

The similarity between the distresses experienced by the several states, visibly quotes a cause common to all. Kentucky and Ohio manufacture more than Virginia and Maryland, and have also suffered more. Manufacturing is, therefore, neither the cause nor the remedy of the general distress. But Kentucky and Ohio pushed the banking member of the eleemosynary system, farther than Virginia and Maryland. If our distresses really proceed from this system, as I have contended, the argument of cruelty can only be settled, by comparing the mass of distresses sustained by the community, under its influence, with the distresses eleemosynarians will sustain by its abolition.

Annuities to bankers and capitalists differ in no respect from the English poor rates, except in being pensions to the rich. What could be said of a nation, which had no mendicant nor poor class at all, but was so enamoured with the English poor laws, as to create one out of rich people? That it imitated the policy of the United States. The several states constitute the community called the United States. Its individuals being states, no mendicant class can exist in this federal nation, except one compounded of states ; and we find no power delegated to congress to provide for poor states. But it has gone out of the federal community into other nations to find a class called poor soldiers, though these individuals are members of state communities, and though there is nothing in the constitution, investing congress with any power over individuals because they are poor, or enabling it to give pensions to poor soldiers, any more than to poor militia men. By a law of congress, poverty is made the criterion of a claim to a pension, and of course, of the right of congress to grant it. What bounds are there to such a power of legislation over persons ? No such boundless power was delegated to congress by the federal constitution, because it was unnecessary to the objects of the union, and that body was wholly unqualified for its judicious exercise. Legislative bodies are less qualified for an exercise of a despotick pensioning power than even kings, and in fact none possess such a power because they are not sovereign. A law granting pensions or sinecures to an individual or class, is simply an exclusive privilege law ; and is evidently of a different character from a general law, making provision for all poor people who may fall within its purview, by an indiscriminate rule ; nor is this latter kind of law an exercise of a judicial function, because it acts, not upon persons or sects, but upon cases only. Neither has a gratuitous pension any resemblance to a pension paid in fulfilment of a contract, or to the right or duty reserved to the states of providing for their poor, not by exclusive individual selections, but by an equal and general law. These cases differing in principle, have been blended by an incorrect application of the word "pension" to both. If our legislatures, and congress in particular, have no power to give away the property of the whole nation by sinecures and exclusive privileges, to individuals and sects, either civil or religious ; the question, whether more cruelty will be produced by restoring our constitutional principles, or by adhering to an error which is oppressive upon industry, sobriety and merit, remains open.

All these sprouts of tyranny and instruments of oppression have sprung from the doctrine of legislative sovereignty, which has elongated the powers of congress from special delegation, into special reservation, and demonstrated that it has become necessary maturely to revise constitutional constructions. What can be a stronger invitation to the exercise of a duty so important to ourselves and our posterity, than the injudicious attempt to convert the federal union into a legal balance of power? If I have construed our constitutions in conformity with their intentions, these sprouts ought to be eradicated without remorse ; but, if I am mistaken, it is then to be considered whether it is best for the nation, that its distresses should be removed or continued. If these have been caused by transferring two thousand millions of national capital to eleemosynary uses, it is obvious that no remedy exists, but a restoration of so much of it, as may not be required for the purposes of a free and moderate government. Should only one half of this capital be now restored to its owners, the other half will bear as heavily on the community, as the whole did when the several burdens were imposed ; if none is restored, it is evident that the weight of the burden will be doubled. This in fact has already happened, and is a most efficient cause of the publick distresses.

Let us, therefore, consider how much of the transferred capital may be restored to the people without injury to the government.

The suppression of banking will restore of
capital, - - - - - - $ 400,000,000
The repeal of all protecting duties, except those
for revenue, do.   - - - -   300,000,000
The suppression of gratuitous pensions, state
and federal, do. - - - -   200,000,000
The renunciation of judicial functions, and
pecuniary patronage by legislatures, by
avoiding bad judgments, partialities and
long sessions, do. - - - -   50,000,000
The suspension of legislative projects, generally catch-penny, and unproductive, do.   25,000,000
The reduction of legislative wages conformably
with present prices, do. - -   25,000,000

$ 1,000,000,000

But as the two first savings, though they will increase the
ability of the people to pay taxes, for the use of government,
are not deductions from them, it is obvious that they would still
bear heavier upon the community, though nominally reduced
by the subsequent articles, than the whole did when property
and products were more valuable. Other items towards libe-
rating national capital must, therefore, be found, or a considerable portion of the existing distresses will remain. No additional retrenchments, sufficient to remove these distresses that
I know of, can be found, except by adverting to the army and
navy. It would be frivolous for our legislatures to waste more
publick money than they would save, by interminable little
wranglings about little sums; and foolish in the people to be
deluded into an opinion, that this was economy. The publick
distresses being great, they can only be removed by great remedies. The European nations exist for the benefit of armies
and navies, and armies and navies do not exist for their benefit.
If this be right, these items, far from affording room for re-
trenchment, require additional hypothecations of national capital; but, if it be wrong, we ought rigidly to examine, whether
these two great sources of expense will not admit of some reduction, beneficial to the community for whose good we yet
suppose them to have been incurred. How is it possible, that

the United States, having trebled their militia and strength, should yet require an army thrice as large, as in the time of Washington? Then they were engaged in a fierce war with several Indian nations; now they are in profound peace. Then the Indians were formidable; now they are feeble. And we are as distant from Europe as we were then. Governments say, that regular troops are cheaper than a militia; but taxes tell a very different tale. Ours have spoken very distinctly to the point. In fact, the idea is collected from partial calculations in time of war, quite inapplicable to times of peace. As to the navy, there may be more difficulty; but I do not know that it is much wiser to oppress the community for the purpose of building ships, which, may probably rot before war comes, than for the keeping of an army which may die without rendering any service. Perhaps it might be a better resource for naval defence, to prepare materials for building ships suddenly in case of war, than to build, man and wear them out in time of peace, by voyages of pleasure. But I leave this subject to those who understand it better.

If the protecting-duty system should be abandoned, and a tariff fabricated with a single eye to revenue, it is objected that consumptions will be increased. This effect is admitted; but I contend, that far from being an evil, it will be highly beneficial to the community. Consumptions are the food of industry; diminish them, she languishes; remove them, she starves; feed her with them, she performs double work; and this double work enables her both to enjoy more pleasures, and to pay more taxes. If half our duties were taken off, it is well established that the other half would produce more revenue than the whole now does. Why? Because industry, consumptions and enjoyments have all increased. Let the rival system face its competitor, and common sense decide which will add most to the happiness of mankind. It is simply this. Increase duties, and you diminish revenue, industry, consumptions and enjoyments. If commodities are a currency, having the effect of enhancing the prices of our commodities, this enhancement will also be a fund compensating for the increase of consumptions. In fact, the extent of consumptions is the true measure of national prosperity and happiness; both are contracted as these are diminished, and both are extended as these are increased. They are a measure of politeness, refinement and civilization; and their diminution to mere necessaries, is constantly attended by savageness. Between the extremes indicated by consumptions, namely, a situation the most exalted or the most debased, lie all the room for the ingenuity of the eleemosynarians.

The ancient appropriation of national capital in England, and the modern one in France, to the use of the clergy, caused severe national mischiefs, which were corrected in both countries by resumptions. The benefits of these resumptions have been acknowledged by most writers, and in the case of France, these benefits are considered by some as an ample compensation for its terrible revolutionary evils. National distresses, in both cases, arose from hypothecations of national capital to unproductive uses, and the remedy in both cases was a restoration. But these mischief-working appropriations of national capital were less oppressive to the people than ours which leave the capital in the hands of its owners, and take away the profit. Although the clerical appropriations consisted of land transferred by legal investitures, and were of a tincture somewhat less flagitious than our gratuitous hypothecations, they became pernicious to national prosperity, and produced evils which caused national uneasiness. The clergy long contended, that the true remedy for these evils was to endow more monastaries or manufactories of religion, and to convert more land into mortmain; and the advice, being followed, conducted the distemper to a paroxysm. We are advised to endow more capitalists, and to transfer more national capital to eleemosynary uses of various kinds. This advice leads us also towards a paroxysm. On the other hand, as the rights of vested property, or the claims of hereditary power, or the venerableness of religious sanctity, do not stand in our way; because, all our hypothecations of national property are legal experiments subject to legal abolition; we can now calmly retrace our steps, and desist from advancing to the gulf of revolution.

There is only one objection to the restoration of the national capital appropriated to banks. What shall we do for the want of a currency? So then, it comes out unequivocally, that bank directors are legislators or lords paramount over the currency of this great community. What shall we do for want of a reli-

gion ? say the priests of established churches. The free industry of the people, if suffered by the government to operate fairly
upon the commercial world, will rapidly supply us with a better
currency than the involving, fluctuating, vanishing, counter-
feited currency of corporations. If banks can pay their debts,
we have a sufficient specie currency in hand ; if they cannot,
their credit ought to cease. But is it possible, that a chain of
aristocracies can give us a national currency, whilst our chain
of republicks are incompetent to effect the object? If this be
true, the haste with which we have been changing our principles, admits of a better defence than I had foreseen. But, for
my part, I do not hesitate to assert, that our republican legislatures are able to give us a better paper currency, if one be
necessary, than the aristocratical legislatures they have put in
commission, can possibly do. The republican paper currency
would collect no dividends, and would not hypothecate four
hundred millions of the national capital for the use of an
eleemosynary family of banks. It would not collect specie for
exportation; and its fund for redemption could never run away
or be concealed. It is incomprehensible to me, how an opinion
came to take root, that paper money issued by a nation ought
to bear interest in favor of those who use it, but that paper
money, issued by a corporation, ought to receive interest from
the same persons. The nation and its territories cannot be
dissipated, stolen, or concealed by directors, cashiers or clerks;
nor its responsibility fail by the disappearance of its stock;
whilst the stock of banks is very often a complete illustration
of Berkeley's philosophy. Do we derive this strange prejudice
from the revolutionary paper money? Well, if that was damn-
ed by experience, we also know that the same upright judge
has at least condemned the paper money of banks to purgatory,
a place requiring the purification by fire. Experience then ad-
vises us to reject both these kinds of paper money most unequivocally; but it has something more to say. It has shewn us
three kinds of paper money; that in use throughout the colonies before the revolutionary war, that in use during the war,
and that now in use. The first did great good and no harm;
the second great good and great harm; and the third great
harm and no good. The first collected no dividends for eleemosynarians, its stock was a colony, its quantity was regulated by

republican legislatures, and its specie for redemption was taxation. The second was driven by the bayonet into the morass of redundancy, was unsustained by taxation, and rested upon the rotten prop of tender laws; but like a patriot, it fought manfully for its country, and disdained to live by infecting it with the eleemosynary policy. The third absorbed four hundred millions of national capital, pretended it had specie to pay its debts, lied, stopt payment, depreciated, aggravated publick expenses and taxation, sometimes became bankrupt, made bankrupts of many individuals, and by causing fluctuations in the prices of property, ruined and reduced to misery thousands of worthy people. Experience has decided that the first was the best and the last the worst. If a paper money was issued by Congress, restricted by a constitutional amendment to one year's amount of all our taxes, state and federal; if it was distributed in portions equal to such taxes, making each state responsible for its portion without interest; if one moiety of all taxes and payments to the publick was allowed to be made in this currency; if it was not made a tender; and if banking was suppressed, a view of the circumstances attending the three paper money experiments seems to justify an expectation that a currency might be produced, infinitely preferable to the eleemosynary currency of corporations, and at least equal to that which flourished for many years before the revolution. But, as we are now wealthy and independent, it is rather to be expected that our republican legislatures would be able to improve upon the example of British colonies. In times of peace the success of this currency would be certain; in times of war, we might still borrow and fund, without being subjected to both interest and dividends for the paper borrowed, so as to hypothecate in fact about six hundred pounds of national capital for each hundred pounds borrowed. But though I believe that the best experimental paper currency was that before the revolution; and that an imitation of it would be our wisest course, if we must have a paper currency, which I do not believe; I do not enter into the subject, because it does not fall within my plan.

The question, however, might be certainly decided by any one state, should the federal government adhere to its hypothecations of national capital to unproductive and eleemosynary

uses. Suppose a single state should make a trial of the policy
of relieving its capital from such destinations as far as possible,
by repealing banking laws; by prohibiting under sufficient
penalties the circulation of every species of paper currency;
by prohibiting with internal protecting duties, the introduction
of all manufactures from other states, sent to collect eleemosynary taxes; by suppressing all gratuitous pensions; by reducing legislative wages; by a legislative forbearance to exercise
judicial functions; by shortening legislative sessions; by suspending improvement and catch-penny projects, until it shall
be ascertained how the suspension will work; by applying all
its resources to the payment of its debts; and by reducing its
taxes down to the rate, which such a policy would justify. It
would then experimentally appear, whether the policy of con-
demning national capital to eleemosynary uses, or of leaving it
to the use of its owners, was most favourable to national prosperity. The discovery of the longitude would be almost nothing, towards advancing human happ   s, compared with the
success of this experiment; and if congress must rival monarchs
in the bounty system, I discern no object so worthy of its liberality. It ought also to be highly gratifying to every state, to
behold an experiment for testing the doctrines of the eleemosynarians; nor could it meet with any constitutional obstructions,
because it falls within the powers reserved to the states. The
state right of taxing both persons and property coming from
other states remains; otherwise, neither would be subject to
state taxation. Some states have prohibited the introduction
of slaves from others, and have also taxed itinerant merchants.
And some may think the introduction of home manufactures to
collect an eleemosynary tax for capitalists, as injurious to their
liberty and prosperity, as the introduction of slaves is thought
to be by others. Both may be right, and both possess a power
to keep off internal and local evil by internal and local laws.

The eleemosynarians endeavour to conceal their pecuniary
speculations, under the general idea too hastily swallowed,
that taxation naturally increases with population. I have no
quarrel with taxation, except that species which hypothecates
national capital for the uses of individuals or combinations,
and not for the use of government. This only gives one man's
property, to another. We have been considering the principle,

and the justice of taxation, and not its rate, though its rate unavoidably came into view, as an illustration of its principle and
its justice. The principle and justice of taxation are equally
applicable to a great or a small, to a rich or a poor nation; and
if an increase of population furnishes any argument applicable
to the subject, it is, that the more numerous we become, the
more people will have bread taken out of their mouths by the
sinecure system, to pamper eleemosynary appetites.

The preceding calculation of the amount of eleemosynary
dislocations of national capital shews, that there is no connexion between the eleemosynary system and population, because the former has greatly outrun the latter. In Washington's
presidency, one hundred and fifty millions of national capital
sufficed to supply the taxes, state and federal, then suggested
by population, without the agency of an eleemosynary system.
Now the single article of pensions, though the smallest item of
that system, absorbs more of the national capital, than the whole
expenses of our governments, state and federal, did then. Protecting duties absorb double as much, and banking still more.
The whole national capital, now hypothecated, is thirteen times
greater than it then was; and experience has determined, that
thirteen nations of the then population of the United States
may be governed for the money, as well as one was at that time.
I do not pretend that my calculations are quite correct; but
they are sufficiently so, to prove that the hypothecation of national capital to eleemosynary uses has far outstript population; and that this artificial system, and not our natural increase, is the true cause of national burdens and national distresses, to a very great extent.

Sir George Staunton in his history of the English embassy to
China in 1793, states " that the taxes of China amounted to 5s
" sterling; of France under the monarchy previously to the re-
" volution, to 16s; and of Britain to 34s; per head, upon their
" respective populations; and that China maintained a stand-
" ing army of one million of infantry and eight hundred thou-
" sand cavalry." In China, corporate pecuniary privileges
were unknown; in France, they were rare; in England, they
were numerous. In the two first cases, the weight of taxation
upon individuals is diminished by population, as it must be,
except for the intervention of an eleemosynary system. These

few facts are credible witnesses to the following conclusions. 1. That the eleemosynary system both conveys the use of national capital to private people, and also greatly increases taxation. 2. That a sovereign power over labour or property is less oppressive in the hands of an absolute monarch, than in those of a representative legislature. 3. That the error of trusting republican governments with this tyrannical power, has probably caused their premature deaths, because they are most likely to push it to excess. 4. That great armies and low taxes are not incompatible; but that exclusive privileges and low taxes are so. Thus many of the states, without any armies to support, have found means to increase their taxes, by entering into partnerships with catch-penny speculations, which hypothecate the capital of the people, and are a losing trade. The eleemosynarians have been for some years our popular patriots, and their projects have already inflicted on us a tax of four dollars a head upon our whole population for the use of government, exclusively of the taxes to banks and manufactory capitalists. A less tax caused a civil war in France. Suppose some individual should offer to reduce the taxes to one dollar, if we would make him our king; politicians and the people would have this question to decide; which is best, a king with one dollar tax, or an eleemosynarian aristocracy, with four to the government and two to bankers and capitalists?

If a plain law were proposed to make tenants pay double rents to capitalist land-owners, every body would see its injustice. A law to make the same tenants pay a second rent to capitalist manufactory owners amounts to the same thing, but its injustice is not seen, because it is not couched in the same words. There are no small tenants who do not pay to capitalists under the protecting-duty system, more than their rents amount to; and who would not make a good bargain by buying of them with a second rent, a freedom of will in exchanges. Yet if a plain law was passed, enacting that all tenants who would pay a second rent to the owners of manufactories should enjoy the right of procuring necessaries without being subjected to the protecting-duty tax, it would open many eyes. But suppose, it could be ascertained how much each person paid to the owners of manufactories under the protecting-duty law, and a new law should be past, abolishing that indirect way to the money, restoring the freedom of exchanges, and enacting that the same sum, now paid in the character of consumers, should be paid by each individual to capitalists by name. The Gipsies, it is said, possess the art of so disfiguring a horse, that it is very difficult to recognize him. One would think, that they drew the protecting-duty laws, and so disguised men's private property, that the owners no longer recognize it.

Our conduct is an enigma. A real hatred of the English policy is united with a real affection for its worst features, against which the English people would rebel, except for the bayonet. The poor system in England, though good in theory, strongly resembles our pension system in its effects. One breeds pauperism; the other pensioners. That is subject to monstrous abuses from cunning, vanity, partiality, benevolence or a love of popularity; so is this. Vestries or overseers, superintending small districts, are unable to prevent these abuses; legislatures, metamorphosed into vestries or overseers, are still more deficient in qualities to correct, and infinitely more copiously replenished with such as cultivate these abuses. Both systems are demoralizing and oppressive; but one is an attempt to discharge a social duty, whilst the other is an usurpation of sovereign power over property. And both have become publick nuisances. England is struggling to get rid of one, and the United States to establish the other. Tithes are taken from worthy and useful ministers of religion, gallant armies are disbanded, and meritorious civil officers are discharged for the publick good; but the pension system claims an exclusive privilege of oppressing a nation. I have no doubt, but that this system receives more than all the civil officers both of the federal and state governments together. Can it be worth as much as civil government? At least it cannot be worth more; and no peculiar merit in any social occupation can possibly deserve, that social liberty should be sacrificed for its reward. If we were carefully to pick out from the superstitions and enthusiasms of mankind, the two by which they have been most frequently oppressed and enslaved, we probably ought to select the notions, that governments are sovereigns over property, and that they may gratuitously transfer it to peculiar merit. The art of magnifying individual power and capital at the publick expense, by the pretext of peculiar merit, is the inchoate feature of those

measures which have terminated injuriously to the happiness
of nations.

The authors of the Federalist appear to think, that in the
division of powers between the federal and state governments,
the largest share had fallen to the latter; but this must have
been a mistake, so far as a capacity for augmentation is considered; because, most or all of the measures complained of as
unconstitutional, have originated with congress; and a capacity
for augmentation naturally encroaches. This symptom is sufficient of itself, to awaken the vigilance of those who think, that
federalism is indispensable for the good government of so large
a country as the United States. Federalism cannot exist
without confederates, and confederates are inefficient without
power. A tacit alliance between congress and a family of eleemosynarians, is a species of federalism inconsistent with the
positive confederation of a family of states. These two kinds
of confederation cannot subsist long together. If the eleemosynarian family should be made strong enough to defend congress against the states, it will be too strong for congress itself;
and as courtiers for pay abhor the vacillancy of election, they
will be always ready to desert from a fluctuating and dependant, to a permanent and hereditary patron. That congress
should for a moment risque the friendship of the states, a federal militia fighting without pay, to cultivate that of a few mercenary troops, sure to desert unless allowed to plunder, is a
policy for which I cannot discern a motive. By weakening the
state governments, congress would weaken itself, since they
are the props upon which its power rests; for if these props
fall, a very different power from that of congress will spring
from the ruins. The notion of a contest for power between
the federal and state governments must therefore have originated from sounds without sense, or from artifices without
honesty. It is like a warfare between two diagrams or two
dogmas, or between two dancing masters about the figure of a
reel, neither of whom can gain any thing by the contest, however they may cripple each other. No federal or state legislator can gain any thing for himself by the success of the
diagram or dogma under which he fights. Had we hereditary
families, the warfare might be accounted for; but as we have
not, we can only ascribe it to the eleemosynarian families,

which may get something by it. The question of course settles into the plain alternative, whether to appease its old friends the states, or to cling to its courtiers, the eleemosynarians, is the best policy for the federal government. The alternative for the state governments is nearly the same; they ought to consider, whether an imitation of the federal eleemosynarian system, or a cultivation of the publick good, will by economy and justice, contribute most to their preservation. Political economists say, in defence of the freedom of property against exclusive privileges, that every man is the best manager of his own affairs. They ought to have added the reason, namely, that no man will form intricate schemes to cheat himself.

As for a balance of power, the other rival of our constitutional federal policy, it may be accurately estimated by considering whether an animal, created with a number of legs, would act wisely in cutting off one half, from a notion that it would walk better with half than with all.

THE END.